THE NEW
Art and Science
OF TEACHING

Writing

KATHY TUCHMAN GLASS   ROBERT J. MARZANO

A joint publication

ASCD   **Solution Tree**

555 North Morton Street
Bloomington, IN 47404
800.733.6786 (toll free) / 812.336.7700
FAX: 812.336.7790

email: info@SolutionTree.com
SolutionTree.com

Visit **go.SolutionTree.com/instruction** to download the free reproducibles in this book.

Printed in the United States of America

Library of Congress Cataloging-in-Publication Data

Names: Glass, Kathy Tuchman, author. | Marzano, Robert J., author.
Title: The new art and science of teaching writing / Kathy Tuchman Glass,
    Robert J. Marzano.
Description: Bloomington, IN : Solution Tree Press, [2018] | Includes
    bibliographical references and index.
Identifiers: LCCN 2017060319 | ISBN 9781945349362 (perfect bound)
Subjects: LCSH: English language--Composition and exercises--Study and
    teaching.
Classification: LCC LB1631 .G5565 2018 | DDC 372.62/3--dc23 LC record available at https://lccn.loc.
gov/2017060319

Solution Tree

Jeffrey C. Jones, CEO
Edmund M. Ackerman, President

Solution Tree Press

President and Publisher: Douglas M. Rife
Editorial Director: Sarah Payne-Mills
Art Director: Rian Anderson
Managing Production Editor: Kendra Slayton
Senior Production Editor: Suzanne Kraszewski
Senior Editor: Amy Rubenstein
Copy Editor: Miranda Addonizio
Proofreader: Elisabeth Abrams
Text and Cover Designer: Laura Cox

Acknowledgments

We would like to thank Douglas Rife and Claudia Wheatley at Solution Tree for providing the opportunity for us to collaborate with each other and share our vision for this book. Thank you, as well, to Suzanne Kraszewski for her exceptional editorial skills and guidance. Additionally, many thanks to Lori Musso and Heather Polcik, two outstanding educators, for their keen insight and astute suggestions.

Visit **go.SolutionTree.com/instruction** to download the free reproducibles in this book.

Table of Contents

About the Authors vii

Introduction 1

    The Overall Model 2

    The Need for Subject-Specific Models 6

    This Book 7

Part I: Feedback

1   Providing and Communicating Clear Learning Goals 11

    Element 1: Providing Scales and Rubrics 11

    Element 2: Tracking Student Progress. 25

    Element 3: Celebrating Success. 26

    Conclusion. 28

2   Using Assessments **29**

    Element 4: Using Informal Assessments of the Whole Class 29

    Element 5: Using Formal Assessments of Individual Students. 32

    Conclusion. 34

Part II: Content

3   Conducting Direct Instruction Lessons **37**

    Element 6: Chunking Content 37

    Element 7: Processing Content 39

    Element 8: Recording and Representing Content 46

    Conclusion. 54

4   Conducting Practicing and Deepening Lessons **55**

    Element 9: Using Structured Practice Sessions. 55

    Element 10: Examining Similarities and Differences 61

    Element 11: Examining Errors in Reasoning 65

    Conclusion. 69

5   Conducting Knowledge Application Lessons **71**

    Element 12: Engaging Students in Cognitively Complex Tasks 71

    Element 13: Providing Resources and Guidance 75

    Element 14: Generating and Defending Claims 82

    Conclusion. 87

6   **Using Strategies That Appear in All Types of Lessons** **89**
        Element 15: Previewing Strategies 89
        Element 16: Highlighting Critical Information 96
        Element 17: Reviewing Content 98
        Element 18: Revising Knowledge 100
        Element 19: Reflecting on Learning 109
        Element 20: Assigning Purposeful Homework 110
        Element 21: Elaborating on Information 112
        Element 22: Organizing Students to Interact 113
        Conclusion 116

Part III: Context

7   **Using Engagement Strategies** **119**
        Element 23: Noticing and Reacting When Students Are Not Engaged 120
        Element 24: Increasing Response Rates 120
        Element 25: Using Physical Movement 123
        Element 26: Maintaining a Lively Pace 124
        Element 27: Demonstrating Intensity and Enthusiasm 126
        Element 28: Presenting Unusual Information 127
        Element 29: Using Friendly Controversy 129
        Element 30: Using Academic Games 130
        Element 31: Providing Opportunities for Students to Talk About Themselves . . 132
        Element 32: Motivating and Inspiring Students 135
        Conclusion 138

8   **Implementing Rules and Procedures and Building Relationships** **139**
        Element 34: Organizing the Physical Layout of the Classroom 139
        Element 39: Understanding Students' Backgrounds and Interests 142
        Conclusion 145

9   **Developing Expertise** **147**
        Step 1: Conduct a Self-Audit 147
        Step 2: Select Goal Elements and Specific Strategies 149
        Step 3: Engage in Deliberate Practice and Track Progress 150
        Step 4: Seek Continuous Improvement by Planning for Future Growth 151
        Conclusion 151

Afterword **153**

Appendix A: Framework Overview **155**

Appendix B: List of Figures and Tables **169**

References and Resources **173**

Index **177**

About the Authors

Kathy Tuchman Glass, MEd, a consultant, is an accomplished author and former classroom teacher with more than twenty-five years of experience in education. She provides professional development services to K–12 educators with a focus on areas concerning curriculum and instruction.

She is recognized for her expertise in differentiated instruction, standards work around English language arts, literacy, instructional strategies, assessments, and backward planning for unit and lesson design. She is a member of the International Literacy Association, the National Council of Teachers of English, the Association for Supervision and Curriculum Development (ASCD), and Learning Forward.

She earned a bachelor's degree from Indiana University–Bloomington and a master's degree in education from San Francisco State University.

To learn more about Kathy's work, visit Glass Educational Consulting (www.kathyglassconsulting.com).

Robert J. Marzano, PhD, is the cofounder and CAO of Marzano Resources in Denver, Colorado. During his fifty years in the field of education, he has worked with educators as a speaker and trainer and has authored more than fifty books and two hundred articles on topics such as instruction, assessment, writing and implementing standards, cognition, effective leadership, and school intervention. His books include *Leading a High Reliability School, The New Art and Science of Teaching*, and *Making Classroom Assessments Reliable and Valid*. His practical translations of the most current research and theory into classroom strategies are known internationally and are widely practiced by both teachers and administrators. He received a bachelor's degree from Iona College in New York, a master's degree from Seattle University, and a doctorate from the University of Washington.

To learn more about Dr. Marzano's work, visit Marzano Resources (www.MarzanoResources.com).

To book Kathy Tuchman Glass or Robert J. Marzano for professional development, contact pd@SolutionTree.com.

Introduction

The New Art and Science of Teaching (Marzano, 2017) is a comprehensive model of instruction with a rather long developmental lineage. Specifically, four books spanning two decades precede and inform *The New Art and Science of Teaching* and its use in the field.

1. *Classroom Instruction That Works: Research-Based Strategies for Increasing Student Achievement* (Marzano, Pickering, & Pollock, 2001)
2. *Classroom Management That Works: Research-Based Strategies for Every Teacher* (Marzano, Marzano, & Pickering, 2003)
3. *Classroom Assessment and Grading That Work* (Marzano, 2006)
4. *The Art and Science of Teaching: A Comprehensive Framework for Effective Instruction* (Marzano, 2007)

The first three books address specific components of the teaching process, namely instruction, management, and assessment. The final book puts all three components together into a comprehensive model of teaching. It also makes a strong case for the fact that research (in other words, science) must certainly guide good teaching, but teachers must also develop good teaching as art. Even if they use precisely the same instructional strategies, two highly effective teachers will have shaped and adapted those strategies to adhere to their specific personalities, the subject matter they teach, and their students' unique needs. Stated differently, we can never accurately articulate effective teaching as a set of strategies that all teachers must execute in precisely the same way.

The comprehensive model in the 2017 book *The New Art and Science of Teaching* (Marzano, 2017) reflects a greatly expanded and updated version of *The Art and Science of Teaching* (Marzano, 2007). One of the unique aspects of *The New Art and Science of Teaching* is that it focuses on what happens in the minds of students by taking a student-outcome perspective as the primary influence. Specifically, when teachers employ instructional strategies, it generates certain mental states and processes in the learner's mind that facilitate student learning. This dynamic that represents the major feature of this new model is depicted in figure I.1 (page 2):

Source: Marzano, 2017, p. 5.

Figure I.1: The teaching and learning progression.

According to figure I.1, the intervening variable between the effective application of an instructional strategy and enhanced student learning is specific mental states and processes in the minds of learners. If teachers do not produce these mental states and processes as a result of employing a given strategy, then that strategy will have little or no effect on students. This implies that teachers should heighten their level of awareness as they use instructional strategies for maximum efficacy.

The Overall Model

The model in *The New Art and Science of Teaching* (Marzano, 2017) is a framework that educators can use to organize the majority (if not all) of the instructional strategies that research and theory identify. It has several parts: three overarching categories, ten design areas, and forty-three specific elements that each serve as an umbrella for a host of instructional strategies.

Three Categories

At the highest level of organization, the model has three overarching categories: feedback, content, and context.

1. ***Feedback*** refers to the all-important information loop teachers must establish with students so that students know what they should be learning about specific topics and their current level of performance on these topics.
2. ***Content*** refers to the sequencing and pacing of lessons such that students move smoothly from initial understanding to applying knowledge in new and creative ways.
3. ***Context*** refers to those strategies that ensure all students meet these psychological needs: engagement, order, a sense of belonging, and high expectations.

Embedded in these three overarching categories are more specific categories (teacher actions).

Ten Design Areas

In *The New Art and Science of Teaching* model, each of the ten design areas is associated with a specific teacher action, as follows:

1. Providing and communicating clear learning goals
2. Using assessments
3. Conducting direct instruction lessons
4. Conducting practicing and deepening lessons
5. Conducting knowledge application lessons
6. Using strategies that appear in all types of lessons
7. Using engagement strategies
8. Implementing rules and procedures
9. Building relationships
10. Communicating high expectations

Table I.1 shows the ten teacher actions within the three categories along with a description of the desirable student mental states and processes for each. For example, the teacher action of conducting direct instruction lessons within the *content* category has the desired effect that when the teacher presents new content to students, they understand which parts are important and how the parts all fit together.

Table I.1: Teacher Actions and Student Mental States and Processes

	Teacher Actions	**Student Mental States and Processes**
Feedback	Providing and Communicating Clear Learning Goals	1. Students understand the progression of knowledge they are expected to master and where they are along that progression.
	Using Assessments	2. Students understand how test scores and grades relate to their status on the progression of knowledge they are expected to master.
Content	Conducting Direct Instruction Lessons	3. When content is new, students understand which parts are important and how the parts fit together.
	Conducting Practicing and Deepening Lessons	4. After teachers present new content, students deepen their understanding and develop fluency in skills and processes.
	Conducting Knowledge Application Lessons	5. After teachers present new content, students generate and defend claims through knowledge application tasks.
	Using Strategies That Appear in All Types of Lessons	6. Students continually integrate new knowledge with old knowledge and revise their understanding accordingly.
Context	Using Engagement Strategies	7. Students are paying attention, energized, intrigued, and inspired.
	Implementing Rules and Procedures	8. Students understand and follow rules and procedures.
	Building Relationships	9. Students feel welcome, accepted, and valued.
	Communicating High Expectations	10. Typically reluctant students feel valued and do not hesitate to interact with the teacher or their peers.

Each of the ten design areas corresponds with a design question. These are a set of questions that help teachers plan units and lessons within those units. Table I.2 shows the design questions that correspond with each design area.

Table I.2: Design Questions

	Design Areas	**Design Questions**
Feedback	1. Providing and Communicating Clear Learning Goals	How will I communicate clear learning goals that help students understand the progression of knowledge they are expected to master and where they are along that progression?
	2. Using Assessment	How will I design and administer assessments that help students understand how their test scores and grades are related to their status on the progression of knowledge they are expected to master?
Content	3. Constructing Direct Instruction Lessons	When content is new, how will I design and deliver direct instruction lessons that help students understand which parts of the content are important and how the parts fit together?
	4. Conducting Practicing and Deepening Lessons	After presenting content, how will I design and deliver lessons that help students deepen their understanding and develop fluency in skills and processes?

continued →

	Design Areas	Design Questions
	5. Conducting Knowledge Application Lessons	After presenting content, how will I design and deliver lessons that help students generate and defend claims through knowledge application?
	6. Using Strategies That Appear in All Types of Lessons	Throughout all types of lessons, what strategies will I use to help students continually integrate new knowledge with old knowledge and revise their understanding accordingly?
Context	7. Using Engagement	What engagement strategies will I use to help students pay attention, be energized, be intrigued, and be inspired?
	8. Implementing Rules and Procedures	What strategies will I use to help students understand and follow rules and procedures?
	9. Building Relationships	What strategies will I use to help students feel welcome, accepted, and valued?
	10. Communicating High Expectations	What strategies will I use to help typically reluctant students feel valued and comfortable interacting with me or their peers?

Source: Marzano, 2017, pp. 6–7.

Within the ten categories of teacher actions, we have organized sets of strategies in even more fine-grained categories, called *elements*.

Forty-Three Elements

The forty-three elements provide detailed guidance about the nature and purpose of a category of strategies. Table I.3 depicts the full complement of elements. For example, we operationally define the category *building relationships* as:

- Using verbal and nonverbal behaviors that indicate affection for students (element 38)
- Understanding students' backgrounds and interests (element 39)
- Displaying objectivity and control (element 40)

Finally, these forty-three elements encompass hundreds of specific instructional strategies. Selected strategies related to writing instruction are the focus of this book.

Over 330 Specific Strategies

At the finest level of detail are over 330 specific instructional strategies embedded in the forty-three elements. For example, element 24—increasing response rates—includes the following nine strategies.

1. Random names
2. Hand signals
3. Response cards
4. Response chaining
5. Paired response
6. Choral response
7. Wait time
8. Elaborative interrogation
9. Multiple types of questions

In effect, there are nine distinctive, specific instructional strategies teachers can use to increase students' response rates, supporting the fact that two different teachers could both effectively improve their students' learning by boosting response rates but with very different techniques. The reader will note that throughout

Table I.3: Elements Within the Ten Design Areas

Feedback	Content	Context
Providing and Communicating Clear Learning Goals 1. Providing scales and rubrics 2. Tracking student progress 3. Celebrating success **Using Assessments** 4. Using informal assessments of the whole class 5. Using formal assessments of individual students	**Conducting Direct Instruction Lessons** 6. Chunking content 7. Processing content 8. Recording and representing content **Conducting Practicing and Deepening Lessons** 9. Using structured practice sessions 10. Examining similarities and differences 11. Examining errors in reasoning **Conducting Knowledge Application Lessons** 12. Engaging students in cognitively complex tasks 13. Providing resources and guidance 14. Generating and defending claims **Using Strategies That Appear in All Types of Lessons** 15. Previewing strategies 16. Highlighting critical information 17. Reviewing content 18. Revising knowledge 19. Reflecting on learning 20. Assigning purposeful homework 21. Elaborating on information 22. Organizing students to interact	**Using Engagement Strategies** 23. Noticing and reacting when students are not engaged 24. Increasing response rates 25. Using physical movement 26. Maintaining a lively pace 27. Demonstrating intensity and enthusiasm 28. Presenting unusual information 29. Using friendly controversy 30. Using academic games 31. Providing opportunities for students to talk about themselves 32. Motivating and inspiring students **Implementing Rules and Procedures** 33. Establishing rules and procedures 34. Organizing the physical layout of the classroom 35. Demonstrating withitness 36. Acknowledging adherence to rules and procedures 37. Acknowledging lack of adherence to rules and procedures **Building Relationships** 38. Using verbal and nonverbal behaviors that indicate affection for students 39. Understanding students' backgrounds and interests 40. Displaying objectivity and control **Communicating High Expectations** 41. Demonstrating value and respect for reluctant learners 42. Asking in-depth questions of reluctant learners 43. Probing incorrect answers with reluctant learners

the text we have addressed only those elements—and strategies within elements—that relate directly to writing instruction. Therefore, the breadth of this book will not extend to explanations and examples related to writing instruction for each of the more than three hundred strategies.

Some strategies use the same or similar terms; for example, the strategy of *summary* appears in element 8 (strategy 40, *summaries*), element 10 (strategy 59, *summaries*), and element 17 (strategy 133, *summary*). This is because teachers will use strategies differently depending on their particular purpose as we show in the following example.

- **Element 8:** In chapter 3 (page 46), "Conducting Direct Instruction Lessons," element 8—recording and representing content—asks that students summarize content briefly and quickly to identify critical information and describe how the pieces fit together.

- **Element 10:** In chapter 4 (page 61), "Conducting Practicing and Deepening Lessons," element 10 focuses on students examining similarities and differences. Students can succinctly summarize the attributes of two opposing topics through a graphic organizer or other method.
- **Element 17:** In chapter 6 (page 98), "Using Strategies That Appear in All Types of Lessons," element 17 suggests that students use summaries to review content. Teachers can furnish a summary for students or ask students to prepare them as the basis for an ensuing discussion.

Figure A.1 in appendix A (page 156) presents an overview of the entire *New Art and Science of Teaching* framework featuring the three overarching categories (feedback, content, and context), ten teacher actions, forty-three elements, and over 330 accompanying strategies. This figure can serve as an advance organizer while reading this book.

The Need for Subject-Specific Models

General models like *The New Art and Science of Teaching* certainly have their place in a teacher's understanding of effective instruction. However, teachers must adapt those models to specific subject areas to produce the most powerful results. That is what we have attempted to do in this book. Specifically, in the following chapters, we address the three overarching categories—(1) feedback, (2) content, and (3) context—with their corresponding ten teacher actions and the embedded forty-three elements. We do so by providing concrete examples for how to apply a generous representation of the hundreds of instructional strategies expressly for writing, with some reading as well, since these areas of literacy closely align and interconnect.

Although this text predominantly provides suggestions to support lesson planning around writing instruction, we encourage readers to explore the foundational book *The New Art and Science of Teaching* (Marzano, 2017). In doing so, they will likely infuse their content areas and grades with additional strategies. For example, element 16—highlighting critical information—encompasses the following eleven strategies.

1. Repeating the most important content
2. Asking questions that focus on critical information
3. Using visual activities
4. Using narrative activities
5. Using tone of voice, gestures, and body position
6. Using pause time
7. Identifying critical-input experiences
8. Using explicit instruction to convey critical content
9. Using dramatic instruction to convey critical content
10. Providing advance organizers to cue critical content
11. Using what students already know to cue critical content

Teachers could wisely incorporate all these strategies into various lessons throughout a unit, as they represent sound instructional practice. For example, when teachers continually repeat important information during a lesson and unit, it alerts students to critical content and helps them remember the information. As well, when teachers intentionally and strategically use their tone of voice, gestures, and body position to emphasize salient information, it again highlights what students should remember and focuses their attention on key content. Instead of focusing our attention on these more pervasive strategies—and other such strategies throughout the model—we provide ideas specific to writing. For example, for element 16, we choose the strategy of using visual activities as an opportunity to show how teachers can apply this strategy to teach a writing skill, which we detail in chapter 6 (page 89). As readers continue through this text, strategies linked to writing and reading take center stage.

This Book

This book is organized into three parts—(1) feedback, (2) content, and (3) context—mirroring the over-arching categories of *The New Art and Science of Teaching* model as described earlier in this introduction. The chapters align with the ten teacher actions and then focus on selected elements (of the forty-three total) within each action and specific strategies for teaching writing.

In part I, chapters 1 and 2 focus on feedback. Chapter 1 pinpoints strategies for providing and communicating clear learning goals, and chapter 2 concentrates on using assessments.

In part II, chapters 3, 4, 5, and 6 focus on content. Chapter 3 looks at conducting direct instruction lessons, chapter 4 on conducting practicing and deepening lessons, and chapter 5 on conducting knowledge application lessons. Chapter 6 focuses on using strategies that appear in all types of lessons.

In part III, chapters 7 and 8 focus on context. Chapter 7 emphasizes using engagement. In chapter 8, readers find a discussion of strategies for implementing rules and procedures and building relationships.

In chapter 9, readers will learn about a four-step process for developing teachers' expertise in an effort to increase students' learning.

Each chapter includes self-rating scales that teachers can use to assess their performance on each element addressed in this book. By doing this, they can determine their areas of strength and the areas in which they might want to improve relative to *The New Art and Science of Teaching*. All scales in this book have the same format for progression of development. To introduce these scales and help readers understand them, we present the general format of a self-rating scale in figure I.2.

Score	Description
4: Innovating	I adapt strategies and behaviors associated with this element for unique student needs and situations.
3: Applying	I use strategies and behaviors associated with this element without significant errors and monitor their effect on students.
2: Developing	I use strategies and behaviors associated with this element without significant errors but do not monitor their effect on students.
1: Beginning	I use some strategies and behaviors associated with this element but do so with significant errors or omissions.
0: Not Using	I am unaware of the strategies and behaviors associated with this element or know them but don't employ them.

Figure I.2: General format of the self-rating scale.

To understand this scale, it is best to start at the bottom with the Not Using row. Here the teacher is unaware of the strategies that relate to the element or knows them but doesn't employ them. At the Beginning level, the teacher uses strategies that relate to the element, but leaves out important parts or makes significant mistakes. At the Developing level, the teacher executes strategies important to the element without significant errors or omissions but does not monitor their effect on students. At the Applying level, the teacher not only executes strategies without significant errors or omissions but also monitors students to ensure that they are experiencing the desired effects. We consider the Applying level the level at which one can legitimately expect tangible results in students. Finally, at the Innovating level, the teacher is aware of and makes any adaptations to the strategies for students who require such an arrangement.

Each chapter ends with a Guiding Questions for Curriculum Design section to help with planning. For easy reference, the strategies we have chosen to feature from the more than 330 appear in bold typeface in figure A.1 (page 156), *The New Art and Science of Teaching* framework overview.

Next, chapter 1 begins part I on feedback by examining how teachers can provide and communicate clear learning goals to students.

PART I
Feedback

CHAPTER 1

Providing and Communicating Clear Learning Goals

When teachers design and communicate learning goals well, students benefit. They not only know what they are supposed to be learning but also know where they stand relative to that targeted content. Additionally, within *The New Art and Science of Teaching*, teachers should communicate clear learning goals so that students understand the progression of knowledge teachers expect them to master and where they are along that progression.

The elements within this first teacher action of providing and communicating clear learning goals include the following.

- **Element 1:** Providing scales and rubrics
- **Element 2:** Tracking student progress
- **Element 3:** Celebrating success

Think of these three elements as a linked set: scales and rubrics are essential for students to track their progress, and tracking progress is necessary for celebrating success.

Element 1: Providing Scales and Rubrics

Scales and rubrics provide the tools for students to understand the progression of knowledge and expectations as the focus for learning.

For element 1 of the model, we selected the following specific strategies to address in this chapter. We list additional strategies for element 1 in figure A.1 in appendix A, on page 156.

- Clearly articulating and creating scales and rubrics for learning goals
- Using teacher-created targets and scales and implementing routines for using them

It is important to note that simply employing a strategy does not ensure the desired effect on students. We recommend that teachers use the scale in figure 1.1 (page 12) to rate their current level of effectiveness with the specific strategies for providing scales and rubrics.

Score	Description
4: Innovating	I engage in all behaviors at the Applying level. In addition, I identify those students who do not have an understanding of the proficiency scales or cannot accurately describe their current level of performance and design alternate activities and strategies to meet their specific needs.
3: Applying	I engage in activities to provide students with rubrics and scales without significant errors or omissions and monitor the extent to which students have an understanding of the proficiency scales, and I can accurately describe their current level of performance on the scales.
2: Developing	I engage in activities that provide students with clear rubrics and scales without significant errors or omissions.
1: Beginning	I engage in activities that provide students with clear rubrics and scales but do so with errors or omissions, such as not systematically referring back to the progression of knowledge in the rubric or scale or explaining how daily assignments relate to the learning goal.
0: Not Using	I do not engage in activities that provide students with clear rubrics and scales.

Figure 1.1: Self-rating scale for element 1—Providing scales and rubrics.

Clearly Articulating and Creating Scales or Rubrics for Learning Goals

A proficiency scale articulates a progression of knowledge or skills and reflects a continuum of learning goals (also referred to as *learning targets*). It includes five levels of proficiency ranging from 0.0 to 4.0 as indicated in the samples for generating narratives for grades 8 and 2 in figures 1.2 and 1.3. Level 3.0 represents at-grade-level work. A score of 2.0 shows foundational skills, and a score of 4.0 reflects the achievement of more complex learning goals. Teachers clarify learning goals using a proficiency scale to identify what students will come to know or be able to do within a unit of study. They explicitly teach items on a scale. However, not all students need instruction for every item on all levels, so teachers preassess and formatively assess students to determine instructional moves they might take that meet the needs of individuals and groups of students.

In order for students to compose any piece of writing, they need to learn general writing skills aside from the characteristics of a specific genre, such as determining task, purpose, and audience; revision (figure 1.4, page 14); editing; and even generating sentences (figure 1.5, page 15) along with spelling skills for primary and elementary students. Therefore, combining several proficiency scales forms the overall focus for any comprehensive writing assignment. Visit marzanoresearch.com/the-critical-concepts to request a free download for examples of other proficiency scales in the document titled *The Critical Concepts* (Simms, 2017). Teachers can compare the provided proficiency scales in this chapter (and others they access on their own) to their standards document. When doing so, they can delete or add line items—particularly from the 2.0 level—to pertain to their teaching situation.

Generating Narratives (GN), Grade 8	
4.0	The student selects events in a plot that hold a reader's interest.
3.5	In addition to score 3.0 performance, the student has partial success at score 4.0 content.
3.0	The student: **GN1—Introduces the conflict, setting, and characters of a narrative** **GN2—Uses description (including sensory details), dialogue, and reflection to develop a narrative**

Generating Narratives (GN), Grade 8	
2.5	The student has no major errors or omissions regarding score 2.0 content and partial success at score 3.0 content.
2.0	**GN1—The student recognizes or recalls specific vocabulary** (for example, *character*, *conflict*, *context*, *description*, *dialogue*, *exposition*, *introduction*, *problem*, and *setting*) and performs basic processes such as: • Explain the purpose of an exposition • Describe how a problem or conflict is developed throughout a narrative • Generate possible characters and settings for a narrative • Generate possible problems characters could encounter in a narrative • Create an outline that lists the characters, settings, and problems to be solved in a narrative • Describe how dialogue and description can introduce a character or communicate a setting or problem • Describe possible events that might lead up to the exposition or main problem of a narrative **GN2—The student recognizes or recalls specific vocabulary** (for example, *description*, *dialogue*, *plot*, *reflection*, *sensory detail*, and *sequence*) and performs basic processes such as: • Generate a list of words that could be used to describe a character • Generate a list of words that could describe an event or location • Describe how dialogue can be used to further the plot or reveal aspects of character • Correctly punctuate dialogue • Properly introduce dialogue • Generate a list of verbs that could be used to describe how a character says something • Create a timeline of events that will occur in a narrative • Describe how a character might feel about the events that will occur in a narrative • Describe what a main character or reader might learn from the events in a narrative
1.5	The student has partial success at score 2.0 content and major errors or omissions regarding score 3.0 content.
1.0	With help, the student has partial success at score 2.0 content and score 3.0 content.
0.5	With help, the student has partial success at score 2.0 content but not at score 3.0 content.
0.0	Even with help, the student has no success.

Source: Simms, 2016.

Figure 1.2: Sample proficiency scale for generating narratives (grade 8).

*Visit **go.SolutionTree.com/instruction** for a free reproducible version of this figure.*

Generating Narratives (GN), Grade 2	
4.0	The student describes how a setting or character positively or negatively impacted a personal experience using descriptive details (for example, when writing a narrative about a favorite summer vacation, he or she recalls that most of one day was spent at the beach, and adds descriptions that explain why that setting made the day more memorable).
3.5	In addition to score 3.0 performance, the student has partial success at score 4.0 content.
3.0	The student: **GN1—Writes about a sequence of at least three events using words that show the order of events** (for example, in a narrative about a character who tries to help a dog find its way home, the student uses words such as *first*, *next*, *then*, and *last* to explain what the character decides to do) **GN2—Uses descriptive details to describe the setting and characters in a narrative** (for example, uses descriptive details to help a reader picture the people and places involved in a favorite holiday celebration)
2.5	The student has no major errors or omissions regarding score 2.0 content and partial success at score 3.0 content.

Figure 1.3: Sample proficiency scale for generating narratives (grade 2). continued →

Generating Narratives (GN), Grade 2	
2.0	The student: **GN1—Recognizes or recalls specific vocabulary** (for example, *beginning, character, conflict, develop, draft, end, event, introduce, middle, narrative, purpose, setting,* and *transition*) and performs basic processes such as: • Describe what kinds of events will be included in a draft using a prompt • Use a graphic organizer to outline the beginning, middle, and end of a narrative • Sketch images of different events from the beginning, middle, and end of a narrative • Describe why transition words and phrases are important • List transition words that show the order of events (such as *first, next, then, after that,* and *finally*) • Draft a sentence using a transition word or phrase • Identify places in a narrative draft where a new event begins **GN2—Recognizes or recalls specific vocabulary** (for example, *adjective, character, characteristic, descriptive detail, event, object, quality, setting,* and *trait*) and performs basic processes such as: • Identify the settings and characters in a narrative • Explain that descriptive details are words and phrases that help a reader picture the setting, characters, objects, and events in a narrative • List qualities or characteristics that adjectives can describe (such as age, size, color, and shape) • Identify examples of descriptive details in a narrative text • List words and phrases that could describe a place in a text • List words and phrases that indicate what time of day or year a narrative takes place (such as *in the summer, that night, during,* and *while*) • List words and phrases that could describe how a character looks and feels during a particular event • List words and phrases that could describe how a character acts • Describe specific actions that could show how a character feels during a particular event (for example, if a character is angry, she might cross her arms and frown) • Sketch how a character looks and acts during a specific event
1.5	Student has partial success at score 2.0 content and major errors or omissions regarding score 3.0 content.
1.0	With help, student has partial success at score 2.0 content and score 3.0 content.
0.5	With help, student has partial success at score 2.0 content but not at score 3.0 content.
0.0	Even with help, the student has no success.

Source: Simms, 2016.

*Visit **go.SolutionTree.com/instruction** for a free reproducible version of this figure.*

Revision (R), Grade 8	
4.0	The student selects revisions that will make a previously written piece stronger (for example, revises a text by rewriting sections that lack clarity or detail, replaces common words with more precise synonyms and combines or rephrases sentences; and explains the reasoning behind the changes).
3.5	In addition to score 3.0 performance, the student has partial success at score 4.0 content.
3.0	The student: **R1—Rewrites sentences so that syntax and sentence forms are varied** (for example, revises sentences that begin with the same phrase or word by adding an adverbial clause or by rephrasing the sentence) **R2—Revises writing to maintain a formal style** (for example, replaces common, overused adjectives, such as *good* or *fun,* and verbs, such as *to be* verbs, with more complex, specific words)
2.5	The student has no major errors or omissions regarding score 2.0 content and partial success at score 3.0 content.

	Revision (R), Grade 8
2.0	The student:
	R1—Recognizes or recalls specific vocabulary (for example, *adverbial clause*, *clause*, *complex sentence*, *compound sentence*, *phrase*, *repetition*, *revise*, *simple sentence*, and *syntax*) and performs basic processes such as:
	• Describe simple, complex, and compound sentences • Annotate simple, complex, and compound sentences in a rough draft in different ways • Annotate a word or phrase that begins multiple sentences within a paragraph or text • Generate strategies for varying and adding interest to sentences with similar lengths and word choices • Add transitions to texts to clarify the relationships between sentences and add interest • Combine two short, simple sentences to create a longer, more complex sentence
	R2—Recognizes or recalls specific vocabulary (for example, *abbreviation*, *casual*, *contraction*, *formal*, *informal*, *quote*, *reference*, *slang*, *summary*, and *synonym*) and performs basic processes such as:
	• Explain the differences between a formal and informal writing style • Explain when a formal style should be used • Annotate slang or words that sound informal • Annotate contractions • Annotate abbreviations that may be too informal for academic writing • Annotate quotes or summarized texts that should be cited • Generate a list of synonyms that could replace simple or over-used vocabulary (for example, the word *great* could be replaced with *impressive*, *excellent*, or *important*)
1.5	The student has partial success at score 2.0 content and major errors or omissions regarding score 3.0 content.
1.0	With help, the student has partial success at score 2.0 content and score 3.0 content.
0.5	With help, the student has partial success at score 2.0 content but not at score 3.0 content.
0.0	Even with help, the student has no success.

Source: Simms, 2016.

Figure 1.4: Sample proficiency scale for revision (grade 8).

Visit **go.SolutionTree.com/instruction** *for a free reproducible version of this figure.*

	Generating Sentences (GS), Grade 2
4.0	The student decides how to make a paragraph more cohesive by adding coordinating conjunctions, details, and linking words (for example, in a paragraph that compares a girl and her brother, the student uses coordinating conjunctions such as *and* or *but* to combine sentences and to show what each does or does not like).
3.5	In addition to score 3.0 performance, the student has partial success at score 4.0 content.
3.0	The student:
	GS1—Generates simple and compound sentences (for example, writes four or more sentences in response to the poem "The Song of the Jellicles" by T. S. Eliot [1939] that describe what the poem says about the cats and what traits the cats have, and uses both simple and compound sentences)
	GS2—Expands and rephrases complete sentences (for example, adds details to change the sentence *The seed grew into a flower* into the sentence *The tiny seed was planted in the ground and soon grew into a marvelous flower*)
2.5	The student has no major errors or omissions regarding score 2.0 content and partial success at score 3.0 content.

Figure 1.5: Sample proficiency scale for generating sentences (grade 2).   continued →

Generating Sentences (GS), Grade 2	
2.0	The student: **GS1—Recognizes or recalls specific vocabulary** (for example, *comma, complete, conjunction, coordinating conjunction, fragment, noun, predicate, punctuation, sentence, subject,* and *verb*) and performs basic processes such as: • Identify the subject and predicate in a sentence • Explain the role of a subject and predicate in a sentence • State that a complete sentence must have a subject and predicate and express a complete thought • Identify sentence fragments that do not state a complete thought • Explain the purpose of conjunctions • List common coordinating conjunctions (such as *for, and, but,* and *so*) • Demonstrate how to combine two simple sentences using a coordinating conjunction and comma • Include appropriate end punctuation for a sentence **GS2—Recognizes or recalls specific vocabulary** (for example, *adjective, adverb, complete, descriptive, detail, noun, object, predicate, rephrase, rewrite, subject,* and *verb*) and performs basic processes such as: • Identify the subject, object, and verb in a sentence • List descriptive details, or adjectives, that could describe a subject in a sentence • List descriptive details, or adjectives, that could describe other nouns or the object in a sentence • Demonstrate where to place adjectives in a sentence • List descriptive details, or adverbs, that could describe the verb in a sentence • Demonstrate where to place adverbs in a sentence • Identify existing descriptive details in a sentence • List additional details that describe why, how, where, or when the main idea in the sentence occurred • Add an additional detail about a topic or main idea using a conjunction or linking word (such as *and, so,* or *because*) • Rewrite a sentence so that the verb comes before the subject • Rewrite a sentence so that the subject comes before the verb
1.5	The student has partial success at score 2.0 content and major errors or omissions regarding score 3.0 content.
1.0	With help, the student has partial success at score 2.0 content and score 3.0 content.
0.5	With help, the student has partial success at score 2.0 content but not at score 3.0 content.
0.0	Even with help, the student has no success.

Source: Simms, 2016.

*Visit **go.SolutionTree.com/instruction** for a free reproducible version of this figure.*

When creating writing units in which students move through the steps of the writing process to produce a comprehensive product, teachers can design analytic rubrics to score students' work. They can base these rubrics on proficiency scales that align to a particular writing genre, providing teachers and students—when they learn how to use them—with concrete information about students' performance on specific skills. Furthermore, this type of rubric is descriptive rather than evaluative, functioning as an instructional tool to explain students' levels of performance. Analytic rubrics can boost student achievement by describing at what level students perform and where they need improvement. This allows for transparency about how the students are doing so they can be advocates for their own learning. Rubrics share these three components (Glass, 2017a).

1. **Scoring criteria:** These refer to the specific elements to assess—such as thesis, reasoning, and evidence—grouped under overarching categories like *Idea and Development*. Each element includes a brief overview of the skills associated with it. For example, *Thesis* might comprise, "Introduce claim through thesis statement, focus on a debatable topic, and use subordinate clause to set up the argument."

2. **Criteria descriptors:** A description accompanies each scoring criterion along a continuum of quality to indicate levels of performance. Teachers use these descriptors to assess students' writing.

When students self-assess, these descriptors enable them to recognize the desirable standard of work they must present and how they can improve.

3. **Levels of performance:** Levels indicate how well a student has performed either numerically, for example, on a six-, five-, four- or three-point scale or with words, such as *advanced proficient, developing, basic,* and *below basic,* or *advanced, proficient, partially proficient,* and *novice.* Sometimes teachers use a combination of both (*5 = advanced*). Teachers should avoid evaluative terms like *outstanding, excellent, competent,* or *poor.* When scoring, assign whole numbers, or half numbers if a student's proficiency is between two levels.

Figure 1.6 features an analytic rubric for an argumentation essay for secondary-level students; figure 1.7 (page 20) shows an opinion writing rubric for the elementary level.

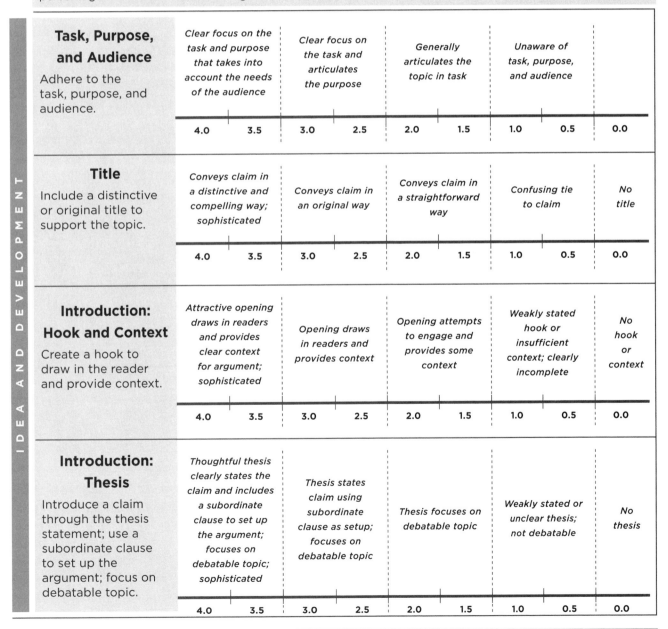

Argument Writing Rubric

Directions: Score the paper by circling the appropriate rubric scale score for each criteria item. To arrive at a single score, determine the mode or median based on all the scores. For items that are weighted double, input the score twice in your calculations. Then use the conversion scale at the end of this figure to arrive at a percentage score and translate to a grade, if needed.

IDEA AND DEVELOPMENT					
Task, Purpose, and Audience Adhere to the task, purpose, and audience.	Clear focus on the task and purpose that takes into account the needs of the audience	Clear focus on the task and articulates the purpose	Generally articulates the topic in task	Unaware of task, purpose, and audience	
	4.0 3.5	3.0 2.5	2.0 1.5	1.0 0.5	0.0
Title Include a distinctive or original title to support the topic.	Conveys claim in a distinctive and compelling way; sophisticated	Conveys claim in an original way	Conveys claim in a straightforward way	Confusing tie to claim	No title
	4.0 3.5	3.0 2.5	2.0 1.5	1.0 0.5	0.0
Introduction: Hook and Context Create a hook to draw in the reader and provide context.	Attractive opening draws in readers and provides clear context for argument; sophisticated	Opening draws in readers and provides context	Opening attempts to engage and provides some context	Weakly stated hook or insufficient context; clearly incomplete	No hook or context
	4.0 3.5	3.0 2.5	2.0 1.5	1.0 0.5	0.0
Introduction: Thesis Introduce a claim through the thesis statement; use a subordinate clause to set up the argument; focus on debatable topic.	Thoughtful thesis clearly states the claim and includes a subordinate clause to set up the argument; focuses on debatable topic; sophisticated	Thesis states claim using subordinate clause as setup; focuses on debatable topic	Thesis focuses on debatable topic	Weakly stated or unclear thesis; not debatable	No thesis
	4.0 3.5	3.0 2.5	2.0 1.5	1.0 0.5	0.0

Figure 1.6: Argumentation writing analytic rubric, secondary level.

continued →

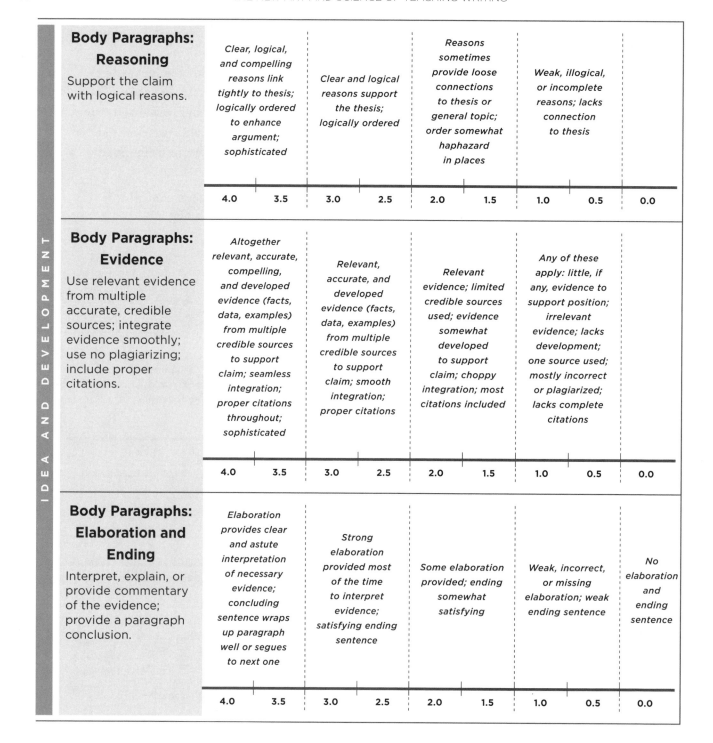

IDEA AND DEVELOPMENT

Body Paragraphs: Reasoning

Support the claim with logical reasons.

Clear, logical, and compelling reasons link tightly to thesis; logically ordered to enhance argument; sophisticated	Clear and logical reasons support the thesis; logically ordered	Reasons sometimes provide loose connections to thesis or general topic; order somewhat haphazard in places	Weak, illogical, or incomplete reasons; lacks connection to thesis

4.0   3.5   3.0   2.5   2.0   1.5   1.0   0.5   0.0

Body Paragraphs: Evidence

Use relevant evidence from multiple accurate, credible sources; integrate evidence smoothly; use no plagiarizing; include proper citations.

Altogether relevant, accurate, compelling, and developed evidence (facts, data, examples) from multiple credible sources to support claim; seamless integration; proper citations throughout; sophisticated	Relevant, accurate, and developed evidence (facts, data, examples) from multiple credible sources to support claim; smooth integration; proper citations	Relevant evidence; limited credible sources used; evidence somewhat developed to support claim; choppy integration; most citations included	Any of these apply: little, if any, evidence to support position; irrelevant evidence; lacks development; one source used; mostly incorrect or plagiarized; lacks complete citations

4.0   3.5   3.0   2.5   2.0   1.5   1.0   0.5   0.0

Body Paragraphs: Elaboration and Ending

Interpret, explain, or provide commentary of the evidence; provide a paragraph conclusion.

Elaboration provides clear and astute interpretation of necessary evidence; concluding sentence wraps up paragraph well or segues to next one	Strong elaboration provided most of the time to interpret evidence; satisfying ending sentence	Some elaboration provided; ending somewhat satisfying	Weak, incorrect, or missing elaboration; weak ending sentence	No elaboration and ending sentence

4.0   3.5   3.0   2.5   2.0   1.5   1.0   0.5   0.0

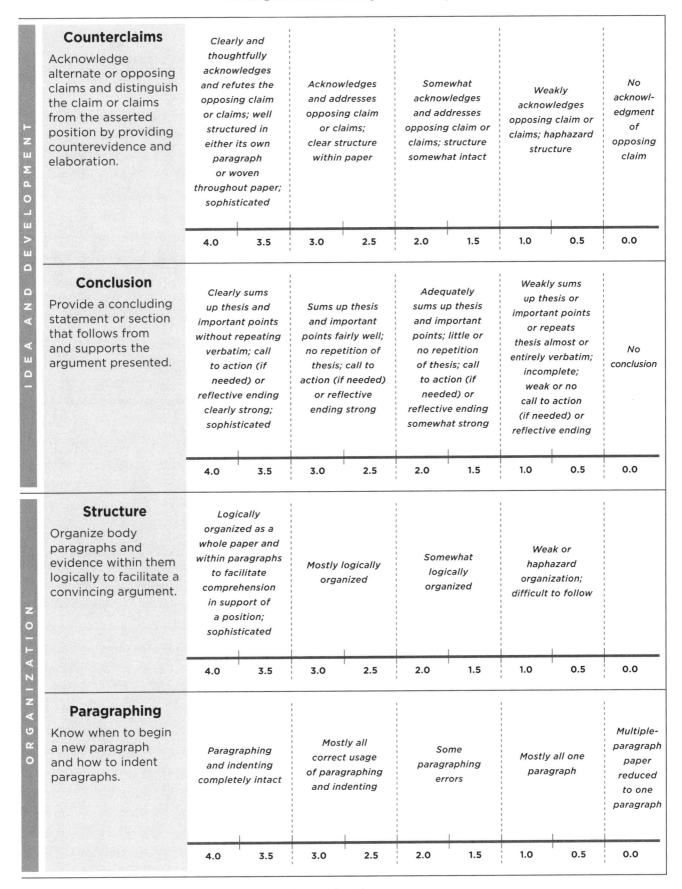

		4.0	3.5	3.0	2.5	2.0	1.5	1.0	0.5	0.0

IDEA AND DEVELOPMENT

Counterclaims

Acknowledge alternate or opposing claims and distinguish the claim or claims from the asserted position by providing counterevidence and elaboration.

- *Clearly and thoughtfully acknowledges and refutes the opposing claim or claims; well structured in either its own paragraph or woven throughout paper; sophisticated* (4.0–3.5)
- *Acknowledges and addresses opposing claim or claims; clear structure within paper* (3.0–2.5)
- *Somewhat acknowledges and addresses opposing claim or claims; structure somewhat intact* (2.0–1.5)
- *Weakly acknowledges opposing claim or claims; haphazard structure* (1.0–0.5)
- *No acknowledgment of opposing claim* (0.0)

Conclusion

Provide a concluding statement or section that follows from and supports the argument presented.

- *Clearly sums up thesis and important points without repeating verbatim; call to action (if needed) or reflective ending clearly strong; sophisticated* (4.0–3.5)
- *Sums up thesis and important points fairly well; no repetition of thesis; call to action (if needed) or reflective ending strong* (3.0–2.5)
- *Adequately sums up thesis and important points; little or no repetition of thesis; call to action (if needed) or reflective ending somewhat strong* (2.0–1.5)
- *Weakly sums up thesis or important points or repeats thesis almost or entirely verbatim; incomplete; weak or no call to action (if needed) or reflective ending* (1.0–0.5)
- *No conclusion* (0.0)

ORGANIZATION

Structure

Organize body paragraphs and evidence within them logically to facilitate a convincing argument.

- *Logically organized as a whole paper and within paragraphs to facilitate comprehension in support of a position; sophisticated* (4.0–3.5)
- *Mostly logically organized* (3.0–2.5)
- *Somewhat logically organized* (2.0–1.5)
- *Weak or haphazard organization; difficult to follow* (1.0–0.5)

Paragraphing

Know when to begin a new paragraph and how to indent paragraphs.

- *Paragraphing and indenting completely intact* (4.0–3.5)
- *Mostly all correct usage of paragraphing and indenting* (3.0–2.5)
- *Some paragraphing errors* (2.0–1.5)
- *Mostly all one paragraph* (1.0–0.5)
- *Multiple-paragraph paper reduced to one paragraph* (0.0)

Source: © 2017 by Kathy Tuchman Glass and Nicole Dimich Vagle.

*Visit **go.SolutionTree.com/instruction** for a free reproducible version of this figure.*

Opinion Writing Rubric, Elementary			
Scoring Criteria		**Descriptors and Levels of Performance**	
Ideas, Content, and Organization	**Title** Include title.	**4**—Original, sophisticated title **3**—Accurate title	**2**—Unrelated or weak title **1**—No title
	Topic Introduce the topic or name of the book as the basis for writing.	**4**—Clear introduction of topic or name of book as the basis for writing **3**—Adequate introduction of topic or name of book as the basis for writing	**2**—Weakly stated introduction of topic or name of book as basis for writing **1**—No introduction to alert reader to the topic or name of book as the basis for writing
	Opinion State an opinion.	**4**—Clearly stated opinion **3**—Somewhat clearly stated opinion	**2**—Weakly stated opinion **1**—Unclear about opinion or not stated
	Reasons Provide reasons that support the opinion.	**4**—Thoroughly developed reasons that clearly support opinion **3**—Somewhat developed reasons that generally support opinion	**2**—Unclear or limited reasons that weakly support opinion **1**—No reasons stated
	Conclusion Provide a concluding statement or section.	**4**—Developed conclusion **3**—Has sense of closure	**2**—Weak conclusion **1**—No conclusion
Word Choice	**Word Choice** Use adjectives and adverbs to modify nouns or verbs.	**4**—Entirely strong, descriptive adjectives and adverbs **3**—Adequate use of adjectives and adverbs	**2**—Weak or minimal use of adjectives or adverbs **1**—No adjectives or adverbs
Voice	**Point of View** Write in consistent first-person point of view throughout paper.	**4**—Consistent use of first-person point of view **3**—May get off track once	**2**—Weak sense of point of view **1**—Whole paper in third person or a combination of first, second (you), and third
	Audience and Purpose Show awareness of audience and purpose.	**4**—Clearly aware of both audience and purpose of writing **3**—Aware of audience or purpose	**2**—Unclear about audience and purpose **1**—Unaware of audience and purpose; off topic

continued →

Opinion Writing Rubric, Elementary (continued)			
Scoring Criteria		Descriptors and Levels of Performance	
Sentence Fluency	**Complete Sentences** Avoid run-ons and fragments.	**4**—All complete sentences **3**—Some run-ons or fragments	**2**—Many run-ons and fragments **1**—Unclear about sentence structure altogether
	Sentence Variety Write sentences with various beginnings, lengths, and structures.	**4**—Thoughtful and consistent use of sentence variety; sophisticated **3**—Sometimes uses sentence variety	**2**—Most sentences with the same sentence structure so there is little cadence **1**—All sentences with the same structure; halted reading
	Linking Words Use linking words (such as *because*, *and*, and *also*) to connect opinion and reasons.	**4**—Thoughtful use of transitions; sophisticated **3**—Some use of transitions	**2**—Weak use of transitions; repetition **1**—No transitions
Conventions	**Spelling** Apply spelling patterns when writing words; consult reference materials, including beginning dictionaries, to check and correct spelling.	**4**—Consistent use of correct spelling **3**—Mostly spells correctly	**2**—Weak command of spelling **1**—No sense of spelling or phonemic rules
	Grammar Writing using standard English grammar and usage	**4**—Consistent use of proper grammar **3**—Mostly uses grammar correctly	**2**—Weak grasp of grammar **1**—No sense of grammar rules
	Capitalization Capitalize names of book titles and people's names, and *I*.	**4**—Consistently capitalizes correctly **3**—Mostly capitalizes correctly	**2**—Weak capitalization **1**—No sense of what to capitalize
	Punctuation Use proper punctuation marks at end of sentences.	**4**—Consistently uses punctuation marks correctly **3**—Mostly uses punctuation marks correctly	**2**—Unclear about how to use punctuation marks **1**—No use of punctuation marks

Source: Adapted from Glass, 2012, pp. 114–115.

Figure 1.7: Opinion writing analytic rubric, elementary level.

Visit **go.SolutionTree.com/instruction** *for a free reproducible version of this figure.*

As stated earlier, rubrics include a descriptor about how students perform against each scoring criteria item. Since a comprehensive written piece comprises myriad items—such as dialogue, logical sequence of plot, setting, characters, and so forth for a narrative—students can use the rubric to ascertain to what degree they have met expectations for each one. Teachers, however, might need to communicate a single score based on the rubric. If this is the case, they can calculate the mode or median (see figure 1.8, page 22). As Susan M. Brookhart (2013) advises in such a situation, "If you do need one overall grade . . . and must summarize an assessment with one overall score, use the median *or* mode, *not* the mean, of the scores for each criterion" (p. 114).

Determine Median and Mode		
For illustrative purposes, a student earns these scores on eleven criteria items on a four-point scale: 2, 2, 4, 3, 4, 2, 3, 4, 3, 3, 1. Here is how to calculate the median and mode.		
Definition	**How to Do It**	**Example**
Median The middle value of a set of numbers	• Rewrite the list of numbers in order from smallest to largest. • Select the middle one. • If there is an odd number of items, the median is the middle entry after sorting the numbers in order. • If the list of numbers is even, calculate the median by adding the two middle numbers and dividing by two.	1, 2, 2, 2, 3, 3,(3,)3, 4, 4, 4
Mode The number in the list that is repeated more often than any other	• Rewrite the numbers in order. • Determine the number that is repeated most frequently. • There can be more than one mode.	1, 2, 2, 2,(3, 3, 3, 3,)4, 4, 4

Source: Glass, 2018, p. 45.

Figure 1.8: Process to determine median and mode.

Using Teacher-Created Targets and Scales and Implementing Routines for Using Them

Once teachers create the scales or rubric, they can generate a checklist to articulate the characteristics that students should include in their writing pieces (see figure 1.9 and figure 1.10, page 24, for a secondary and primary example). Although they lack a rubric's descriptions or a scale's learning targets for each level of performance, checklists can serve as a useful guide to students as they write because they detail the requirements of an assignment.

It is incumbent upon teachers to be transparent in their expectations. Preparing and presenting the criteria against which teachers will score students at the outset of writing readies them for achievement. For this purpose, teachers can conduct the activity we outline in What do you think you know? (element 15 in chapter 6, page 89) to introduce students to a proficiency scale, rubric, or checklist that articulates the writing goals. Doing so creates a sense of ownership as students move forward fully aware of what their teachers expect them to eventually produce. Plus, it paves the way for using these mechanisms as instructional tools formatively during each lesson in the unit. To this point, teachers routinely refer to specific items on the scale, checklist, or rubric to set the purpose for learning, constantly reminding students of a lesson's targeted goals. Because clearly defined learning goals are essential for designing any unit, lesson ideas within this book all emanate from these pieces. For example, students measure worked examples (element 9 in chapter 4, page 55)—student and published writing samples—against the criteria, and complete a revision sheet aligned to the criteria to self-assess and review a peer's writing against the expectations (element 18 in chapter 6, page 100).

Argument Student Writing Checklist

Directions: Use this checklist to guide you while responding to the following writing task.

_____

_____

Idea Development

☐ I show I'm aware of the **task, purpose,** and **audience**.

☐ I include a distinctive or original **title** to support my topic.

Introduction:

☐ My introduction **engages** readers and provides a **context** for my argument. ☐ I stake a **claim** for my argument by a clear **thesis statement** that begins with a subordinate clause.	☐ My argument is based on a **debatable topic** or issue.

Body paragraphs:

☐ Each topic sentence is a logical and valid **reason** that supports my argument and connects to the thesis. ☐ I support each reason with **relevant, accurate,** and **sufficient evidence** (such as facts, data, and examples) that is smoothly integrated into my paper. ☐ I use **multiple, credible sources** to collect evidence.	☐ I give proper attribution to my sources through **in-text citations**. ☐ I **interpret, analyze,** or **comment** about evidence to explain what it means in favor of my argument. ☐ I briefly **summarize** the main points of each paragraph.

Conclusion:

☐ I write a strong ending that is **not abrupt**. ☐ My conclusion **sums up** my most important points without exactly repeating the thesis.	☐ If appropriate, I suggest **solutions** or ways readers can **take action**. ☐ I include a **reflective ending**.

Counterargument:

☐ I **acknowledge** alternate or **opposing viewpoints**. ☐ I provide **a reason or reasons, evidence,** and **elaboration** for the weakness in the opposing view to further my argument.	☐ I devote a **body paragraph** to the counterargument or **weave** this text into other body paragraphs.

Organization

☐ I **organize** each paragraph in an order that promotes a convincing argument. ☐ The **evidence** within each paragraph is logically structured.	☐ I know when to begin a new **paragraph** and **indent** properly.

Language and Style

☐ I write in a **consistent point of view**. ☐ I establish and maintain a **formal style** appropriate for my task, purpose, and audience. ☐ I use a **reasonable tone** that shows I'm fair-minded and objective.	☐ I do not include **emotionally charged** words. ☐ I use **precise and accurate vocabulary**. ☐ If I use **repetition**, I do it for effect.

Figure 1.9: Argumentation writing checklist (secondary).

continued →

Argument Student Writing Checklist	
Transitions and Sentence Structure	
☐ I use appropriate and varied **transitional strategies** to link sections of my paper and create cohesion. ☐ I use appropriate **transitions between sentences** so my writing flows.	☐ I have **no run-ons or fragments**. ☐ My **sentences begin in different ways**. ☐ I use a **variety of sentence structures**.
Format, Grammar, and Conventions	
☐ I properly **format** my paper with a centered title, left and right margins, and a proper heading. ☐ If **typed**, I use Times New Roman or Arial twelve-point font, black type, and double spacing. If **handwritten**, I neatly write all words. ☐ I compile a **Works Cited page** and **format** it using MLA or APA style.	☐ I use correct **grammar** (such as active voice and consistent verb tense). ☐ I use correct **capitalization**. ☐ My **punctuation** is accurate including for quoted text and in-text citations. ☐ I **spell** all words correctly.

Source: Glass, 2017b, pp. 34–35.

*Visit **go.SolutionTree.com/instruction** for a free reproducible version of this figure.*

Opinion Writing Checklist, Primary
Why?
☐ I tell my **opinion**.   ☐ My **pictures match** my **words**.   ☐ I use the word *because*.   ☐ I retell **why** at the end.
Spelling
☐ I spell **sight words** correctly.   ☐ I **sound out words to help me spell**.
Punctuation
☐ I use **end marks**. . ? !   ☐ My **sentences begin** with an uppercase letter.   ☐ All **names begin** with an uppercase letter.   ☐ The **word I** is capitalized.
Penmanship/Neatness
☐ My handwriting is **neat**.   ☐ I use two-finger **spacing**.

Figure 1.10: Opinion writing checklist (primary).

*Visit **go.SolutionTree.com/instruction** for a free reproducible version of this figure.*

When teachers use scales or rubrics to identify what they want students to know and be able to do, it enables them to squarely focus learning. Utilizing them as instructional tools sets students up for success as expectations are well-defined and students can track their progress against clearly defined goals.

Element 2: Tracking Student Progress

With proficiency scales or rubrics in place, the teacher can help provide each student with a clear sense of where he or she started relative to a topic and where he or she is currently. Figure 1.11 presents the self-rating scale for element 2, tracking student progress.

Score	Description
4: Innovating	I engage in all behaviors at the Applying level. In addition, I identify those students who are not aware of what they must do to improve and design alternate activities and strategies to meet their specific needs.
3: Applying	I engage in activities to track student progress without significant errors or omissions and monitor the extent to which students are aware of what they must do to improve their current status.
2: Developing	I engage in activities to track student progress without significant errors or omissions.
1: Beginning	I engage in activities to track student progress but do so with errors or omissions, such as not keeping track of the progress of individual students and not making students aware of their individual progress.
0: Not Using	I do not engage in activities to track student progress.

Figure 1.11: Self-rating scale for element 2—Tracking student progress.

This section illustrates the following concrete examples for writing instruction associated with strategies about tracking progress. (For all the strategies related to this element, see figure A.1, page 156, in appendix A.)

- Designing assessments that generate formative scores
- Using different types of assessments

Designing Assessments That Generate Formative Scores

Using a proficiency scale or analytic rubric line item as a learning focus, teachers design formative assessments to gauge students' level of understanding. As a guide to generate them, teachers can implement a variety of instructional strategies from other elements featured throughout this book. For example, they can conduct a concept attainment activity (element 7, page 39) or ask students to write a summary or complete a graphic organizer (element 8, page 46). The detailed suggestions in chapter 3 (page 37) illustrate these particular strategies and how they can function well as formative assessments. As readers go through the book, they can consider other strategies that serve as effective opportunities to formatively assess students' progress and incorporate those strategies into their lessons.

Using Different Types of Assessments

Teachers can administer different types of formative assessments—unobtrusive, obtrusive, or student-generated—to check for students' understanding of targeted learning goals. Together these assessments formulate a picture and reflect student growth toward learning.

Unobtrusive assessments, as the name implies, do not interrupt the flow of a lesson as students barely, if at all, realize that teachers are assessing them. Informally and unobtrusively, teachers watch and listen for time on task, group work involvement, or students who are stuck and those speedily finishing a task. During whole-class discussion and interaction, teachers also pay attention to the quality of students' responses and their engagement levels. For specific examples, teachers can notice and gauge students at work, making entries on a recordkeeping sheet to inform future planning. For example, teachers might notice what parts of the text a student annotates, where a student places a prepared, labeled card on a student writing sample that indicates a characteristic of a genre (for example, *thesis*, *reason*, or *evidence*), a student's detailed drawing that reflects an author's sensory details about a character, or the organization of a student's notes while he or she listens to a lecture.

Obtrusive assessments are actions teachers take that interrupt an activity as students stop to participate or complete the task. Some are relatively quick and simple, for example, exit slips or cards (see element 19 in chapter 6, page 109) and active-participation activities such as hand signals or response cards (see element 24 in chapter 7, page 120). Others require more intense attention and investment of time for students to address either in or outside of class. After delivering formal instruction on a skill, process, or subject, teachers collect the work, assess it, provide feedback, input a score or notes, and plan next steps in instruction. Here are examples.

- After leading instruction about how to construct a sentence with parallel structure, the teacher asks students to practice finding examples in a complex text and write their own sentences with parallelism.
- To assess how well students know the characteristic elements of a genre, the teacher distributes sample papers and asks students to circle and label parts of the paper (for example, in a mystery identify *detective, suspect, clue,* and *red herring*). The teacher would also expect students to indicate those elements that are missing.
- The teacher instructs students to annotate a paper for an express purpose, such as highlighting instances of figurative language and interpreting the meaning. Or, students underline examples of evidence and annotate in the margin the degree to which each piece supports each reason.
- To determine understanding of content, the teacher asks students to draw a diagram of the digestive system and write an explanation about how it works.
- When targeting forms of verbs, the teacher provides students with a list of verbs to conjugate. Students then write sentences with proper grammar using the words.
- After instruction on a specific grammar or convention skill, students review a peer's paper and make corrections based on what they have learned. They use standard proofreaders' marks when editing (for further elaboration and a chart of proofreading marks, see chapter 6, page 89).

Using scales and rubrics as instructional tools allows students and teachers to track progress and celebrate student success, the focus of element 3.

Element 3: Celebrating Success

Once a strong system for tracking student progress is in place, the teacher and students have a great deal of rich information with which to celebrate success. Figure 1.12 presents the self-rating scale for this element.

Score	Description
4: Innovating	I engage in all behaviors at the Applying level. In addition, I identify those students who do not exhibit a sense of pride in their accomplishments and design alternate activities and strategies to meet their specific needs.
3: Applying	I engage in activities to celebrate students' success without significant errors or omissions and monitor the extent to which students have a sense of pride in their accomplishments.

Score	Description
2: Developing	I engage in activities to celebrate students' success without significant errors or omissions.
1: Beginning	I engage in activities to celebrate students' success but do so with errors or omissions, such as acknowledging students' status but not growth and not providing continual verbal encouragement.
0: Not Using	I do not engage in activities to celebrate students' success.

Figure 1.12: Self-rating scale for element 3—Celebrating success.

To instill a sense of pride in accomplishing goals, teachers orchestrate situations to celebrate students' success. At any moment when students do well or when they have exhibited growth along the way from one point to another on a proficiency scale or rubric, classmates and teachers can take notice verbally, in writing, or by other means, such as by ringing a bell, standing to snap fingers or applaud, or playing an upbeat current song and dancing to it. Teachers and students can do this for one student, a small group, or the whole class. When celebrating the whole class, teachers—with the help of students—can organize a get-together and invite parents or school administrators to attend. Students can even write about their own accomplishments in their gratitude journals to mark the occasion (see element 32, chapter 7, page 135).

When celebrating, cultivate a growth mindset (Dweck, 2006/2008) by encouraging students to celebrate the persistence, hard work, dedication, and risk taking that earned improved results for them. For example, a teacher might say, "I see you continued to work hard when the assignment got tough. That persistence seemed to pay off for you," "It's clear you got the hang of it by taking risks and learning from your mistakes," or "You showed that you can grow your intelligence through hard work." Comments about the preceding characteristics spur learning and contribute to achievement much more than those that focus on praise, such as "Good job," "Exactly right," "Superior work," or "You are one smart kid." In fact, research has shown that praise can discourage effort and produce a negative effect:

> After seven experiments with hundreds of children, we had some of the clearest findings I've ever seen: Praising children's intelligence harms their motivation and it harms their performance. . . . Yes, children love praise. They especially love to be praised for their intelligence and talent. It really does give them a boost, a special glow—but only for the moment. The minute they hit a snag, their confidence goes out the window and their motivation hits rock bottom. If success means they're smart, then failure means they're dumb. (Dweck, 2006/2008, p. 175)

Hattie and Yates (2014) state that "in teaching contexts, it is more responsible to increase informational feedback while going lean on praise. Students need clear indications that the worthwhile target they are harbouring is becoming real" (p. 68). Therefore, when celebrating success, teachers should judiciously measure their words to emphasize the process of achievement and effort—kudos for engagement, tenacity, and risk-taking—and concretely indicate where students have made growth in their learning goals.

GUIDING QUESTIONS FOR CURRICULUM DESIGN

When teachers engage in curriculum design, they consider this overarching question for communicating clear goals and objectives: *How will I communicate clear learning goals that help students understand the progression of knowledge I expect them to master and where they are along that progression?* Consider the following questions aligned to the elements in this chapter to guide your planning.

- **Element 1:** How will I design scales or rubrics?

  _____
  _____
  _____
  _____
  _____
  _____
  _____
  _____

- **Element 2:** How will I track student progress?

  _____
  _____
  _____
  _____
  _____
  _____
  _____
  _____

- **Element 3:** How will I celebrate success?

  _____
  _____
  _____
  _____
  _____
  _____
  _____

Conclusion

Effective feedback—the first of three overarching categories in this model—begins with clearly defined and articulated learning goals. When teachers make expectations transparent so that students understand what they are to learn within a lesson or unit, they can determine how well they are performing and what they need to do to improve. Once teachers focus on providing and communicating clear learning goals, they direct their attention to using effective assessments.

CHAPTER 2

Using Assessments

During writing instruction, some teachers use assessments only as evaluation tools to quantify students' current status relative to mastery of specific writing skills. While this is certainly a legitimate use of assessments, their primary purpose should be to provide students with feedback they can use to improve. When teachers use assessments to their full capacity, students understand how their test scores and grades relate to their status on specific progressions of knowledge and skill they are expected to master.

There are two elements within this category.

- **Element 4:** Using informal assessments of the whole class
- **Element 5:** Using formal assessments of individual students

Element 4: Using Informal Assessments of the Whole Class

Rather than formal assessments of individual students—the emphasis of element 5—the focus here is on informally assessing the whole class. This provides the teacher with a barometer of how students are progressing with specific skills along a continuum of growth to inform their instructional moves. Figure 2.1 presents the self-rating scale for this element so teachers can gauge their professional performance.

Score	Description
4: Innovating	I engage in all behaviors at the Applying level. In addition, I identify those students who are not using the whole-class feedback to set personal and group goals and design alternate activities and strategies to meet their specific needs.
3: Applying	I engage in activities to informally assess students without significant errors or omissions and monitor the extent to which students use the feedback to set personal and group goals.
2: Developing	I engage in activities to informally assess the class as a whole without significant errors or omissions.
1: Beginning	I engage in activities to informally assess the class as a whole but do so with errors or omissions, such as not focusing on content important to students' learning or not providing feedback regarding the class's status on specific progressions of knowledge.
0: Not Using	I do not engage in activities to informally assess the class as a whole.

Figure 2.1: Self-rating scale for element 4—Using informal assessments of the whole class.

Within this element, we show how teachers can directly apply the following specific strategies to the writing classroom.

- Voting techniques
- Response boards

As mentioned earlier, refer to figure A.1 in the appendix (page 156) for a complete listing of all strategies related to each of the forty-three elements.

Voting Techniques

Teachers can pose questions with multiple-choice responses, and students reply by using clickers or displaying fingers. Prompts are based on items in a proficiency scale, such as this one for example A in the list that follows: "Describe what types of details can act as evidence in a text" (Generating Claims, Evidence, and Reasoning 5 ELA, GCER2, 2.0; Simms, 2016).

There are innumerable options for using voting to informally check for understanding of skills related to writing. For example, teachers consider depth of knowledge (DOK) when crafting prompts to require a range of thinking. Examples A through C focus on recall whereas D and E exemplify more rigor.

- **Example A:** Which of the following is NOT a type of evidence?
    1. Quotes
    2. Facts
    3. Examples
    4. Reason
- **Example B:** Which is NOT a reason to start a new paragraph?
    1. Change the time or place.
    2. Introduce a new idea or topic.
    3. Insert evidence.
    4. Change dialogue between speakers.
- **Example C:** A dependent clause construction includes . . .
    1. Subordinating conjunction + subject + verb
    2. Coordinating conjunction + subject
    3. Preposition + subject
    4. Subject + verb + adverb
- **Example D:** Which sentence from Natalie Babbitt's (1975) *Tuck Everlasting* is a simile?
    1. "Disconnected thoughts presented themselves one by one" (p. 32).
    2. "The first week of August was reasserting itself after a good night's sleep" (p. 86).
    3. "I got a feeling [our secret] is going to come apart like wet bread" (p. 59).
    4. "The parlor came next, where the furniture, loose and sloping with age, was set about helter-skelter" (p. 51).
- **Example E:** What can you infer about the boy from this passage? *The filthy, unkempt ten-year-old boy ravenously devoured the meal with such eagerness that he attacked each morsel swiftly and clumsily. When finished, his plate looked as clean as if it had just been lifted from the dishwasher.*
    1. He loves food so much that he eats quickly.
    2. His home life is questionable since he is dirty and seems like he's starving.
    3. He ignores his appearance and has bad table manners.
    4. He might have been in an eating contest.

Voting techniques can also overlap with other elements. For example, asking students to vote using their fingers aligns with the hand-signal strategy (element 24, chapter 7, page 120). If teachers pose a series of questions that they phrase like examples A and B, the activity would be more akin to an academic game (see element 30, chapter 7, page 130), and we would classify it under the strategy "Which one doesn't belong?"

Response Boards

In this strategy, teachers can quickly ascertain students' degree of understanding or how they're applying a skill by posing a question or prompt that elicits a brief student response. For example, in an opinion paper, teachers can ask K–2 students, "What is your favorite farm animal in this book?" For upper elementary, "Write one reason for your opinion. Or, list one fact you will use in your paper." For older students, "Write a thesis statement for your argumentation essay that includes a subordinate clause to set up the claim."

Once teachers present the question or prompt, they allow sufficient time for each student or pair to write an answer on an erasable mini-whiteboard or chalkboard, type on an electronic device, or input their response on an app (such as www.padlet.com). When typing their responses, teachers tell students to add their names in parentheses so they can determine the originator of each contribution. As students write responses or enter them on a device, the teacher gathers input and clarifies as needed. As is true for all strategies, a targeted line item or items on a proficiency scale drive the focus.

Teachers can ask rudimentary questions, such as "What is the first step of the writing process?" "Where and when will your story take place?" or "What source will you first use to research your topic?" Here are other suggestions from the countless options that can support writing instruction.

- "Write a compound sentence that relates to the text we are reading."
- "Write a dependent clause. Circle the subordinating conjunction, and underline the verb."
- "Read the sentence on the board from our text and notice the pattern. Then write a sentence using this pattern." (For example, teachers can share a sentence that reflects parallel construction or one that includes dialogue or a speaker tag positioned in the middle of a sentence.)
- "What specific pronouns could you use if you write a piece from third (or first) person point of view?"
- "Write a sentence using proper mechanics of dialogue with a middle (or beginning or end) speaker tag. Write something that a character in your story would say."
- "Correctly format the book information that you see on the front board for a works cited document."
- "After listening to the article (speech, essay, or other), write the author's purpose."
- "I will say a title of a book (article, chapter, poem title, and so forth). Write it using proper conventions."
- "Write a personality trait for the protagonist (main character) in your story."
- "Draw a plot diagram for the narrative you plan to write."
- "Write a synonym for the word _____."
- "Draw a symbol or simple picture for the word _____."
- "What two things are being compared in the metaphor (or simile) I will read?"
- "Read the paragraph on the board. Which words show alliteration?"
- "Identify the rhyme scheme of the stanza you see on the front board."

Teachers can also use more formal assessments of individual students, as we discuss in the following section.

Element 5: Using Formal Assessments of Individual Students

To individually show evidence that students can demonstrate their understanding of an item or a set of related items on a proficiency scale, the teacher issues formal assessments. Figure 2.2 presents the self-rating scale teachers can utilize for this element.

Score	Description
4: Innovating	I engage in all behaviors at the Applying level. In addition, I identify those students who are not independently using their scores on these assessments as information with which to improve their learning and design alternate activities and strategies to meet their specific needs.
3: Applying	I engage in activities to formally assess individual students without significant errors or omissions and monitor the extent to which students are independently using their scores on these assessments as information with which to improve their learning.
2: Developing	I engage in activities to formally assess individual students without significant errors or omissions.
1: Beginning	I engage in activities to formally assess individual students but do so with errors or omissions, such as not using the information gained by these assessments to provide individual students with helpful feedback regarding how to improve.
0: Not Using	I do not engage in activities to formally assess individual students.

Figure 2.2: Self-rating scale for element 5—Using formal assessments of individual students.

To address this element, teachers might use the following strategies from the seven aligned to this element.

- Common assessments designed using proficiency scales
- Student demonstrations
- Student-generated assessments

Common Assessments Designed Using Proficiency Scales

Collaborative teams responsible for the same content at a particular grade level can devise common writing assessments around items on a proficiency scale, such as the following examples focused on generating text organization and structure at level 2.0.

- **Grades 9–10:** Write an introduction for a text that identifies the topic and thesis, previews the rest of the text, and summarizes the context for a reader.
  Assessment example: After reading Jane Austen's (1996) *Pride and Prejudice*, write an introduction for an argumentation essay in which you engage the reader, provide context, and stake a claim through a thesis statement.

- **Grade 5:** Generate a thesis statement that explains the focus of a text.
  Assessment example: After reading *Tuck Everlasting* by Natalie Babbitt (1975), write a thesis statement that provides your opinion to this guiding question—"Is Winnie right in deciding not to drink the water?"

- **Grade 2:** Draft a sentence that states a response's main idea or opinion using wording from a question or prompt.
  Assessment example: After reading *My Five Senses* by Aliki (2015), write your opinion about the sense you think is most important.

See the section Student-Designed Tasks in element 12, chapter 5 (page 72) for more comprehensive examples and support.

Student Demonstrations

Students can prepare presentations that demonstrate to teachers their level of understanding, plus teach their classmates in the process. This learning experience serves as a formative assessment as teachers listen and observe students engaging in the preparation and presentations. For example, teachers can focus on students' learning of skills associated with writing an opinion or argument. Secondary students can select a debatable topic (such as animal testing, the death penalty, or euthanasia) and then collect and review evidence from a site like ProCon.org or another reputable source. They present an example of key evidence along with accompanying commentary to show how it furthers their claim.

Elementary students read or listen to a picture book about a protagonist who asserts a position and goes about justifying it. They prepare a presentation to demonstrate to teachers how they can identify an opinion and support it. Here are some titles teachers can use for this purpose.

- *Animals Should Definitely Not Wear Clothing* by Judi Barrett (1970)
- *Earrings!* by Judith Viorst (1990)
- *I Wanna New Room* by Karen Kaufman Orloff (2010)
- *I Wanna Iguana* by Karen Kaufman Orloff (2004)
- *I Want a Dog!* by Helga Bansch (2009)
- *A Pig Parade Is a Terrible Idea* by Michael Ian Black (2010)
- *The Perfect Pet* by Margie Palatini (2003)
- *Red Is Best* by Kathy Stinson (1982)

Student-Generated Assessments

Teachers can invite students to propose ways to provide evidence of their understanding. The choices are endless. Students might suggest completing a graphic organizer that shows the causes and effects of a relationship among characters or write a paragraph that explains this association. They can write a self-reflection, draw and explain a diagram or model they create, or write and perform a monologue. In studying allusion in preparation for incorporating it into a written piece, students might annotate a text that includes allusion or discuss and record a conversation with a partner about the presence of this literary device. They can write about the degree to which they feel they are mastering a skill and explain what more they need to do to be fully proficient. Or, they can score their written work on a rubric and compare it to what the teacher has scored. By looking at the discrepancy, they can determine what support they need to improve their paper.

GUIDING QUESTIONS FOR CURRICULUM DESIGN

This overarching question can guide teachers when using assessments: *How will I design and administer assessments that help students understand how their test scores and grades are related to their status on the progression of knowledge I expect them to master?* Consider the following questions aligned to the elements in this chapter to guide your planning.

- **Element 4:** How will I informally assess the whole class?

_____

_____

_____

_____

_____

_____

_____

_____

_____

_____

_____

_____

_____

- **Element 5:** How will I formally assess individual students?

_____

_____

_____

_____

_____

_____

_____

_____

_____

_____

_____

_____

_____

Conclusion

Assessments are feedback tools for both students and teachers. Used well, they serve as instructional and evaluation mechanisms by offering students information about how to advance their understanding of content and providing teachers a vehicle for assisting students to do so. By informally assessing the whole class and formally assessing individual students in various ways, teachers can support students in this progression of knowledge. To master new content, teachers design and deliver direct instruction lessons as explained in the subsequent chapter.

PART II
Content

CHAPTER 3

Conducting Direct Instruction Lessons

Students benefit greatly from direct instruction on new content. This type of instruction commonly suffers from the perception that it is straight presentation in lecture format. This is far from the truth. As this chapter illustrates, direct instruction has a number of essential components that teachers can deliver in a wide variety of ways. Regardless of the specific strategies that a teacher uses, the net effect of direct instruction should be that students understand the key parts of the new content and how together they form a unified whole.

This teacher action includes the following elements.

- **Element 6:** Chunking content
- **Element 7:** Processing content
- **Element 8:** Recording and representing content

Element 6: Chunking Content

Learning new information can be overwhelming; however, breaking it down into manageable increments can facilitate student learning. Figure 3.1 presents the self-rating scale for teachers to use.

Score	Description
4: Innovating	I engage in all behaviors at the Applying level. In addition, I identify those students for whom the chunking process is not helping them understand the content and design alternate activities and strategies to meet their specific needs.
3: Applying	I engage in activities to chunk content when presenting new information without significant errors or omissions *and* monitor the extent to which the chunking process is helping students understand the new content.
2: Developing	I engage in activities to chunk content when presenting new information without significant errors or omissions.
1: Beginning	I engage in activities to chunk content presenting new information but do so with errors or omissions, such as not breaking the new content into small enough chunks that students can easily process or breaking content into chunks that are too small.
0: Not Using	I do not engage in activities to chunk new content when presenting new information.

Figure 3.1: Self-rating scale for element 6—Chunking content.

In this section, we specifically highlight these strategies.

- Using preassessment data to plan for chunks
- Allowing for processing time between chunks

Using Preassessment Data to Plan for Chunks

When introducing new content and information—whether through reading complex text, listening to a speech or video, watching a demonstration, or another way—dividing it into manageable parts offers advantages. By conducting a preassessment, teachers can use the data they collect about students' prior knowledge to help determine how to chunk the material. If teachers learn that students are somewhat familiar with the information, the amount of content they present at a time can be larger than if it is uncharted territory, in which case smaller sections suffice.

To illustrate, consider figurative language, which includes simile, metaphor, hyperbole, personification, and imagery (or sensory details). Figures 3.2 (secondary), 3.3 (upper elementary), and 3.4 (elementary, page 40) show examples of formal preassessments that can reveal to what degree students can identify, interpret, and write using forms of figurative language. Teachers can also issue informal preassessments to gauge students' understanding which can inform how teachers divide new learning into manageable parts, for example, telling students that they will write a research paper and asking them to discuss with teachers how they will conduct and document research.

Figurative Language Preassessment, Secondary	
1. **Annotate:** Read Anthony Doerr's (2014) passage from *All the Light We Cannot See* and underline one or two examples of figurative language that he uses. In the Notes column, provide an interpretation of what you underline including the name of the type or types of figurative language.	
Text	**Notes**
There are cadets who do everything right—perfect posture, expert marksmanship, boots polished so perfectly that they reflect clouds. There are cadets who have skin like butter and irises like sapphires and ultra-fine networks of blue veins laced across the backs of their hands. For now, though, beneath the whip of the administration, they are all the same, all Jungmänner. They hustle through the gates together, gulp fried eggs in the refectory together, march across the quadrangle, perform roll call, salute the colors, shoot rifles, run, bathe, and suffer together. They are each a mound of clay, and the potter that is the portly, shiny-faced commandant is throwing four hundred identical pots.	
2. **Write using figurative language:** Write a paragraph using at least two examples of figurative language that continues to describe the cadets and their experience. Underline each example of figurative language that you craft.	

Source: Doerr, 2014, p. 139.

Figure 3.2: Secondary figurative language preassessment.

*Visit **go.SolutionTree.com/instruction** for a free reproducible version of this figure.*

Figurative Language Preassessment, Upper Elementary	
1. **Annotate:** Read the passage and underline one or two examples of figurative language that author Pam Muñoz Ryan (2000) uses in her book *Esperanza Rising*. In the Notes column, provide an explanation of what you underline including the name of the type or types of figurative language.	
Text	**Notes**

Esperanza smoothed her dress and knelt down. Then, like a caterpillar, she slowly inched flat next to him, their faces looking at each other. The warm sun pressed on one of Esperanza's cheeks and the warm earth on the other.
    She giggled.
    "Shhh," he said. "You can only feel the earth's heartbeat when you are still and quiet."
    She swallowed her laughter and after a moment said, "I can't hear it, Papi."	

2. **Write using figurative language:** Write a paragraph using at least two examples of figurative language that continues to describe Esperanza's feelings and actions. Underline each example of figurative language that you craft.	

Source: Ryan, 2000, p. 2.

Figure 3.3: Upper elementary figurative language preassessment.

Visit **go.SolutionTree.com/instruction** *for a free reproducible version of this figure.*

Armed with the information gleaned from the preassessment, teachers can aptly divide the content into sections based on students' readiness for the new material. For instance, teachers can split a complex text rich in targeted figurative techniques into parts based on the interpretive depth required and the length of these passages.

Allowing for Processing Time Between Chunks

Once teachers collect and review preassessment data, they design structured learning experiences for students to work together to process chunks of information. To do so, they organize students into groups and stop at strategic points to engage them in a collaborative exercise designed for them to keenly study each segment of material. For instance, in the previous example about figurative language, teachers can introduce each type one at a time and ask students to define, identify, and interpret examples. They also go deeper by analyzing an author's use of figurative language, interpret passages that include a combination of forms, and eventually write their own passages incorporating intentional figurative language for an express purpose.

In a direct instruction lesson, teaching something rather large and breaking it into manageable parts increases the likelihood that students will retain and apply the targeted skills. However, doing that alone will not contribute to success. Teachers must also help students process content.

Element 7: Processing Content

When students pause between chunks as previously described, teachers must create opportunities for students to process each part to help ensure that they understand and effectively use what they have learned. If teachers forego dedicated situations to engage students in meaningful activities that help them analyze and process the material, they shortchange students' learning. Figure 3.5 (page 41) presents the self-rating scale to guide teachers in implementing this element.

Figurative Language Preassessment, Elementary

1. Draw a picture for each of these sentences from the book *Swimmy* by Leo Lionni (1991).

Swimmy saw a lobster, who walked about like a water-moving machine.	Swimmy saw sea anemones, who looked like pink palm trees swaying in the wind.

2. Circle the words in the two sentences that are the same and that show a pattern. Write your own sentence using this pattern and draw a picture for it.

Your sentence:	Your picture:

Source: Lionni, 1991.

Figure 3.4: Elementary figurative language preassessment.

Visit go.SolutionTree.com/instruction for a free reproducible version of this figure.

Score	Description
4: Innovating	I engage in all behaviors at the Applying level. In addition, I identify those students who are not using the processes to better understand the content and design alternate activities and strategies to meet their specific needs.
3: Applying	Along with adequate guidance and support, I engage students in activities that help them process new information by making predictions, summarizing, and asking clarifying questions and monitor the extent to which students are using the processes to better understand the content.
2: Developing	I engage students in activities that help them process new information by making predictions, summarizing, and asking clarifying questions and provide adequate guidance and support.
1: Beginning	I engage students in activities that help them process new information by making predictions, summarizing, and asking clarifying questions but do not provide adequate guidance and support, such as modeling the use of these processes and providing students with adequate time to engage in these processes.
0: Not Using	I do not engage students in activities that help them process new information by making predictions, summarizing, and asking clarifying questions.

Figure 3.5: Self-rating scale for element 7—Processing content.

It is imperative to employ effective strategies so students can aptly process and internalize the material to facilitate their understanding. In this section, we focus on these strategies relevant to this element.

- Perspective analysis and thinking hats
- Concept attainment

Perspective Analysis and Thinking Hats

Two strategies—perspective analysis and thinking hats (de Bono, 1985/1999)—afford students the opportunity to thoughtfully examine all sides of an issue, topic, idea, character, or individual as a vehicle to foster deeper understanding. These strategies are effective when students read all sorts of complex texts while accumulating information and researching for writing tasks. Specifically, students can access either technique when identifying and examining their own and others' viewpoints and their ramifications for an opinion or argumentative paper. Even though younger students in earlier grades do not include counterarguments, they still need to determine a debatable topic that has a contrary viewpoint, so recognizing others' perspectives is a prudent goal. The prewriting stage, when students gather research, is a good time to introduce one or both of these strategies in an opinion or argument unit.

Perspective analysis allows students to process information by identifying different vantage points plus concrete examples. It entails five steps with corresponding questions that form the structure teachers can follow when designing tasks. See figure 3.6 (page 42) for elementary, upper elementary, and secondary examples. Notice that the grade cluster examples emanate from the Process Steps column, which teachers use as a guide to create the age-appropriate tasks.

Teachers can organize thinking hats, featured in figure 3.7 (page 43), by color, whereby each represents a different aspect of an issue, problem, or topic that students need to explore. Like the Process Steps column in figure 3.6, the Description column in this figure helps teachers devise their question tasks. The column Addressing a Problem can be used for students to look at all sides of an issue they personally face and write about them in a journal. They can also share their impressions with others to assist them in a resolution. This column can also be adapted to help students develop a character for a story they will write. For example,

Perspective Analysis Examples			
Process Steps	**Elementary** (Turn Taking)	**Upper Elementary** (American Revolution)	**Secondary** (Prose or Poetry)
1. Identify your position on a controversial topic. **What do I believe about this topic?**	What do I believe about following rules such as taking turns?	What do I believe about the Loyalists' (Tories') position during the American Revolution?	What do I believe about expressing personal feelings through poetry versus prose?
2. Determine the reasoning behind your position. **Why do I believe that?**	Why do I believe in taking turns?	Why do I believe in the Loyalists' viewpoint?	Why do I believe poetry can convey feelings better than prose?
3. Identify the opposing position or positions. **What is another way of looking at this topic?**	What happens when people don't take turns?	What was the position of the Patriots during the American Revolution?	What are other written options for conveying feelings besides poetry?
4. Describe the reasoning behind the opposing position. **Why might someone else hold a different opinion?**	Is there a reason someone might not take turns?	Why did the Loyalists, Patriots, and Neutralists believe in their causes?	Why might a writer prefer to express personal feelings in genres of prose?
5. When you are finished, summarize what you have learned. **What have I learned about this topic?**	What have I learned about taking turns?	What have I learned about the opposing sides during the American Revolution?	What have I learned about written options for communicating personal feelings?

Figure 3.6: Perspective analysis examples.

*Visit **go.SolutionTree.com/instruction** for a free reproducible version of this figure.*

"What are the facts about a problem you face?" can be revised to read "What are the facts about a problem the protagonist faces?"

For elementary students, not all questions will apply, so delete those that may not align to a particular topic or aren't grade appropriate. For instance, when using this strategy to juxtapose the presence and absence of classroom rules, teachers can ask, "What are the rules of our classroom?" (white), "What can happen if someone doesn't follow this rule: _____?" (black), and "What classroom rule might we need to change and why?" (green). Although students process the new information by imagining themselves wearing any one of the six thinking hats, teachers can certainly convert this strategy by creating tangible colored hats for this activity. For example, teachers of elementary students can say, "Let's put our green thinking hat on now."

As students participate in perspective analysis or thinking hats, they can work individually or in small groups. Each group can focus on the same or different subjects and respond to all questions, or the same subject and focus on different questions. After they broaden their understanding of the content, teachers can encourage them to share and compare their responses with classmates. Additionally, students can access either strategy to scrutinize a published or student-written sample of an opinion or argumentation essay to determine if the author provides sufficient evidence of his or her position as well as address and acknowledge opposing claims.

Thinking Hats		
Description	**Examples**	
	Addressing a Problem	**Determining a Position**
1. **White (Facts):** Facts and details; neutral and objective perspectives—What are the facts about . . . ?	What are the facts about a problem you face?	What are the facts about using animals for scientific or commercial testing?
2. **Black (Cautions):** Cautious or careful perspectives—What are the negatives about . . . ? What doesn't work or could go wrong?	What could go wrong if you choose to . . . ?	What are the negatives about using animals for scientific or commercial testing? What do opponents believe?
3. **Yellow (Benefits):** Optimistic perspectives—What are the positives or benefits about . . . or what will people gain from . . . ?	What are the advantages if you choose to . . . ?	What are the positives about animal testing? What do proponents say?
4. **Red (Emotions):** Emotional perspectives and feelings—How does . . . make . . . feel?	How would it make you feel if you . . . ?	How do I feel about animal testing?
5. **Green (Creative Ideas):** Imaginative thinking and creative perspectives—What could be changed to make . . . more accessible or appealing? What are alternatives?	What are your choices or alternatives?	What could be changed to make animal testing more acceptable?
6. **Blue (Conclusions):** Reflection and metacognition; organizational perspectives—How does . . . have an impact on . . . ?	How will your decision have an impact on others?	How does animal testing have an impact on people?

Figure 3.7: Thinking hats.

Visit **go.SolutionTree.com/instruction** *for a free reproducible version of this figure.*

Concept Attainment

In concept attainment, teachers orchestrate a situation in which students productively struggle to process content. Like many other strategies, teachers can use it across disciplines. When focusing on writing skills, teachers can use concept attainment to help students recognize an author's purpose for writing, distinguish formal from informal style, learn mechanics rules for treating titles and dialogue, identify types of figurative language or parts of speech, ascertain types of evidence used in an opinion or argument, and myriad other options. This section presents steps that teachers can use to lead a pair or small-group concept attainment exercise for teaching content, skills, or strategies.

To personalize the steps of this strategy, we geared the featured example toward teaching parallelism for upper elementary and secondary students. For elementary students, teachers can focus on simplistic parallel construction, including items in a series, and alter the steps accordingly.

Parallelism, as the term denotes, is a sentence with a parallel—or balanced—structure that contains a series or pair of elements that are grammatically similar, such as words (adjectives, nouns, and so forth), phrases, or clauses. Authors use this technique in literary works as well as informational texts for a variety of reasons. For example, they use it to repair ungrammatical (or maintain grammatical) construction, as a rhetorical device when they intend repetition for effect and emphasis, to create rhythm and cadence, or to compare or contrast ideas. We've underlined and bolded the sentence parts that exemplify this skill in the following examples.

- "He hardly got the words out before Father **jumped over to the man**, **jerked him out of his chair** and **pushed him through the door** into the mud of the street." (Collier & Collier, 1984, p. 39)
- "And if there isn't anything else to do, there's **scrubbing the floors** and **washing the windows** and **keeping everything clear** generally." (Collier & Collier, 1984, p. 41)
- "Rabbits come out of the brush to sit on the sand in the evening, and the damp flats are covered **with the night tracks of 'coons**, and **with spread pads of dogs from the ranches**, and **with split-wedge tracks of deer** that come to drink in the dark." (Steinbeck, 1965)

Elementary students can detect the pattern and try to emulate it, as in these examples from *Kitten's First Full Moon* by Kevin Henkes (2006).

- "So she **closed her eyes** and **stretched her neck** and **opened her mouth** and **licked**."
- "So she **pulled herself together** and **wiggled her bottom** and **sprang from the top step of the porch**."
- "But Kitten only tumbled—**bumping her nose** and **banging her ear** and **pinching her tail**."

Here are the six steps for leading a concept attainment exercise related to parallelism. It is important to note, however, that teachers lead exercises around the content of the complex text prior to diving into grammar in isolation. Essentially, students read the text first for different purposes, such as to analyze a literary device, use evidence to justify a character's perspective, or interpret a passage. They then return to the text to study an author's craft, for example, how authors construct sentences and the effect of their technique. Teachers can use these concept attainment steps as is for a parallelism exercise or adapt them for a different purpose.

1. **Examine and group a set of common items:** Provide each small group with a set of text excerpts to sort into two piles. Instruct students to read all the excerpts and notice which ones share something in common regarding sentence structure. Explain that at the end of this first part of the exercise, they will have a group of like items and another group of random excerpts that belong in their own pile of nonexamples. After some minutes of productively struggling, mention to groups that need a hint that they are looking for sentences that contain a pattern of some sort. It is best to use actual excerpts from a complex text that is the center of instruction. Figure 3.8 shows excerpts from *My Brother Sam Is Dead* (Collier & Collier, 1984) and figure 3.9 from *Of Mice and Men* (Steinbeck, 1965).

2. **Identify the specific attributes of this grouped set:** Instruct students to focus only on the sentences they grouped together and make a list of their common attributes, or distinguishing characteristics. When finished, each student group shares these features to compile a class list. Verify that the items on the class-generated list are all examples of *parallel structure,* or *parallelism.* Continue to use this term so students become familiar with it. In figure 3.8, the first eight strips include parallelism; in figure 3.9 the first seven are examples.

3. **Provide a definition:** Together with their small group, ask students to define *parallelism* by carefully reviewing the examples from the grouped set and the list of attributes. Students share the definition with the class to arrive at a consensus. They might record the attributes and definition in a student journal or academic notebook.

4. **Create another example:** Students review the items in the grouped set, their list of attributes, and the definition to help them construct new examples. Teachers might ask students to create parallelism examples based on the complex text they are reading to check for understanding both of this skill and of the content of the reading material.

5. **Find and critique examples:** Direct students to a source, such as a literary text, textbook, print or digital article, or website to find examples of parallelism. In their groups, instruct them to discuss and critique the effect these examples have on the writing passages in which they appear, then share their observations with the class.

6. **Apply the skill:** Ask students to independently practice applying the skill of parallelism within their own argumentation essay, literary critique, realistic fiction, creation myth, or other piece of writing.

Once teachers divide sections of content and engage students in orchestrated activities to analyze and process each increment, element 8 comes into play.

My Brother Sam Is Dead Excerpts
He tripped on a headstone and the farmer fell off and broke his neck and was dead a minute later.
So finally he had to stop; and we finished up the service, and I breathed a sigh of relief and got up and started to file toward the stairs.
Covering the poles were hides and rags and . . . patches of straw thatch.
He hardly got the words out before Father jumped over to the man, jerked him out of his chair and pushed him through the door.
Running a farm is terrible hard work—plowing and hoeing and milking cows.
Carefully I slid my hand down the barrel until I got to the stock, gripped it, and gave it a little pull.
Sam was bigger and stronger and faster than me.
Then suddenly he waved, jumped down from the wall, and disappeared into the woodlot.
At first I thought he would come in a few days, but he didn't.
The geese flew south in long, wavering V's.
The door to the taproom was mostly closed, but there was a crack where it was hinged onto the wall.
My father wasn't around, and Mother said, "Tim will bring it right over, Mr. Heron."

Figure 3.8: Parallelism activity (upper elementary).

*Visit **go.SolutionTree.com/instruction** for a free reproducible version of this figure.*

Of Mice and Men Excerpts
Rabbits come out of the brush to sit on the sand in the evening, and the damp flats are covered with the night tracks of 'coons, and with spread pads of dogs from the ranches, and with split-wedge tracks of deer that come to drink in the dark.
He took off his hat and wiped the sweat-band with his forefinger and snapped the moisture off.
His huge companion dropped his blankets and flung himself down and drank from the surface of the green pool.
Then he replaced his hat, pushed himself back from the river, drew up his knees and embraced them.
He pushed himself back, drew up his knees, embraced them, looked over to George to see whether he had it just right.
A big carp rose to the surface of the pool, gulped air and then sank mysteriously into the dark water again, leaving widening rings on the water.
Lennie hesitated, backed away, looked wildly at the brush line as though he contemplated running for his freedom.
In a moment Lennie came crashing back through the brush.
Immediately Lennie got up and did the same with his bed.
The boss stepped into the room with the short, quick steps of a fat-legged man.
Lennie cried out suddenly—"I don't like this place, George. This ain't no good place. I wanna get outa here."

Figure 3.9: Parallelism activity (secondary).

*Visit **go.SolutionTree.com/instruction** for a free reproducible version of this figure.*

Element 8: Recording and Representing Content

This element of direct instruction asks that students have an opportunity to record and represent the new content in ways that are personally meaningful. They do so linguistically and nonlinguistically. Figure 3.10 presents the self-rating scale for this element.

Score	Description
4: Innovating	I engage in all behaviors at the Applying level. In addition, I identify those students for whom the process does not help them discover and remember new distinctions they have made about the content and design alternate activities and strategies to meet their specific needs.
3: Applying	Along with adequate guidance and support, I engage students in activities that help them record and represent their thinking regarding new content and monitor students to ensure that their actions help them discover and remember new distinctions they have made about the content.
2: Developing	I engage students in activities that help them record and represent their thinking regarding new content and provide adequate guidance and support.
1: Beginning	I engage students in activities that help them record and represent their thinking regarding new content but do not provide adequate guidance and support, such as allowing and encouraging students to record and represent their thinking in ways that are most comfortable for them individually, modeling the different ways to record and represent their thinking, and providing adequate time to record and represent their thinking.
0: Not Using	I do not engage students in activities that help them record and represent their thinking regarding new content.

Figure 3.10: Self-rating scale for element 8—Recording and representing content.

This section provides specific examples geared toward teaching writing for these strategies within element 8.

- Summaries
- Graphic organizers
- Academic notebooks
- Mnemonic devices

Summaries

Summarizing is a key comprehension strategy that helps readers understand and remember a text. It's an effective critical thinking exercise requiring students to identify the core of an author's work and succinctly write about it. Students can summarize the whole text or topics within a larger work. They might write a simplistic one-paragraph summary that includes a topic sentence and supporting details or a lengthier multiple-paragraph summary.

In longer works, proficient readers can summarize sections at a time; collectively these interval summaries help to formulate the overall essence of a text. For any length of text students encounter, writing a summary contributes to comprehension on a deeper level as they encode the information in their own words to help anchor the content. A more formal summary includes the following points.

> A Traditional Summary . . .
>
> - Is a type of expository writing
> - Identifies the author and title that are the basis for the summary
> - Includes the main idea and key supporting details written in a reader's own words
> - Shows what readers glean from any printed text, audio, or video (or part of it) to demonstrate understanding and inform others

Summaries can be in different formats and are not always traditional. Sometimes teachers migh[t] [stu]dents to write a one sentence or a limited word summary, which can be deceptively challenging.

Teachers can even ask students to fashion a summary using a template like the one in figure 3.11 [...] for a fictional piece. It includes an example based on R. J. Palacio's (2012) *Wonder*. Teachers from [...] Intermediate School in Arkansas created it to use as a model for their students. The template's fo[rm...] be adapted for a summary of a nonfiction text to reflect a historical figure or an individual. In t[h...] students focus on key events in lines five, six, and seven. For a narrative, students should include [...] climax in one of these lines.

Template

Formula
Line 1: Write the character or individual.
Line 2: Write two words describing the character or individual.
Line 3: Write three words describing the setting.
Line 4: Write four words stating the central conflict.*
Line 5: Write five words associated with one event in the narrative.*
Line 6: Write six words associated with a second event.*
Line 7: Write seven words associated with a third event.*
Line 8: Write eight words associated with the solution to the central conflict or the theme.*

Example
Auggie
Courageous humorous
Beecher Prep home camp
August attends Beecher Prep.
August overhears Jack dismiss friendship.
Classmates defend August from camp bullies.
Auggie earns award; friendship and appreciation abound.
Inner character reveals one's essence rather than appearances.

* Or a ____-word sentence—for example, "Write a six-word sentence describing a second event."

Source: Adapted from Glass, 2018.

Figure 3.11: Story summary template and example: *Wonder*.

*Visit **go.SolutionTree.com/instruction** for a free reproducible version of this figure.*

Additionally, poetry can effectively capture the main idea and details of a text, such as with an acrostic poem in which each line begins with a significant letter in order to spell a word vertically. This key word or term is also an opportunity to represent the main idea.

Teachers might also share a summary pattern and ask students to emulate it as in Margaret Wise Brown's (1977) *The Important Book*. Each page of this picture book features a topic; the main idea of each one appears at the beginning and repeats in the last line of the stanza with details in between. The following poem is written in the style of Brown.

> The important thing
>
> about a leaf is that it is green.
>
> It blows in the wind, and is shiny,
>
> with a smooth, glossy texture
>
> But the important thing about a leaf
>
> is that it is green.

Teachers can create a template for elementary students for Brown's picture book. Add more lines for the details based on students' readiness levels, and provide word labels, if needed. Although older students can dispense with a template, they can still use this book's pattern based on subtopics of a larger topic or concept. For example, summarize the different planets by stating what is important about each, causes of a conflict that led to a war, or significant aspects in a novel (for example, what is important about a particular character, setting, event, or use of a literary device or figurative language). In the following template, students can repeat the middle sentence several times to capture key details.

> The important thing about _____ is that it is _____.
>
> It _____ and _____.
>
> But the important thing about _____ is that it is _____.

Graphic Organizers

Graphic organizers are an excellent strategy for recording and representing content. Not only can students use them to summarize text, demonstrate knowledge, organize what they learn, and make sense of material, but they have also long served as an effective strategy during the writing process. For example, when students conduct research in the prewriting stage, they can create an outline to organize their notes either electronically or by hand. They can fashion a plot diagram to map out their storyline for realistic fiction or a mystery. In science, they can record the causes and effects during a lab demonstration or one they conduct themselves. Additionally, teachers should create learning experiences using graphic organizers that help students recognize text structures, specifically these common ones: compare-contrast, problem-solution, cause-effect, sequence, and description. In doing so, students can better grasp the content, plus emulate a text structure in their own writing. Figure 3.12 features a list of online tools for finding and downloading graphic organizers for different purposes.

Graphic Organizers
• BrainPOP Educators (https://bit.ly/2xbYMeX)
• edHelper.com (www.edhelper.com/teachers/graphic_organizers.htm)
• Education Oasis (www.educationoasis.com)
• everythingESL.net (www.everythingesl.net/inservices/graphic_organizers.php)
• Freeology (http://freeology.com/graphicorgs)
• Houghton Mifflin Harcourt Education Place (www.eduplace.com/graphicorganizer)
• Teacher Files.com (www.teacherfiles.com/resources_organizers.htm)
• TeacherVision (www.teachervision.com)
• Teachnology (www.teach-nology.com/web_tools/graphic_org)

Figure 3.12: Graphic organizers.

Visit **go.SolutionTree.com/instruction** *for a free reproducible version of this figure.*

Academic Notebooks

During direct instruction lessons, students keep academic notebooks—either a traditional version with handwritten entries or one they create electronically. In them, they record notes of new information both linguistically and nonlinguistically to catalog what they have learned and need to remember and organize the material into sections. When students express themselves nonlinguistically, they can create graphic representations, physical models, pictures, pictographs, or other expressions tied to visual imagery or kinesthetic modes. Here are some examples of entries they can make to support and enhance their understanding of writing.

- **Vocabulary lists:** As they encounter unknown words when reading complex text, students log new vocabulary. Each word should include a nonlinguistic representation (such as illustrations or symbols) and a combination of any of these: example, nonexample, explanation, definition, synonym, antonym, part of speech, and sentence. Students devise an organizational system for the words to help them retain and apply them orally and in their writing. For example, students can categorize or color-code words by part of speech; words for personality traits, like *industrious*, *accomplished*, or *evil*; alternatives to the word *said*; or sensory words.

- **Genre characteristics and expectations:** As students learn to write in different genres throughout the year, teachers expose them to the genres' characteristic elements and structure. Teachers should also provide rubrics and checklists to reveal expectations of what the finished written product should entail. Students can house these criteria pieces in their academic notebooks with accompanying published and student samples that exemplify stellar writing.

- **Sentence patterns:** After receiving instruction on various sentence patterns—for example, compound and compound-complex—students record the construction of each type, input authors' examples, and draft their own varied sentences for practice and reference.

- **Grammar, conventions, and formatting:** Grammar and mechanics (or conventions) rules can be entries in an academic notebook. Students use what they learn and record as a writing reference, such as dialogue punctuation, treatment for titles, or ways to use a comma. They might also include relevant guidelines from MLA or APA, for example, how to properly format in-text citations and works cited documents, plus protocols dictated by a department, school, or district (such as headings, papers, margins, and so forth).

- **Bookmarks:** Teachers tell students who use electronic devices to add bookmarks that support their writing in any category, such as websites for vocabulary, resources for grammar or proper formatting, a literary devices glossary, writing samples, and so forth. If students have a hard copy academic notebook, they can reference these electronic resources.

Teachers encourage students to regularly revisit their academic notebooks to make adjustments or additions as they refine their thinking or consider new ideas or examples for existing entries. Element 18 in chapter 6 (page 100) explicitly addresses these actions. To accommodate these changes, for those not using an electronic device, we suggest a three-ring binder.

Mnemonic Devices

Mnemonic—or memory—devices can be an effective technique for information retention. People of all ages can use and even invent their own mnemonic devices for various situations in and out of school. This can involve reciting information that should be remembered by singing it to a familiar tune like "Mary Had a Little Lamb," using acronyms such as HOMES to recall the Great Lakes (Huron, Ontario, Michigan, Erie, and Superior), or inventing a sentence where the first letter of each word triggers something that needs remembering. For example, in mathematics, this familiar sentence helps people recall the order of solving algebraic operations: *Please excuse my dear Aunt Sally* (parenthesis, exponents, multiplication, division, addition, subtraction). When one author, Kathy Glass, moved to San Francisco, she developed a mnemonic device to remember the order of various streets: *Gray old ladies buy wide full skirts* stood for Gough, Octavia, Laguna, Buchanan, Webster, Fillmore, and Steiner streets. Incidentally, many confuse the meaning of acronyms, which occur when the first letters of several words together form their own new word, like HOMES discussed earlier, OPEC, NATO, STEAM, or scuba. When people use the first letter and say each one—like FBI or IRS—we do not technically call it an acronym (but rather *initialism*).

Other mnemonic devices can serve as useful retention techniques. Songs can support people's memory of information, such as this one for determining how many days in each month: "Thirty days hath September, April, June, and November . . . all the rest have thirty-one except for February. . . ." Jingles can also activate recall, like how to tighten or loosen a jar—*righty tighty, lefty loosey*—or for daylight saving time adjustment—*spring forward, fall back*.

There is value in using this strategy for areas of writing, such as helping with spelling rules: *i* before *e* except after *c*. <u>D</u>inner <u>MINTS</u> can help with what to capitalize—days of the week, months of the year, the pronoun *I*, names, titles, and starts of sentences. The acronym *fanboys* represents the beginning letter of coordinating conjunctions that can form compound sentences by combining simple sentences for fluency and to avoid run-on sentences: *for, and, nor, but, or, yet*, and *so*. Table 3.1 identifies these conjunctions and the purpose for each.

Table 3.1: Coordinating Conjunctions

for, so	Shows a cause-effect relationship
and	Joins things or ideas that are alike or similar; implies a continuation of thought
nor	Continues a negative thought
but, yet	Shows a contrasting relationship
or	Indicates a choice between things or ideas

Teaching mnemonic devices helps students remember content that they use to advance their learning. For example, once students recall *fanboys*, they can apply what they have come to know about coordinating conjunctions to devise compound sentences. For elementary students, simple and compound sentences that include *and* and *but* will prepare them for future grades when they will use more sophisticated coordinating conjunctions like *yet* and *for*. Students will ultimately progress to detect and use complex and compound-complex sentences by incorporating subordinating conjunctions (for example, *when, since, while, even though,* and *until*) to construct dependent clauses.

- **Compound sentences** combine two independent clauses (or simple sentences). This can be done in one of two ways: (1) with a comma and a coordinating conjunction or (2) with a semicolon.
- **Complex sentences** include one dependent and one independent clause.
- **Compound-complex** sentences include two or more independent clauses and one or more dependent clauses.

Here are activity ideas to embed in lessons about sentence patterns and conjunctions. When students compose their own work, teachers can tell them that a criteria item is to write using sentence variety, and these exercises can prepare them for this goal. Teachers can use these guiding questions to set the purpose for learning, "How does sentence variety contribute to fluency and rhythm? How can you apply this strategy to your own writing?"

- **Scavenger hunt:** Ask students to find examples in print or online text (from magazines, independent reading books, newspapers, mentor texts, and so forth) of sentence variety and identify each type—simple, compound, complex, or compound-complex.
- **Combine sentences:** Give each student an index card with various simple sentences from a familiar text. For older elementary students, add dependent clauses. Instruct students to combine the cards to form compound, complex, and compound-complex sentences. Have them compare their sentences with each other and then with the author's original work. Discuss and justify which sentences are stronger—those students invented or those the author wrote.
- **Manipulatives:** Type parts of sentences—independent and dependent clauses—onto different cards, and make word labels of coordinating or subordinating conjunctions like the following example for a compound sentence.

she chose the perfect gift for him	and	he appreciated the kind gesture

Place the clauses and conjunctions in an envelope so there are enough to distribute to each small group. Add elbow macaroni to use as commas and dried beans for periods; students can stack beans over macaroni to make semicolons. Instruct groups to formulate compound, complex, and compound-complex sentences using the cards, conjunction labels, and punctuation items. Teachers can use excerpts from the text they are reading at the center of instruction. For an activity around compound sentences, teachers can visit **go.SolutionTree.com/instruction** to download and use figures 3.13 (elementary, page 52), 3.14 (upper elementary, page 52), and 3.15 (secondary, page 53). In these examples, we purposefully omitted some punctuation marks and uppercase letters so students can think more critically about the placement of a clause. In sharing with their classmates, students might discover that they have switched the order but the sentence still works. When students agree on a well-formulated sentence, they can discuss proper use of mechanics. Present the formula for each sentence pattern prior to this activity, or ask students to determine it after constructing sentences. They can enter each sentence pattern and an example in their academic notebooks.

Compound Sentence Excerpts From *Charlotte's Web* by E. B. White (1952/1980)		
then Mr. Zuckerman leaned lazily on the fence	and	Mr. Zuckerman scratched Wilbur's back with a stick
she saw him from the kitchen window	and	she immediately shouted for the men
the cocker spaniel heard the commotion	and	he ran out from the barn to join the chase
he tried to follow the instructions his friends were giving him	but	he couldn't run downhill and uphill at the same time
it was still only about four o'clock	but	Wilbur was ready for bed
his back itched	so	he leaned against the fence and rubbed against the boards
then he pulled the loose board away from the fence	so	there was a wide hole for Wilbur to walk through

Source: White, 1952/1980.

Figure 3.13: Compound sentence examples (elementary).

*Visit **go.SolutionTree.com/instruction** for a free reproducible version of this figure.*

Excerpts From *Tuck Everlasting* by Natalie Babbitt (1975)		
she might not have noticed it	for	it looked more like a mushroom than a living creature sitting there
a pair of green suspenders, more decorative than useful, gave the finishing touch	for	he was shoeless
her mother's voice, the feel of home, receded for the moment	and	her thoughts turned forward
"Where's the child?" he demanded	for	Winnie was hidden behind his wife
"The bed's no better	or	I'd switch with you," he said
he didn't seem to know how to finish the conversation	but	then he bent and kissed her quickly on the cheek
there wasn't time to wonder	for	at that moment someone knocked at the door
his face was without expression	but	there was something unpleasant behind it that Winnie sensed at once
something made her instantly suspicious	yet	his voice was mild

Source: Adapted from Babbitt, 1975.

Figure 3.14: Sentence examples (upper elementary).

*Visit **go.SolutionTree.com/instruction** for a free reproducible version of this figure.*

Excerpts From *Of Mice and Men* by John Steinbeck (1965)		
the water is warm too	for	it has slipped twinkling over the yellow sands in the sunlight before reaching the narrow pool
both men glanced up	for	the rectangle of sunshine in the doorway was cut off
he paused and looked toward the open door	for	the horses were moving restlessly and the halter chains clinked

Excerpts From *Of Mice and Men* by John Steinbeck (1965)		
rabbits come out of the brush to sit on the sand in the evening	and	the damp flats are covered with the night tracks of 'coons, and with the spread pads of dogs from the ranches
they had walked in single file down the path	and	even in the open one stayed behind the other
Lennie looked startled	and	then in embarrassment he hid his face against his knees
far off toward the highway a man shouted something	and	another man shouted back
"A guy on a ranch don't never listen	nor	he don't ast no questions."
"We run. They was lookin' for us	but	they didn't catch us."
George said coldly, "You gonna give me that mouse	or	do I have to sock you?"
Lennie dabbled his big paw in the water and wiggled his fingers	so	the water arose in little splashes
George said, "Say it over to yourself, Lennie	so	you won't forget it."
in front of the low horizontal limb of a giant syc-amore there is an ash pile made by many fires	;	the limb is worn smooth by men who have sat on it
Lennie's hands remained at his sides	;	he was too frightened to defend himself

Source: Steinbeck, 1965.

Figure 3.15: Sentence examples (secondary).

*Visit **go.SolutionTree.com/instruction** for a free reproducible version of this figure.*

GUIDING QUESTIONS FOR CURRICULUM DESIGN

This design question pertains to conducting direct instruction lessons: *When content is new, how will I design and deliver direct instruction lessons that help students understand which parts are important and how the parts fit together?* Consider the following questions aligned to the elements in this chapter to guide your planning.

- **Element 6:** How will I chunk the new content into short, digestible bites?

_____

_____

_____

_____

_____

_____

- **Element 7:** How will I help students process the individual chunks and the content as a whole?

_____

_____

_____

_____

_____

_____

_____

- **Element 8:** How will I help students record and represent their knowledge?

_____

_____

_____

_____

_____

_____

Conclusion

Within the second major category of this model—content—teachers effectively use strategies within four design areas in an intentionally coordinated way to help students learn the information and skills at the center of instruction. As mentioned in the introduction, these design areas include direct instruction, practicing and deepening, and knowledge application lessons, plus strategies applicable to all types of lessons. Direct instruction, the focus for this chapter, is essential when teachers introduce new learning to students whether it be a new skill, process, strategy, or content information. Teachers then design and conduct lessons that allow students to practice and deepen their understanding of the new learning.

CHAPTER 4

Conducting Practicing and Deepening Lessons

Practicing and deepening strategies are different for procedural and declarative knowledge. This is a very important distinction to keep in mind when considering the use of specific instructional strategies. *Procedural knowledge* involves large comprehensive processes and the basic skills and tactics that are the components of the larger processes. Certainly, writing qualifies as an example. While we can describe the overall phases of writing, the process includes many embedded skills and strategies like brainstorming for ideas, revising for overall logic and attention to word choice, editing for correct spelling and punctuation, and the like. Students must practice procedural knowledge to the point where they can execute fluently and without significant error.

Declarative knowledge is informational in nature. It involves details such as facts and terminology, but also more broad information about generalizations, principles, and concepts. Subject areas like history largely comprise declarative knowledge because they involve learning about people, events, concepts, and generalizations. However, even procedural topics contain a fair amount of declarative knowledge. For example, to effectively engage in the writing process, students must understand appropriate ways to cite sources, information about types of narrative and expository structures, characteristic elements of specific genres, and so on. We must practice procedural knowledge, while we must deepen our declarative knowledge.

These elements pertain to practicing and deepening lessons.

- **Element 9:** Using structured practice sessions
- **Element 10:** Examining similarities and differences
- **Element 11:** Examining errors in reasoning

Element 9: Using Structured Practice Sessions

Students need to practice procedural knowledge. Therefore, teachers should plan and conduct learning situations for students to practice the new skill, process, or procedure so they can apply it autonomously in a novel way. Figure 4.1, page 56, presents the self-rating scale to guide teachers in addressing this element.

Score	Description
4: Innovating	I engage in all behaviors at the Applying level. In addition, I identify those students who are not systematically developing fluency and accuracy and design alternate activities and strategies to meet their specific needs.
3: Applying	I engage in activities that provide students with structured practice sessions without significant errors or omissions and monitor the extent to which students are systematically developing fluency and accuracy.
2: Developing	I engage in activities that provide students with structured practice sessions without significant errors or omissions.
1: Beginning	I engage in activities that provide students with structured practice sessions but do so with errors or omissions, such as assigning independent practice for which students are not adequately prepared and not providing enough practice over time.
0: Not Using	I do not engage in activities that provide students with structured practice sessions.

Figure 4.1: Self-rating scale for element 9—Using structured practice sessions.

We focus specifically on the following strategies aligned to this element that represent ways teachers can assist students in honing procedural knowledge.

- Modeling
- Guided practice
- Worked examples

Modeling

Figure 4.2 details how teachers might model a lesson involving writing a description. It includes the think-aloud strategy, which teachers use to orally communicate to students what they are thinking. By doing so, teachers speak out loud to reveal what is going on in their brains as they work so students can emulate this thought process. We use the following learning progressions related to narrative text—likely included in standards documents at various grades—for illustrative purposes to show modeling and guided practice in action.

- Generate a list of descriptive details about a character.
- Use sensory language to describe a character.

If teachers need an example of what to draft during modeling, they can review the student samples in figure 4.3 (page 58) for inspiration. (The modeling centers on one trait; whereas, most samples include more than one trait per character.) In guided practice, which teachers conduct after the modeling session, we discuss activity options using these samples.

Think Aloud (What the Teacher Says)	Modeling (What the Teacher Does)
Preview the task. The task is to write a paragraph with sensory details about my protagonist that I'll eventually incorporate into my story. My goal is to write so descriptively that the personality trait I assign to this character is implied rather than stated directly. Before I can begin, I need to refer to the assignment sheet, which outlines these three steps. 1. Identify traits for my protagonist that reflect how he or she develops throughout the story. Choose one as the focus for this task. 2. Brainstorm a list of detailed phrases like actions, thoughts, and emotions that support the trait. Later, I can repeat this exercise to reflect other traits my character exhibits as he or she changes throughout my story. 3. Draft a character sketch using these phrases to vividly describe my character at some point in the plot.	• Prepare in advance an assignment sheet on a handout or electronic device and distribute or transmit it to students. • While thinking aloud, point to the associated parts of the task. Highlight or circle important words or phrases of the task.
First, I brainstorm traits for my protagonist that I can express as adjectives. If the word can fit into this construct, then I know it's an adjective: The very _____ man. Let's see, *courageous, honorable, appreciative, free-spirited, gracious, supportive.* They all fit, so I need to select one that matches the pro-tagonist I want to create at some point in the story.	• Write "the very _____ man" for students to see. Ask them to turn and talk with each other to provide other traits to engage them and check for understanding. • Make a T-chart. Label the left column *Traits* and the right column *Support.* • Enter personality traits in the *Traits* column. Circle one that appeals to the protagonist and will be the focus for modeling.
Next, I create supporting phrases to show this trait. I want to include imagery, so I must rely on words that appeal to the senses. I don't necessarily need to use all five, but I should be mindful of them. Also, I may want to include other forms of figurative language like simile or metaphor. [The teacher might recite the definitions of imagery, simile, and metaphor.]	• Write phrases that are appropriate for the tar-geted trait in the *Support* column. Use imag-ery and other forms of figurative language as appropriate. • When inventing phrases, say aloud: What would a _____ (enter the trait) person do? • Invite students to turn and talk about other examples. Call on a few volunteers to share; add their phrases to the T-chart.
Finally, I use the support that I brainstormed to draft a character sketch based on the trait. I need to avoid using the character trait in my paragraph. Therefore, my details need to be descriptive enough that some-one can infer the trait based on my writing. I'm going to review all the entries and circle those that I think are most descriptive. I'll determine which phrases I want to circle based on those that create visuals in my head as I read them. Now that I've circled several, I need to figure out an order that makes sense. (*Teacher explains rationale for order.*) Okay, I'm ready to draft my paragraph using this order and adding transitions to make it flow.	• Read and circle phrases from the *Support* entries in the T-chart that are particularly descriptive because they foster mental images. • Number the phrases in a logical order. • Use these phrases to draft a descriptive paragraph that includes transitions.

Figure 4.2: Modeling example.

*Visit **go.SolutionTree.com/instruction** for a free reproducible version of this figure.*

Guided Practice

In preparation for writing their own character sketches, students engage in one of the following guided practice activities. As an optional activity focusing on word choice, students can revisit figure 4.3 and revise each draft to eliminate the overuse and redundancy of pronouns.

- **Option 1:** In pairs, students critique the teacher's draft from the modeling exercise. They can share their impressions with another pair, then report out to the whole class.
- **Option 2:** Teachers arrange students in pairs or trios and distribute a student draft of a protagonist or antagonist from a row in figure 4.3. Together, they read, discuss, and revise the draft to better capture one of the intended traits, then pass their comments to another group to enter comments or revisions.
- **Option 3:** Teachers distribute one student draft from a row in figure 4.3 to pairs who color code each trait, such as *graceful* in yellow and *elegant* in pink. They then find phrases that describe each trait and use the same color to show the accompanying support. The teacher invites students to revise or write additional supporting details on the student sample to better reflect one of the identified traits.

Personality Traits	Support	Character Sketch
Elegant **Graceful** **Confident**	• Gliding with perfect rhythm • Elegance and superiority of a model • Linger as if to enchant • Dazzling light that danced on face • Glistening and reflecting light	When Cassandra passed by, she seemed to glide as if ice skating with the poise and superiority of a model strutting with long legs down a runway. Behind her, the scent of a light and natural smelling perfume would linger and enchant others. The beguiling scent would coax anyone to run after her and get the chance to meet her. Her gentle face glowed as if there were a dazzling light dancing upon her face. The winter fairy had given her intelligent blue eyes, and they glistened and reflected light with every intentional movement.
Outgoing **Assertive** **Independent**	• Caught every ray of light • Vivid teal-blue eyes • Assurance and pride • Relaxed and sure of himself • Uncommon sense of independence	Malcolm had a great sense of humor. He was able to cajole the most unpleasant, malcontent person to break into a smile and start rolling around on the floor like a pig in a nest of mud. The young man's sandy-blonde hair caught every ray of light, and it radiated. His pale face was obviously a great gift from the snow king and it made his extraordinary vivid teal-blue eyes jump out of his face. He walked with a sense of assurance and pride. He smiled freely and it made people feel that they were known, lifting many a load off their weary shoulders. He was always relaxed and sure of himself, and he contained an uncommon amount of independence which really showed off in the way he dressed.
Hostile	• Stentorian, thunderous voice • Heavy breathing fills the air • Beady eyes search the room • Violently pounds the table	As his thick eyebrows lower in fury, his stentorian voice raises over everyone else's in the room. His heavy breathing fills the air and his beady eyes search the room until everyone is silent. His thunderous voice begins the lecture, and he gesticulates with his arms to show his anger. He violently pounds the table he is standing by, and it shakes unsteadily. The audience trembles with fear as he storms out of the room muttering words of profanity under his breath.

Personality Traits	Support	Character Sketch
Loving **Innocent**	• Sparking blue eyes twinkle with delight • Hugs her leg in a childlike way • Hands stained brown with dirt • Mouth is stretched into a loving smile	As he raises his hand and offers the brightly colored array of flowers to his mother, I can see the huge grin he is trying to hold back. His sparkling blue eyes twinkle with delight when he sees the pleasure he has brought to her. In a loving gesture, he hugs her leg in a childlike way. He happily brushes back his scraggly hair with a hand that is tainted brown with dirt and then wraps his chubby arm back around her knee. His eyes raise to meet hers and his mouth is stretched into a loving smile. He murmurs a soft "I love you, Mommy," and she replies, "I love you, too, sweetheart."

Figure 4.3: Student character sketches.

*Visit **go.SolutionTree.com/instruction** for a free reproducible version of this figure.*

Worked Examples

When learning a new skill or process, it is helpful to see correct and strong examples. Student athletes or amateurs watch demonstration tapes to study the strategies and maneuvers of experienced professionals who play their sport adeptly. Scientists watch other experts in their field conduct a laboratory experiment and examine each step carefully so they can replicate it. So, too, do writers benefit from examining the work of authors who have mastered the skill or process well. The strategy of worked examples fulfills this purpose. It involves students reading and critiquing student and published exemplary writing samples to see a clear picture of what works well to positively direct and influence their own writing.

There are myriad skills specific to each writing type or genre—as well as general writing habits—that students learn and incorporate into their products. In a narrative, for example, students need to develop a plot, build suspense, use methods of characterization, invent imagery to devise a setting, and more. For a research report, students conduct research, write a thesis, organize ideas, display information on charts or graphs, and so on. For general writing, students combine sentences; signal a new paragraph; use transitions to create rhythm, indicate shifts in time and place, and connect ideas; provide a context for reading; and so forth. Individual skills or a set of aligned skills create opportunities for learning experiences that should include worked examples—exemplary student and published samples. Not only should teachers feature these model samples, they should also incorporate mediocre and weak versions into their instruction. By doing so, they can encourage students to juxtapose them with quality work to clearly articulate and pinpoint the differences to determine what to forego and qualities they aim to emulate in their own writing.

To guide students in using these worked examples in the classroom, teachers conduct lessons to sharpen their proficiencies around skills that focus instruction. The teacher vets and finds myriad writing samples of papers in which the author performs the skill (or set of related skills) well and those that are weak or nonexistent. Student pairs or small groups can sort papers based on the presence or absence of the skill or rank them from strongest to weakest. They can also critique a section or the whole writing sample against a proficiency scale or a rubric to determine levels of performance based on the criteria descriptors and compare their impressions. As well, students can use the writing checklist to determine which characteristics are present or omitted (see element 1, chapter 1, page 11). Teachers ask students to provide textual evidence to defend their sorting, ranking, and scoring and make clear the quality aspects of the worked examples.

Resources for Student and Published Writing Samples

These resources can help teachers search and find the appropriate writing samples to embed within an instructional program. This first list includes various collections of student work. Peruse them carefully to identify worked examples (exemplary) and those that fall short to determine how selected papers can be used for teaching purposes. Visit **go.SolutionTree.com/instruction** for live links to these resources.

- **Achieve the Core's Student Writing Samples** (http://achievethecore.org/category /330/student-writing-samples)

- **Brown's Student Learning Tools** (www.mesacc.edu/%7Epaoih30491/Argument SampleEssays.html)

- **Common Core State Standards for English Language Arts and Literacy in History/Social Studies, Science, and Technical Subjects: Appendix C— Samples of Student Writing** (www.corestandards.org/assets/Appendix_C.pdf)

- **Holt, Rinehart and Winston's Holt Online Essay Scoring—Writing Prompts** (https://my.hrw.com/support/hos/host_models_list_Fall_2006 .html#MSExpository)

- **Literacy Design Collaborative's Student Work Samples** (for scientific research papers) (https://coretools.ldc.org/mods/b8b888e2-e0f7-484d-a5b7-6bb6a27de747)

- *New York Times's* **The Learning Network Editorial Contest Winners** (http:// learning.blogs.nytimes.com/2015/08/26/announcing-our-2015-16-student -contest-calendar *and* http://learning.blogs.nytimes.com/tag/editorial-winner)

- **Oregon Department of Education's Writing Scored Student Work and Writing Work Samples**
  - Grades 3–8 (www.oregon.gov/ode/educator-resources/assessment/Pages /Writing-Scored-Student-Work.aspx)
  - High School (www.oregon.gov/ode/educator-resources/essentialskills/Pages /Writing-Work-Sample-Tasks.aspx)

- **Roane State Community College Sample Essays for Narrative and Descriptive Writing** (www.roanestate.edu/owl/Describe.html)

- **Teachers College Reading and Writing Project (TCRWP): Student Writing** (http://pfaulconer.staging.readingandwritingproject.com/resources/student-work)

- **Teen Ink** (www.teenink.com/Contests/Winners1516)

- **Thoughtful Learning** (https://k12.thoughtfullearning.com/resources/studentmodels)

Teachers can also use published writing as work samples for students to critique and examine based on a particular purpose for learning. Review any of the following resources to find the right text—or even a passage within a longer work.

- **Ebooks:** Access these websites to find free ebooks to download.
  - **Project Gutenberg** (www.gutenberg.org)
  - **East of the Web** (www.eastoftheweb.com/short-stories/indexframe.html)
  - **The Literature Network** (www.online-literature.com)
  - **Fullreads** (http://fullreads.com/literature)
  - **Gleeditions** (www.gleeditions.com/collections-titles.html)

- *Hippocampus Magazine* (www.hippocampusmagazine.com)

- **The Moth** (https://themoth.org/stories)

- **The *New York Times Magazine*'s "Lives" section** (http://goo.gl/vM9R3P)

- **ProCon.org** (www.procon.org)

- *The Sun* (http://thesunmagazine.org)

The category of conducting practicing and deepening lessons includes element 10 which contributes to students developing knowledge.

Element 10: Examining Similarities and Differences

Taking a critical look at the similarities and differences of two items related to procedural or declarative knowledge deepens students' understanding. For example, students can compare and contrast purposes for writing, text structures, phrases and clauses, or types of irony. Figure 4.4 presents the self-rating scale for this element.

Score	Description
4: Innovating	I engage in all behaviors at the Applying level. In addition, I identify those students who are not gaining new and deeper insights into the content they compare and design alternate activities and strategies to meet their specific needs.
3: Applying	Along with adequate guidance and support, I engage students in activities that help them identify similarities and differences in content and monitor students to ensure that they gain new and deeper insights into the content they compare.
2: Developing	I engage students in activities that help them identify similarities and differences in content and provide adequate guidance and support.
1: Beginning	I engage students in activities that help them identify similarities and differences in content but do not provide adequate guidance and support, such as ensuring that students identity important attributes on which to compare content and ensuring that students accurately identify the extent to which elements possess the identified attributes.
0: Not Using	I do not engage students in activities that help them identify similarities and differences in content.

Figure 4.4: Self-rating scale for element 10—Examining similarities and differences.

Teachers can implement the following strategies to create learning opportunities for students with regard to this element. After students engage in any activity using one of these strategies, teachers emphasize the similarities and differences between the topics as the basis for the exercise.

- Sentence-stem comparisons
- Summaries, Venn diagrams, and T-charts
- Sorting, matching, and categorizing

Sentence-Stem Comparisons

Thinking carefully about the similarities and differences between aspects of writing skills helps prepare students for their own writing projects. Consider these examples.

- Similes and metaphors are similar because _____. They are different because _____.
- Complex sentences are similar to compound-complex sentences because _____. They are different because _____.
- Memoirs and personal narratives are similar because _____. They are different in this way: _____.
- Myths and legends share these similarities: _____. They are different because _____.
- A thesis statement and topic sentence are similar because _____. They are different because _____.
- Periods and exclamation marks are similar because _____. They are different because _____.

Summaries, Venn Diagrams, and T-Charts

Students can create summary tables, Venn diagrams, or T-charts to identify the similarities and differences between two objects, ideas, events, people, characters, or topics. These strategies work well when students decipher and internalize reading material by comparing and contrasting—for example, two characters, historical events, religions, biomes, or economies. They can even juxtapose objects like two different sculptures, baking products, or woodworking projects. Or, students can examine the distinction between narrative genres, text structures, sentence types, poetry formats, or punctuation marks.

Summaries within the context of this element are three-column tables. Students list attributes specific to topic A in the first column and those of topic B in the third. They reserve the middle column for a list of similarities common to both entities along with a summary statement. A Venn diagram represents a different graphic organizer with a similar purpose. Instead of a table format, students format this organizer in two overlapping circles. The intersecting portion of the two circles contains information about the similarities between two topics, which is the function of the middle column in a summary table. Where the circles do not intersect, students record characteristics unique to each topic. In a T-chart, students input the comparison items as the subheading for each column, like *science fiction* and *historical fiction* or *persuasive essay* and *argumentation*. They enter the details that describe each topic within the columns. When finished, they review, assess, and discuss their lists to determine the similarities and differences between the two items. Students can also highlight what is specific about two opposing topics by writing a diamante poem. After they complete it, teachers can ask students to identify the similarities, as well. (See the formula and example in figure 4.5.)

Sorting, Matching, and Categorizing

Teachers can prepare picture or word cards, sentence strips, paragraphs, objects, or other elements like punctuation marks for students to sort, match, or categorize. They can match two items or sort various items into predetermined groups. When categorizing, students group elements into two or more sets and identify the name of the category, for example, written on sticky notes, and their reasoning for grouping them together.

The list that follows details some of the many opportunities for implementing this strategy. The sorting examples ask that students provide category titles, which makes the exercise more challenging. However, teachers can furnish prepared titles, and students sort the items accordingly. Teachers do not necessarily conduct them with cards or other items that students manipulate tactilely on desks, tables, or the floor. Teachers can also distribute cards and lead a kinesthetic activity whereby students walk around the classroom and find their partner or group.

- Match titles of short stories with associated themes.
- Match character profiles or descriptions with their types (for example, *dynamic, static, round, flat,* and so on).
- Match a cause with an effect, such as events in a narrative.
- Match a sentence (void of a period, exclamation point, or question mark) with the proper end punctuation mark.
- Match a word with its synonym, a word with a picture or symbol, a word with an example, and so forth.
- Match a thesis statement with its type of claim, such as *factual, definitional, claims of value,* and so on (see element 14 in chapter 5—generating and defending claims, page 82).
- Sort text excerpts into groups that share the same method of characterization and provide a title for each category (such as what a character does, what a character says, what others say about the character, and so on).

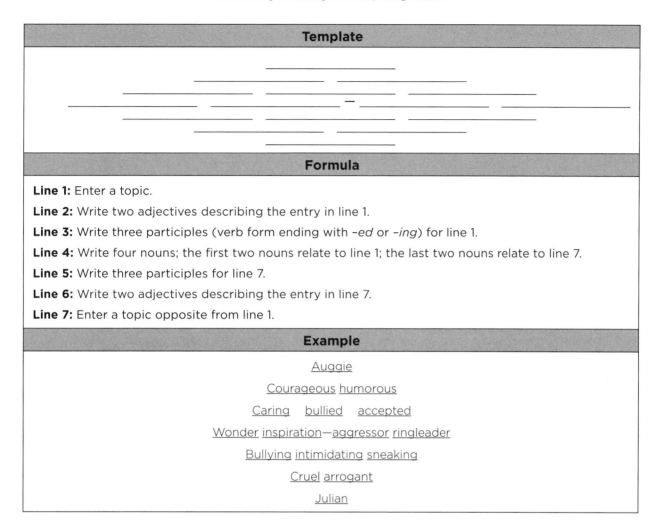

Template

Formula

Line 1: Enter a topic.

Line 2: Write two adjectives describing the entry in line 1.

Line 3: Write three participles (verb form ending with *–ed* or *–ing*) for line 1.

Line 4: Write four nouns; the first two nouns relate to line 1; the last two nouns relate to line 7.

Line 5: Write three participles for line 7.

Line 6: Write two adjectives describing the entry in line 7.

Line 7: Enter a topic opposite from line 1.

Example

Auggie

Courageous humorous

Caring   bullied   accepted

Wonder inspiration—aggressor ringleader

Bullying intimidating sneaking

Cruel arrogant

Julian

Source: Adapted from Glass, 2018.

Figure 4.5: Diamante template and example: *Wonder*.

*Visit **go.SolutionTree.com/instruction** for a free reproducible version of this figure.*

- Sort sample paragraphs according to a similar purpose for writing and provide a category title (for example, to inform, to explain, or to describe).
- Sort worked examples by text structure and identify the name of each structure (for example, cause and effect or problem and solution).
- Sort student samples that are weak in supporting an argument and identify the types of errors, such as errors of faulty logic or weak reference (see element 11 in the upcoming section on page 65).
- Sort words by part of speech and provide the category title.

Targeting fluid writing to promote cadence, teachers can use the categorizing strategy as students focus on beginning sentences in different ways, such as with a dependent clause, adjective, prepositional phrase, and so forth. To lead such an activity, teachers prepare sentences with different beginnings from familiar classroom texts like those in figure 4.6 (page 64)—sentences from E. B. White's (1952/1980) *Charlotte's Web*—or figure 4.7 (page 64)—excerpts from Shirley Jackson's (1948) short story "The Lottery." They cut off the answers in the left column, place a collection of sentence strips in an envelope to make a set, and distribute one set to each pair or small group. Then, teachers provide these directions: "Empty and read the sentences in the envelope. Sort them by grouping together sentences that begin in the same way. Name the way sentences in each group begin, if you can, and explain your reasoning."

Type of Beginning	Sentence Excerpt
Common Noun	The barn was very large.
	The goose took command and began to give orders.
	The sheep soon got to know her and trust her.
	Pigs need warmth, and it was warm and comfortable down there in the barn cellar on the south side.
	The board gave way.
Pronoun	It was very old.
	It smelled of hay and it smelled of manure.
	She found an old milking stool that had been discarded, and she placed the stool in the sheepfold next to Wilbur's pen.
	He put his head down, shut his eyes, and pushed.
	They will never-never-never catch you in the woods.
Proper Noun	Wilbur looked through the fence and saw the goose standing there.
	Mrs. Zuckerman screamed at Lurvy.
	Mr. Zuckerman knew that a manure pile is a good place to keep a young pig.
	Fern came almost every day to visit him.

Source: White, 1952/1980.

Figure 4.6: Sorting exercise sentence excerpts 1.

*Visit **go.SolutionTree.com/instruction** for a free reproducible version of this figure.*

Type of Beginning	Sentence Excerpt
Dependent Clause	Although the villagers had forgotten the ritual and lost the original black box, they still remembered to use stones.
	When he arrived in the square, carrying the black wooden box, there was a murmur of conversation among the villagers.
	Although Mr. Summers and everyone else in the village knew the answer perfectly well, it was the business of the official of the lottery to ask such questions formally.
Common Noun	The women, wearing faded house dresses and sweaters, came shortly after their menfolk.
	The morning of June 27th was clear and sunny, with the fresh warmth of a full-summer day.
	A tall boy in the crowd raised his hand.
	School was recently over for the summer, and the feeling of liberty sat uneasily on most of them.
	Chips of wood, Mr. Summers had argued, had been all very well when the village was tiny.

continued →

Type of Beginning	Sentence Excerpt (continued)
Pronoun	They stood together, away from the pile of stones in the corner, and their jokes were quiet and they smiled rather than laughed.
	His father spoke up sharply, and Bobby came quickly and took his place between his father and his oldest brother.
	He was a round-faced, jovial man and he ran the coal business, and people were sorry for him because he had no children and his wife was a scold.
	She tapped Mrs. Delacroix on the arm as a farewell and began to make her way through the crowd.
	It had a black spot on it, the black spot Mr. Summers had made the night before with the heavy pencil in the coal company office.
Proper Noun	Bobby Martin ducked under his mother's grasping hand and ran, laughing, back to the pile of stones.
	Mr. Summers spoke frequently to the villagers about making a new box, but no one liked to upset even as much tradition as was represented by the black box.
	Mrs. Hutchinson craned her neck to see through the crowd and found her husband and children standing near the front.

Source: Jackson, 1948.

Figure 4.7: Sorting exercise sentence excerpts 2.

Visit go.SolutionTree.com/instruction for a free reproducible version of this figure.

After the sorting exercise, teachers lead a discussion and verify or provide the types of ways sentences can begin using the proper terminology. Next, they focus on teaching each kind of construction to increase students' ability to use sentence variety in their writing.

In the next element, students examine errors in reasoning.

Element 11: Examining Errors in Reasoning

When students thoughtfully examine their own logic or the information teachers impart to them, they deepen their understanding of content. Figure 4.8 presents the self-rating scale for this element so teachers are better equipped to determine how they can support students to examine potential errors in reasoning.

Score	Description
4: Innovating	I engage in all behaviors at the Applying level. In addition, I identify those students who are not recognizing errors in their own thinking or that of others and those who are taking steps to rectify those errors and design alternate activities and strategies to meet students' specific needs.
3: Applying	Along with adequate guidance and support, I engage students in activities that help them examine errors in reasoning and monitor students to ensure that they recognize errors in their own thinking or that of others and take steps to rectify these errors.
2: Developing	I engage students in activities that help them examine errors in reasoning and provide adequate guidance and support.
1: Beginning	I engage students in activities that help them examine errors in reasoning but do not provide adequate guidance and support, such as explicitly teaching common types of errors in reasoning and providing practice in identifying such errors.
0: Not Using	I do not engage students in activities that help them examine errors in reasoning.

Figure 4.8: Self-rating scale for element 11—Examining errors in reasoning.

The following strategies present a wide array of options for teachers to aid students in examining their own or others' errors in reasoning. In the first section under this element, we focus on the following strategies to support teaching students how to write an argument or speech.

- Identifying errors of faulty logic
- Identifying errors of attack
- Identifying errors of weak reference
- Identifying errors of misinformation
- Finding errors in the media
- Examining support for claims
- Judging reasoning and evidence in an author's work
- Identifying statistical limitations

In the next section within this element, we examine anticipating student errors, a more generalized strategy that doesn't pertain to just argumentation.

Identifying Errors in Argumentation

When secondary students write arguments, such as essays, literary critiques, or speeches, they must support their claims with clear and valid reasoning and sufficient, accurate, and relevant evidence. To prime them for success, teachers plan myriad learning experiences using a variety of strategies for producing a well-developed and effective piece. For example, teachers should expect students to examine student and published samples to identify the claims and critique the grounds (reasons), backing (evidence), and qualifiers (counterclaims) to determine their validity, relevancy, and sufficiency. Additionally, they devise lessons that compel students to critically examine the work of others and detect faulty logic, attack, weak references, misinformation, and statistical limitations. When they can detect these errors in others' writing, they are positioned to conscientiously avoid emulating these missteps in their own work that could potentially derail their arguments. See figure 4.9 for an explanation of strategies teachers can employ to support this type of writing. Additionally, augment the discussion here with information from element 14 in chapter 5 (page 82) on generating and defending claims.

Strategy	Description
Identifying errors of faulty logic	The teacher asks students to find and analyze errors of faulty logic. Errors of faulty logic refer to situations in which a conclusion is not supported by sound reasons. Specific types of errors in this category include contradiction, accident, false cause, begging the question, evading the issue, arguing from ignorance, composition, and division.
Identifying errors of attack	The teacher asks students to find and analyze errors of attack. Errors of attack happen when a person focuses on the context of an argument, rather than the argument itself, in trying to refute the other side.
Identifying errors of weak reference	The teacher asks students to find and analyze errors of weak reference. Specific types of these errors include using sources that reflect biases, using sources that lack credibility, appealing to authority, appealing to the people, and appealing to emotion.
Identifying errors of misinformation	The teacher asks students to find and analyze errors of misinformation. Two types of misinformation errors are confusing the facts and misapplying a concept or generalization.

Strategy	Description
Finding errors in the media	The teacher provides students with footage of political debates, televised interviews, commercials, advertisements, newspaper articles, blogs, and other sources and asks them to find and analyze errors in reasoning that underlie the messages therein.
Examining support for claims	The teacher asks students to examine the support provided for a claim by analyzing the grounds, backing, and qualifies that support it. Grounds are the reasons given to support a claim and backing is the evidence, facts, or data that support the grounds, while qualifiers address exceptions or objections to the claim.
Judging reasoning and evidence in an author's work	The teacher asks students to apply their knowledge of reasoning and argumentation to delineate and evaluate the arguments present in a text. Students read a text and identify the claim, grounds, backing, and qualifiers. Students must decide whether the reasoning is valid or logical (containing no errors) and whether the supporting evidence is sufficient and relevant.
Identifying statistical limitations	The teacher asks students to find and analyze errors that commonly occur when using statistical data to support a claim. The five major types of statistical limitations for students to be aware of are (1) regression toward the mean, (2) conjunction, (3) base rates, (4) the limits of extrapolation, and (5) the cumulative nature of probabilistic events.

Source: Marzano, 2017, pp. 41–42.

Figure 4.9: Types of errors in arguments.

Anticipating Student Errors

When teaching an argument, teachers can conduct lessons that implement the strategies discussed earlier (see figure 4.9). For writing in general, teachers should identify common mistakes students make to alert them about potential problems in reasoning. For example, when writing using figurative language, sometimes students compare topics that are too similar when inventing metaphors or similes, such as comparing a couch to a sofa. Also, K–5 students might mistake using *like* as a verb versus using it to signal a comparison for a simile. Or students might confuse closely aligned genres, such as an allegory with a parable. Teachers can share examples of each and point out specifically that in an allegory nearly every element, like each character and action, has symbolic meaning. A parable reveals a religious principle, moral, lesson, or general truth like the prodigal son or the Good Samaritan. When these errors are pointed out during a lesson, students can write with clearer intentions and avoid possible pitfalls.

Another common issue is when students fail to connect their topic sentences to their thesis statement in expository writing. In doing so, it results in a disjointed product. Teachers can use an exemplary and a weak sample paper to model and avert this possible error by deconstructing each and comparing them. To do so, they can use the graphic organizer in figure 4.10 (page 68) for an informational paper. Teachers can use this same strategy and alter the figure for an opinion or argumentation by replacing topic sentences with reasons. It is important to also note that there do not have to be three prescribed body paragraphs. Writers can determine how many supporting points or reasons are necessary to produce a well-developed paper.

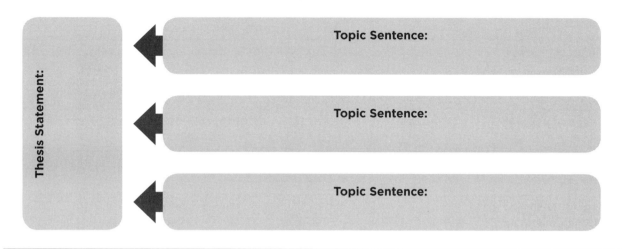

Figure 4.10: Thesis and aligned topic sentences.

*Visit **go.SolutionTree.com/instruction** for a free reproducible version of this figure.*

GUIDING QUESTIONS FOR CURRICULUM DESIGN

This design question focuses on practicing and deepening lessons: *After presenting content, how will I design and deliver lessons that help students deepen their understanding and develop fluency in skills and processes?* The following questions, which are aligned to each of the elements in this chapter, can guide teachers to plan instruction. Each represents distinct activities rather than a sequential order when planning. In other words, if the content the teacher presents is on procedural knowledge (skills, strategies, and processes), structured practice is necessary. If it's more declarative in nature (terminology, facts, generalizations, and principles), teachers use strategies in which students examine similarities and differences.

- **Element 9:** How will I help students engage in structured practice?

  _____
  _____
  _____
  _____
  _____

- **Element 10:** How will I help students examine similarities and differences?

  _____
  _____
  _____
  _____
  _____

- **Element 11:** How will I help students examine errors in reasoning?

  _____
  _____
  _____
  _____

Conclusion

When teachers plan lessons to help students practice and deepen what they learn, they first need to consider whether the content is procedural knowledge—skills, strategies, and processes—or declarative which involves terminology, facts, generalization, principles, or concepts. If procedural content is the focus for instruction, teachers select strategies that involve structured practice. For learning that is more declarative, teachers design lessons around examining similarities and differences. When choosing strategies for examining errors in reasoning, activities can be geared toward both types of knowledge. Next, teachers create opportunities for students to apply what they learn.

Conducting Knowledge Application Lessons

Once students experience the content from direct instruction lessons and engage in practicing and deepening lessons, they are ready to apply the newly acquired information and skills. During knowledge application lessons, teachers require students to use what they have learned in unique situations. By definition, this means students must go beyond what they have learned in class. Also by definition, knowledge application tasks generate new awareness in students about the content. The following elements are important to this type of lesson.

- **Element 12:** Engaging students in cognitively complex tasks
- **Element 13:** Providing resources and guidance
- **Element 14:** Generating and defending claims

Teachers should use these elements in conjunction with one another. That is, they should typically employ all three when assigning knowledge application tasks.

Element 12: Engaging Students in Cognitively Complex Tasks

Cognitively complex tasks are those that require students to use the content teachers have addressed in class in unique ways. Figure 5.1 contains the self-rating scale for this element.

Score	Description
4: Innovating	I engage in all behaviors at the Applying level. In addition, I identify those students who are not accurately carrying out the important parts of those tasks and design alternate activities and strategies to meet their specific needs.
3: Applying	Along with adequate guidance and support, I engage students in activities that help them apply their knowledge through cognitively complex tasks and monitor students to ensure that they accurately carry out the important parts of those tasks.
2: Developing	I engage students in activities that help them apply their knowledge through cognitively complex tasks and provide adequate guidance and support.
1: Beginning	I engage students in activities that help them apply their knowledge through cognitively complex tasks but do not provide adequate guidance and support, such as clearly articulating the steps in the complex task and modeling the steps to the task.
0: Not Using	I do not engage students in activities that help them apply knowledge through cognitively complex tasks.

Figure 5.1: Self-rating scale for element 12—Engaging students in cognitively complex tasks.

The strategies associated with engaging students in cognitively complex tasks require several mental steps for students as they think deeply about newly learned content and apply it in novel situations.

- Experimental-inquiry tasks
- Decision-making tasks
- Student-designed tasks

Experimental-Inquiry Tasks

Students can write to reflect on their thinking process, convey information about acquired material, or draw conclusions based on investigation or research. For example, in science students participate in experimental-inquiry tasks using the scientific method, which involves asking a question, conducting research, constructing and testing a hypothesis, analyzing data, and drawing a conclusion. Stanford History Education Group's Reading Like a Historian curriculum (http://sheg.stanford.edu/rlh) engages students in historical inquiry. With their resources, students investigate historical questions and use primary and secondary source documents to evaluate multiple perspectives and make claims backed by evidence. For example, one inquiry activity revolves around the question, Why were Japanese Americans interned during World War II? In another one, students examine whether or not Abraham Lincoln believed in racial equality.

Decision-Making Tasks

Participating in decision-making tasks is another strategy under this element. In language arts, teachers can ask students to determine alternative actions in response to conflicts a character faces other than those the text presents. For each option, students write what the outcome might be, such as reactions from others, changes in plot, or altered beliefs, and choose the most feasible one. They can write a revision to the narrative based on what eventually happens given this new direction. In doing so, students enhance their understanding of narrative elements and the content of the text they are reading. In social studies, students can identify possible solutions to a problem a politician faced in the past or a current-day issue using researched evidence, the consequences for each option, and the most viable alternatives. They can compare their recommended decision with the circumstances of the actual one. This comparison and contrast exercise deepens their content knowledge.

Student-Designed Tasks

In any subject, students can design their own writing task aligned to a learning goal and respond to it (or swap with a peer to respond to each other's) to deepen their understanding of a topic that interests them. To assist them in generating prompts, teachers can provide students with a choice of templates—which in and of itself fosters critical thinking as they select appropriate ones for a writing task they will address.

An effective source for both students and teachers to generate tasks is through Literacy Design Collaborative (LDC; 2014). This nonprofit organization offers a collection of K–12 writing frameworks aligned to the argumentation and informational or explanatory Common Core text types. Even for those in non–Common Core states or provinces, the task templates (and other resources on the website accessible at https://coretools.ldc.org/home) are worthwhile as LDC aims to provide educators with tools for literacy instruction across core subject areas by integrating reading and writing skill development.

Figure 5.2 features sample templates and examples of writing tasks for the secondary level; later in the section, we have included those geared to elementary. When accessing other task templates from the LDC link, teachers will find optional demands they can use to add rigor to a prompt. These are three of many examples of supplemental expectations the site offers. Teachers can choose one or more demands to suit a particular task: "In your discussion, address the credibility and origin of sources." "Include _____ (charts, tables, illustrations, or stylistic devices) to help convey your message to your readers." "Include a _____ (retelling,

Task Templates (LDC, 2014)	Sample Writing Tasks (Glass, 2017a)
[Insert optional question] After (reading or researching) _____ (literary texts or informational text on _____ content), write _____ (product) in which you examine causes of _____ (content) and explain the effects of _____ (content). Support your discussion with evidence from the texts.	**What are the effects of hydraulic fracking?** After reading informational texts about fracking, write an informational report in which you examine causes of alternative energy sources, specifically hydraulic fracking, and explain the effects of fracking. Support your discussion with evidence from the texts including examples from current events to illustrate or clarify your position.
[Insert optional question] After (reading or researching) _____ (literary texts or informational texts on _____ content), write _____ (product) in which you argue _____ (content). Support your position with evidence from the texts.	**Should animals be used for scientific or commercial testing?** After researching informational texts on animal testing, write a letter to the editor of the local newspaper in which you argue your viewpoint in response to the question. Support your position with evidence from the texts. Be sure to acknowledge competing views.
	Can photographs fuel change? After researching and studying pictures from the civil rights movement (or another movement), write an argumentation essay in which you argue whether photographs can be as compelling as words to fuel action and change. Support your position with evidence from the photographs and any accompanying captions or texts. Include citations.
[Insert optional question] After (reading or researching) _____ (literary texts or informational texts on _____ content), write _____ (product) in which you explain _____ (content). Support your discussion with evidence from the texts.	**How can writers use authentic cultural characters and conflicts they encounter to foster empathy and realism?** After reading two culturally centered short stories or autobiographies, write an essay in which you explain the experience of the protagonists and address the guiding question. Support your discussion with evidence from the texts.

Source: Glass, 2017a; LDC, 2014.

Figure 5.2: Sample secondary templates and tasks.

Visit **go.SolutionTree.com/instruction** *for a free reproducible version of this figure.*

recounting, summary) in your response." The last option applies to grades K–1 and 2–5 tasks. Since each task requires students to create a product, figure 5.3 (page 74), Assessments A to Z, includes suggestions. Teachers should model how students can use the templates as tools for framing tasks that they can address to deepen their understanding of content.

Students can also position guiding questions within a prompt, such as this narrative task example based on informational text.

> After researching the Westward Expansion during the early 1800s, write a personal narrative from the point of view of someone who journeys west. Write a developed storyline that includes descriptive details so readers can experience what life was like during this period in history through this individual's eyes. Address these questions somewhere within your story.
> - What obstacles do you face on your journey?
> - How do you or your family overcome obstacles, or don't you?
> - What route have you or others with you decided to take and why?
> - Do you encounter Native Americans or others? If so, how does this experience affect you and those with you?

Assessments A to Z With Writing

A	B	C	D	E
• Advertisement (newspaper, TV, magazine, and radio) • Advice column • All-about paper • Allegory • Anagram • Anecdote • Announcement • Anthem • Application • Argumentation essay or speech • Associations • Autobiography	• Bibliography • Billboard • Biography • Blog • Book • Book cover • Brochure • Bulletin board • Business letter • Business plan (proposal)	• Cartoons • Case study • Catalog • Chapter • Character sketch • Collage with captions • Comedy (play or script) • Comic book • Convention program • Course outline • Creation myth • Critique	• Dictation • Drama • Dictionary with pictures and words • Directions • Documentary	• Editorial • Essay • Eulogy

F	G	H	I	J–K
• Fable • Fairy tale • Fantasy or fictional story • Feature story • Future scenario	• Glossary • Graph with analysis • Graphic organizer • Greek myth • Greeting card	• Handbook • Headlines • Historical fiction • How-to paper	• Informational or explanatory paper or report • Interview • Invitation (personal or business)	• Job descriptions • Joke book • Journal (personal or historical accounts)

L	M	N	O	P
• Lab report • Labels • Laws for organization • Legal document • Legend • Lesson plan • Letter (personal or business, resume cover letter) • Letter of recommendation • Letter to the editor • Literary critique or analysis	• Magazine article or layout • Manual • Memoir • Menu • Multimedia project • Mural • Myth (creation, Native American, or Greek)	• Narrative • Nature log • News story • Newsletter • Newspaper • Notes (Cornell notes, observational notes) • Novel • Novella	• Obituary • Opinion piece • Organization bylaws; vision or mission statement • Outline	• Pamphlet • Parody • Pattern book • Personal narrative • Petition • Poem • Political cartoon • Portfolio • Poster • Pourquoi tale • PowerPoint, Keynote, Prezi • Prediction • Press release • Program

Q–R	S	T–V	U–V	W–X–Y–Z
• Reader's theater • Recipe • Research report or project • Resume • Review of book, movie, experiment, or presentation	• Satire • Scrapbook (annotated) • Short story (mystery, realistic fiction, fantasy, or other) • Song lyrics • Speech • Storyboard • Summary	• TED Talk or television script • Timeline (with visuals and text) • Travelogue • Trickster tale	• Venn diagram • Video • Vignette	• Writing prompt and responses

Figure 5.3: Options for written products.

Visit go.SolutionTree.com/instruction for a free reproducible version of this figure.

Additionally, teachers can encourage students to write in a genre that interests them but that still allows them to show understanding of the content—like the two choices that follow for either an informational or narrative piece. Teachers can also instruct students to incorporate subject-matter terms as a requisite when writing and responding to prompts.

- **What is the mechanism that causes plate tectonics?** After researching informational texts on plate tectonics, write an **informational report** in which you define and explain the process that causes plate tectonics. Incorporate these terms in a clear way that shows your understanding of these phenomena: subduction zone, cooling, convection, mid-ocean ridge, and continental plate. Support your discussion with evidence from multiple resources.
- **What is the mechanism that causes plate tectonics?** After researching informational texts on plate tectonics, write a **story** in which you explain the process that causes plate tectonics. Feel free to use personification, such as turn inanimate objects into characters, and be sure the setting reflects your understanding of the content. Use descriptive language, develop a plotline that tells a dramatic story of the phases of this process, and include suspense at critical points to entice readers. Incorporate these terms in a clear way to show your understanding of these phenomena: *subduction zone*, *cooling*, *convection*, *mid-ocean ridge*, and *continental plate*. Support your discussion with evidence from multiple resources.

Teachers help elementary students create writing prompts that they address as well. For instance, see this task template from Literacy Design Collaborative (2014) for grades 2–5 and the examples that follow: "[Insert optional question] After (reading or researching) _____ (literary texts, informational texts on _____ content, or both), write _____ (product) in which you explain or describe _____ (content). Support your response with evidence from the texts."

- **How can people participate in government?** After reading informational texts about citizenship and government, write a pamphlet to explain how people can get involved and participate in local or state government. Support your response with evidence from the text.
- **How do authors describe characters?** After reading "The Pudding Like a Night on the Sea" by Ann Cameron (1981), write a character sketch to describe the boys' father. Support your response with evidence from the story.

In order to engage in cognitively challenging tasks, students require resources and guidance, the focus of element 13.

Element 13: Providing Resources and Guidance

Engaging in cognitively complex tasks is challenging for many students. Consequently, teachers must be available and prepared to provide adequate resources and guidance. The self-rating scale for this element is depicted in figure 5.4 (page 76).

This section addresses the following strategies for providing resources and guidance.

- Using proficiency or scoring scales
- Providing resources and informational handouts
- Teaching research skills
- Offering feedback

Score	Description
4: Innovating	I engage in all behaviors at the Applying level. In addition, I identify those students who are not gradually taking over responsibility for the completion of the complex tasks and design alternate activities and strategies to meet their specific needs.
3: Applying	I engage in activities to provide resources and guidance to students as they engage in cognitively complex tasks without significant errors or omissions and monitor the extent to which students are gradually able to take over responsibility for the completion of the tasks.
2: Developing	I engage in activities to provide resources and guidance to students as they engage in cognitively complex tasks without significant errors or omissions.
1: Beginning	I engage in activities to provide resources and guidance to students as they engage in cognitively complex tasks but do so with errors or omissions, such as not being readily available to students and not having critical resources available to students as they work on their complex tasks.
0: Not Using	I do not engage in activities to provide resources and guidance to students as they engage in cognitively complex tasks.

Figure 5.4: Self-rating scale for element 13—Providing resources and guidance.

Using Proficiency or Scoring Scales

When students work on a comprehensive writing project, they monitor their progress as they seek proficiency on various writing skills that collectively contribute to the whole piece. For example, during an opinion or argumentation unit, they stake a claim, provide reasons, collect and organize evidence, and establish a formal writing style. When conducting research, they determine a query, narrow their search, determine credible sources, and take notes.

The discussion within element 1 (providing scales and rubrics) in chapter 1 (page 11) focuses on the necessity of scales and rubrics. These mechanisms help students understand the progression of knowledge that teachers expect them to learn and make the writing expectations transparent. They also serve to ground teachers in what they plan to teach. Here our emphasis turns to providing support for students to use and apply scales or rubrics for their own advantage with some relative independence to grow as writers. Specifically, teachers can model for students how to use scales or rubrics as instructional tools. To do so, they instruct students to focus on one criteria item at a time (the visual strategy of color coding is appropriate) and find evidence of it in their papers. We detail an aligned strategy in chapter 6 (page 87) in which students use a revision sheet that matches the rubric. They find evidence in their papers of expectations on the rubric and catalog this proof on a prepared revision sheet expressly designed as a self-assessment and peer review tool (see element 18, page 100).

Providing Resources and Informational Handouts

To facilitate success in composing written products, teachers provide a host of resources and informational materials for students to examine and use. These are some of the many options that teachers might supply.

- **Technology:** Teachers make computer devices available so students can take advantage of myriad technology options, such as accessing the internet to conduct research, finding websites for formatting (such as for works cited documents) or grammar and convention support, posting writing drafts for feedback from a remote community, or offering input to classmates for writing revision.

- **Worked examples:** As discussed within element 9 in chapter 4 (page 55), students benefit from examining stellar examples of published and student work to identify specific strengths. This serves to guide them in their own writing.
- **Graphic organizers:** Although students can generate their own organizers, teachers can also select and download specific ones to distribute to students for different purposes or ask them to complete an organizer electronically. (Refer to the discussion of graphic organizers in element 8, chapter 3, page 46.)
- **Vocabulary resources:** Depending on the students' age group, teachers provide picture or other beginning dictionaries and thesauri, or more advanced vocabulary resources in print or electronically.
- **Writing tools for handwritten work:** These tools differ according to the task and students' age and readiness levels. For primary and elementary students, teachers supply a variety of paper (for example, white, colored, unlined, lined, or decorated), blank books, alphabet charts for spelling help, dry-erase boards and markers, and student- and teacher-generated word walls and charts. They can have drawing tools available for students to create illustrations. Students of all levels need lined or blank paper for prewriting webs or other idea-generation organizers, sticky notes for making editing comments and inserts, writing implements for handwritten work, and other tools to support writing in all its forms.
- **Paper or electronic handouts:** Throughout the writing process, teachers physically or electronically distribute various handouts and resources, such as the writing task along with a checklist and rubric that articulate the criteria, peer response sheets, editing and revision suggestions, portfolio contents and self-reflection sheets, plot diagrams, dialogue punctuation rules, formatting examples and rules, and so forth.

Teaching Research Skills

When students write an informational report, opinion or argumentation paper, or even a historical fiction piece, they will need to conduct research. Teachers can use the suite of differentiated search lessons from Google Search Education, which are accessible at www.google.com/intl/en-us/insidesearch/searcheducation /lessons.html (developed by author Kathy Glass in collaboration with Tasha Bergson-Michelson for Google). The compilation of five comprehensive lessons focuses on a gamut of skills related to research, such as determining search terms, evaluating search results, selecting and utilizing appropriate search strategies, validating sources, ascertaining the credibility of sources, and so forth. Although the lessons include embedded links for those classrooms with internet access, screenshots of sites support those without internet availability. Through these lessons—or others that teachers conduct—students should ultimately learn how to independently find resources and information to vet and use within their writing projects.

Offering Feedback

When advancing through the writing process, the feedback based on clear criteria that students receive supports them in moving from where they currently are in their learning proficiency to a higher level of achievement. Teachers' input in the form of concrete suggestions proves critical so each draft is an improvement upon the previous one. As well, it is imperative that students self-assess, plus solicit and receive input from peers. It is through this iterative process of revisionary support that students ultimately produce effective writing pieces. (To augment the discussion here, see the elaborative interrogation strategy, element 21, chapter 6, page 112.)

Grant Wiggins (2012) suggests abiding by these key elements when providing feedback to students. Feedback should be:

- **Goal referenced**—Students must know the goal of the feedback and how it will help accomplish a task. Criteria via scales, rubrics, and checklists identify and reinforce goals, so teachers should use these tools instructionally within feedback sessions. Students can also pinpoint areas in their papers where they need specific feedback.

- **Tangible and transparent**—The feedback must be concrete and comprehensible so students can use it to make the necessary improvements. Comments such as "awkward" or "wrong word" confuse students and don't provide clear direction.

- **Actionable**—Feedback that is actionable gives information that helps students revise, such as: "You write about many events that happen in your story. Work on creating tension as you describe them so you build suspense." "This quote with statistics clearly connects to your topic. What's missing is the elaboration. Explain how this piece of evidence connects to the thesis and furthers your argument." "Good job on naming your favorite sense. Now tell readers why you like the sense of sight best."

- **User-friendly**—Too much feedback can overwhelm students, so teachers are wise to be judicious in how much to offer based on the grade level and characteristics of each student. Additionally, the input must be in language suitable for the level of learners. If they cannot understand the feedback, they will not heed it.

- **Timely**—So that students can apply the feedback as soon as possible, teachers should strive for a quick turnaround time on suggestions for improvement. This proves challenging, especially for secondary English language arts teachers who interface with many students and read comprehensive, lengthy pieces. Students can ask teachers (and peer reviewers) for specific areas they need feedback on so that the readers can target their input. Students can do this by highlighting areas on the rubric or checklist and attaching this to their drafts to purposefully direct teachers and reviewers for feedback. Another option is to use or adapt figures 5.5 and 5.6 (page 80) for a narrative and argumentation piece respectively that students can complete to target input. When responding to student queries and offering other comments, teachers can access platforms such as Google Docs.

- **Ongoing**—A continuous cycle of input at all stages of the writing process from a variety of individuals besides teachers—self, classmates, online community members, and parents or guardians—can facilitate learning and progress. These comments can come orally, electronically, and written by hand during class and at other times.

- **Consistent**—A consistent understanding of what constitutes quality is important for both students and teachers. Within instruction, teachers should show sample papers that reflect different performance levels on a rubric so students can work toward meeting expectations that are clear to them. (Review worked examples in element 9 in chapter 4 [page 55] for a list of resources for student samples and suggestions for using them.) Teachers within a school and even a district should score papers together to identify anchor papers that represent attributes of a performance level. This will help ensure consistency and reliability as teachers score papers independently from their own classrooms. To collect anchor papers, teachers conduct calibration sessions to help colleagues come to agreement or common understanding about examples of proficiency levels. To conduct calibration sessions and collect anchor papers for instructional and grading purposes, plus additional information in this area, teachers can access any of these resources. Visit **go.SolutionTree.com/instruction** to access direct links to these resources.

- "Writing Calibration Protocol" (Rhode Island Department of Education, 2013; http://bit.ly/2F32QO5)
- "Calibration Protocol for Scoring Student Work: A Part of the Assessment Toolkit" (Rhode Island Department of Education, n.d.; http://bit.ly/1gkBPb7)
- "Selecting Anchor Papers: A Guide" (SCALE, n.d.; www.performanceassessmentresource bank.org/resource/10491)
- *The Fundamentals of (Re)designing Writing Units* (Glass, 2017a)
- *FAST Grading: A Guide to Implementing Best Practices* (Reeves, 2016)

Narrative Feedback Sheet				
Writer Directions: Highlight or place a check next to the questions you want a reviewer to concentrate on when reading and providing you with input. Enter any additional questions in the blank spaces at the end of this sheet, if necessary.				
Writer: _____ Reviewer: _____				
Questions to Guide Revision	**Check Appropriate Column:**			**Comments**
	Yes	Somewhat	No	
Is my **introduction** compelling enough to engage you?				
Is the **central conflict** intriguing?				
Do I build enough **suspense**?				
Is the story **sequenced** and **well paced** to facilitate reading and avoid confusion?				
Does the **climax** create tension and put you on the edge of your seat?				
Is the **resolution** satisfying and does it answer any questions you might have?				
Are the **characters** realistic? Do I provide enough information about them?				
Is the **dialogue** important to the story, and does it represent characters well?				
Are there areas that are **too wordy** or **long**? If so, what can I delete?				
Is there a section of the story that I need to **develop** more?				

Figure 5.5: Narrative feedback sheet.

continued →

Questions to Guide Revision	Check Appropriate Column:			Comments
	Yes	Somewhat	No	
Are there **confusing parts** that interfere with following the story?				
Do I include enough **figurative language** and strong **vocabulary** to provide vivid **descriptions about characters**, **setting**, or **events**?				

Source: Glass, 2018, pp. 106–107.

*Visit **go.SolutionTree.com/instruction** for a free reproducible version of this figure.*

Argumentation Feedback Sheet
Directions: Highlight or place a check next to the questions you want a reviewer to concentrate on when reading and providing input. Enter any additional questions in the blank spaces at the end of this sheet, if needed.

Writer: _____   Reviewer: _____

Questions to Guide Revision	Check Appropriate Column:			Comments
	Yes	Somewhat	No	
Is the **introduction** compelling and does it provide enough **context**?				
Is the **thesis** strong and does it clearly stake a claim?				
Do the **topic sentences** support the thesis by providing clear and compelling **reasons**?				
Is there enough **evidence**? Is the evidence relevant?				
Is there clear **elaboration** to explain the evidence?				
Is the paper **organized** in a way that facilitates understanding?				
Do any paragraphs or parts need to be **reordered**?				
Is the **counterargument** acknowledged and addressed in a compelling way to support the argument?				
Is the text sometimes **too wordy**? If so, what information can the writer delete?				
Do words and phrases unnecessarily **repeat**, detracting from the message?				
Are there **inflammatory**, **judgmental**, or **biased words** or phrases the writer should delete or change?				

Are there **confusing parts** that interfere with building a cogent argument?			
Is the writing geared to the intended **audience** and written in an appropriate **tone** and **style** for these readers?			
Does the **conclusion** leave a strong impression and restate the major premise and points?			
Is there an image, graphic, or other **text feature** that can enhance the piece?			
Are there appropriate **transitional words and phrases** to make the writing flow?			

Source: Glass, 2017b, pp. 94–95.

Figure 5.6: Argumentation feedback sheet.

*Visit **go.SolutionTree.com/instruction** for a free reproducible version of this figure.*

Teachers can ask K–3 students to read their papers aloud or explain their pictures then offer feedback to guide revision. For example, they might suggest that students add words like adjectives or prepositional phrases for more detail. To generate these phrases, teachers can make cards from figure 5.7 and use them as props to help students with the skill of elaborating. Additionally, students may need support with time sequence, transitions, a consistent focus, capitalizing the first word of a sentence, end punctuation, or spacing. Or, teachers can suggest that students add more detail to their pictures or verify that the words match their drawings.

Figure 5.7: Prepositional phrase cards.

*Visit **go.SolutionTree.com/instruction** for a free reproducible version of this figure.*

Supporting students as they tackle cognitively complex tasks helps students prepare for element 14, generating and defending claims.

Element 14: Generating and Defending Claims

The ultimate goal of cognitively complex tasks is to give students the ability to generate new conclusions and defend their claims by providing evidence. Figure 5.8 contains the self-rating scale for this element.

Score	Description
4: Innovating	I engage in all behaviors at the Applying level. In addition, I identify those students who are not developing logical arguments regarding their claims and design alternate activities and strategies to meet their specific needs.
3: Applying	Along with adequate guidance and support, I engage students in activities that help them generate and defend claims and monitor students to ensure that they have developed logical arguments regarding their claims.
2: Developing	I engage students in activities that help them generate and defend claims and provide adequate guidance and support.
1: Beginning	I engage students in activities that help them generate and defend claims but do not provide adequate guidance and support, such as providing a clear model of the nature of an effective argument with its related parts and providing adequate practices in analyzing and constructing arguments.
0: Not Using	I do not engage students in activities that help them generate and defend claims.

Figure 5.8: Self-rating scale for element 14—Generating and defending claims.

The strategies for this element revolve around components of a well-structured and developed argument.

- Introducing the concept of claims and support
- Presenting the formal structure of claims and support
- Generating claims
- Providing grounds
- Providing backing
- Generating qualifiers
- Formally presenting claims

Introducing the Concept of Claims and Support and Presenting the Formal Structure

To prepare students for the rigor of writing a formal argumentation product in middle and high school, such as essays, literary critiques, or speeches, elementary teachers begin with introducing opinion writing. In early elementary grades, this entails students stating an opinion about a topic and providing reasons for it. The topic could be a favorite book, author, farm animal, or place. As they progress through the grades and eventually tackle argumentation pieces, students learn that this form of writing revolves around controversial topics or issues, and their job is to provide support for their claims through logical reasoning and relevant evidence culled from credible sources. They eventually incorporate counterarguments to acknowledge and address opposing viewpoints.

Key characteristics, featured in figure 5.9, form the basis for an argument, which we explain in detail in subsequent sections. The structure is shown in figure 5. To introduce opinion writing to elementary students, see figure 5.11 (page 84).

Argumentation Characteristics		
Characteristic Elements	**Question Prompts**	**Example**
Claim	What do you believe?	Requiring students to wear school uniforms would rob them of their individuality and cause discontent.
Grounds (reason)	Why do you think your claim is true? Why should I believe you?	The mandate to wear uniforms denies students freedom of expression.
Backing and warrants (evidence and elaboration)	How do you know this is true? What is your evidence, and how does it connect to your claim?	In the 1970 case Richards v. Thurston, the U.S. First Circuit Court of Appeals sided with a boy who refused to cut his hair shorter stating "compelled conformity to conventional standards of appearance" does not "seem a justifiable part of the educational process" (United States Court of Appeals for the First Circuit, Richards v. Thurston, ahcuah.com, April 28, 1970). Upholding the boy's right to keep his hair long provides a clear defense for how students should be able to make their own decisions about what clothing to wear.
Qualifiers (counterargument)	What are the opposing views and their weaknesses?	Proponents of mandatory school uniforms believe students can express themselves in other ways, for example through hairstyles, nail polish, backpack accessories, or shoes. However, these other means of individuality might have the reverse effect by increasing peer pressure or even encouraging theft.

Figure 5.9: Argumentation characteristics.

*Visit **go.SolutionTree.com/instruction** for a free reproducible version of this figure.*

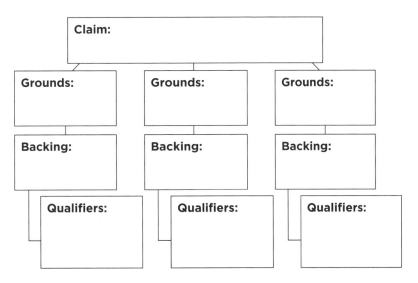

Source: Marzano, 2017; Marzano Resources, 2016.

Figure 5.10: The structure of an argument.

Introducing Argumentation Structure to Elementary Students
Although claims, grounds, backing, and qualifiers reflect ideas that are too sophisticated for younger students, teachers can still introduce them to the basic argumentation structure. To do so, Marzano (2012) recommends these sentence starters to frame an opinion paper; for kindergarten, the first prompt alone might suffice.
• **"My new idea is . . .":** These sentence starters help students learn to generate a claim. Home or school can serve as the impetus for topics, such as "My new idea is that dogs should not have to wear a leash," and "My new idea is that kids should decide their own bedtime."
• **"I think this is true because . . .":** Students can learn about grounds or reasons with this prompt. For example, "I think this is true because dogs can run faster and farther without a leash," and "I think this is true because some kids can read or play longer and still get up in time for school."
• **"I actually saw . . .":** If students are ready to tackle this prompt, they can begin to learn the concept of backing or evidence. They might augment what they witnessed firsthand with an anecdote or a quote from someone. For instance, "I actually saw dogs on short leashes at the park. These dogs seemed like they wanted to take off and run but couldn't. Then there were other dogs without leashes that were catching Frisbees and running all over the park happily." And "I actually saw my brother stay up late to color and he wasn't even cranky. In the morning, he popped out of bed for breakfast and got dressed easily."
• **"But I don't know . . .":** Students can try identifying qualifiers or evidence counter to their claim. For instance, "I don't know whether leashes must be on dogs in all neighborhoods, but I will try to find out," and "I don't know if some children get in bad moods when they wake up tired from going to bed too late. I'll have to ask my friends."

Source: Marzano, 2012.

Figure 5.11: Introducing the structure of an argument to elementary students.

*Visit **go.SolutionTree.com/instruction** for a free reproducible version of this figure.*

Generating Claims

Teachers explain that a claim for an argument is the position, belief, or conclusion that students set out to prove or argue hoping to compel readers to accept the position or take some sort of action. Claims are debatable and defensible; thus, they require support. When generating a claim, writers articulate it in a thesis statement. There are five types of claims writers typically make, and sometimes an argument involves more than one (Glass, 2017b).

1. **Factual claims** assert some realistic truth that readers can verify.
   Thesis example—Since approximately 17 percent of Americans ages two to nineteen years old suffer from obesity, the government should intervene and sanction the sale of certain unhealthy foods.
2. **Definitional claims** argue how to define, characterize, or categorize something, even an individual or character, to avoid unwanted connotations or implications.
   Thesis example—Even though people claim it is a compassionate way to die, euthanasia is clearly murder.
3. **Claims of value** are based on worthiness and argue that a topic, issue, character, or leader is, for example, better than, more honest than, more influential than, or more accomplished than something or someone else.
   Thesis example—Since evidence shows that involvement in the arts is associated with student gains across subject areas, instructional programs would be more effective if they incorporated arts education into their curricula.
4. **Claims associated with solutions or policies** focus on what people or organizations should do or avoid.

Thesis example—Because hospitals are a hotbed of germs that leave patients vulnerable to serious illnesses, healthcare workers should not interface with patients unless they receive flu shots.

5. **Claims of cause and effect** (or vice versa) involve propositions stating that a person, event, situation, or thing caused something to happen on a short- or long-term basis.

   Thesis example—If people conscientiously change their lifestyles by limiting their power usage and travel, we could reduce the effects of climate change.

Providing Grounds

After students make a claim, they need to supply grounds—or reasons—to answer the questions: *Why do you think your claim is true? Why should I believe you?* In a paper of multiple paragraphs, reasons are typically the topic sentences for each body paragraph, and each one must support the thesis statement or overarching claim.

Students must strategically position their body paragraphs of grounds along with the backing to further their arguments. Some place the strongest reason and supporting evidence first to attract readers to their position from the start. Others save the strongest for last in hopes of leaving an enduring impression. Although opinions are split on this decision, what remains is the consistent finding that writers should not situate the strongest body paragraph in the middle (Zarefsky, 2005).

Providing Backing

Backing provides information by way of textual evidence and accompanying references to substantiate the grounds and establish their validity in support of a claim. It answers questions such as *How do you know this is true? What is your evidence?* and *How does it connect to your claim?* It essentially delivers the hard-core proof. Evidence falls into four general categories:

1. **Specific instances or examples:** Events or case studies illustrative of a specific situation (for instance, brief or developed examples of the ways Mother Teresa showed compassion); might be a hypothetical situation

2. **Statistics:** Facts with numbers (or data), such as raw numbers (1,264,000 soldiers died during the Civil War), percentages (39.8 percent of the electoral vote went to Abraham Lincoln), ratios (the Union forces outnumbered the Confederates roughly 2:1), index numbers, averages, mean, median, or mode. Writers may display statistical evidence through graphs, charts, maps, diagrams, or surveys. (Civil War Trust, 2014)

3. **Testimony:** Eyewitness (firsthand account from people who directly observe or experience something; anecdotal) or expert testimony (someone deemed credible with formal knowledge, expertise, or training who can attest to something); might be a combination where an expert relays an experience he or she encountered firsthand

4. **Tangible objects:** Actual things or pictures of them, such as documents, maps, or artifacts. Proficient writers selectively choose the most relevant and salient evidence to convince readers of their positions. In addition, they carefully supply ample evidence. (Glass, 2017b, p. 11)

Once students offer data, quotes, examples, or other evidentiary support, they need to provide commentary, interpretation, or discussion to illustrate how this evidence furthers a point in connection to the argument. This elaboration—or warrants—helps readers better understand why the evidence matters, minimizes any likelihood of misinterpretation, and respectfully cajoles readers to accept or agree with a writer's position.

Generating Qualifiers

After students articulate their reasons and provide relevant and sufficient evidence with elaboration or interpretation, they acknowledge what others might say who oppose the writer's position. Then they address these contrary assertions. Qualifiers answer these types of questions: *What are the exceptions to your claim? What are the opposing views and their weaknesses?* Figure 5.10 (page 83) reflects an argument structure in which the writer presents qualifiers in each body paragraph. Writers can also dedicate a separate body paragraph to one or more oppositional viewpoints and countering them. To help students craft this part of their arguments, teachers can model and share sentence frames, like those in figure 5.

Acknowledge the Opposition (Part 1) [Opposing party] + [verb] that . . .		Counter the Opposition (Part 2)
Opposing Party Examples	**Verb Options**	
• Specific individual (Dr. _____, Professor _____, Senator _____) • Type of individual or group (opponents, proponents, critics, parents, politicians, environmentalists) • Name of organization (National Institutes of Health, Facebook, North Central High School)	• affirm • argue • assert • believe • claim • complain • concede • contend • contradict • counter • demonstrate • deny • disagree • disbelieve · disprove • dispute • do not deny • emphasize • forbid • insist • invalidate • maintain • negate • oppose • refute • reject • show • suggest	• On the other hand, _____. • However, there is little research to support _____. • Alternatively, consider _____. • Alternatively, other sources state that _____. • The weakness in _____ is that _____. • Contrary to X's position is the fact that _____. • Nevertheless, the evidence concerning _____ refutes the _____. • Rather than adopt this view, consider _____.

Source: Adapted from Glass, 2017b, p. 86.

Figure 5.12: Counterargument sentence frames.

*Visit **go.SolutionTree.com/instruction** for a free reproducible version of this figure.*

Formally Presenting Claims

When students finish and submit their written opinion or argumentation papers, teachers can extend exposure for their work by asking them to present orally or summarize them in a format like a PowerPoint, Prezi, or Keynote. They can present to peers in small groups or to the whole classroom. Or students can share with members of the greater school community, such as students in other classrooms, the principal, or school board members. Perhaps the task and topics address a community issue in which case students can present to public officials or business leaders whom they want to convince of their positions and take action. Students can even submit their work to the school or local print or online newspaper. After they have an opportunity to share with others, students can reflect on what they learn from peers.

GUIDING QUESTIONS FOR CURRICULUM DESIGN

To implement knowledge application lessons, this is the design question: *After presenting new content, how will I design and deliver lessons that help students generate and defend claims through knowledge application?* Consider the following questions aligned to the elements in this chapter to guide your planning.

- **Element 12:** How will I engage students in cognitively complex tasks?

  _____
  _____
  _____
  _____
  _____
  _____
  _____
  _____

- **Element 13:** How will I provide resources and guidance?

  _____
  _____
  _____
  _____
  _____
  _____
  _____
  _____

- **Element 14:** How will I help students generate and defend claims?

  _____
  _____
  _____
  _____
  _____
  _____
  _____
  _____

Conclusion

After leading lessons to introduce new content, teachers must also design experiences for students to apply what they learned in a novel situation so they can demonstrate mastery. The ultimate goal of cognitively complex tasks, a hallmark of knowledge application lessons, involves students generating their own claims and providing evidence for their conclusions. Teachers can employ a host of instructional strategies within the three types of lessons—direction instruction, practicing and deepening, and knowledge application—which is the topic of the upcoming chapter.

CHAPTER 6

Using Strategies That Appear in All Types of Lessons

Chapters 3, 4, and 5 represent specific types of lessons each with unique purposes and unique strategies. Chapter 3 deals with direct instruction lessons, chapter 4 with practicing and deepening lessons, and chapter 5 with knowledge application lessons. The instructional strategies we discuss in those chapters would most probably appear in the context of their respective lessons. For example, teachers use chunking primarily when they are introducing new content, they use structured practice sessions primarily when they wish to develop fluency in a procedure, and they use cognitively complex tasks primarily when they wish to have students apply their knowledge.

In contrast, there are a number of strategies that teachers can and should use within all three types of lessons previously discussed. As a set, these strategies help students continually integrate new knowledge with old knowledge and revise their understanding of the content accordingly. The following elements and the strategies embedded within them in this chapter help students perform these functions.

- **Element 15:** Previewing strategies
- **Element 16:** Highlighting critical information
- **Element 17:** Reviewing content
- **Element 18:** Revising knowledge
- **Element 19:** Reflecting on learning
- **Element 20:** Assigning purposeful homework
- **Element 21:** Elaborating on information
- **Element 22:** Organizing students to interact

As mentioned previously, to see all strategies within every element, refer to figure A.1 in appendix A, page 156.

Element 15: Previewing Strategies

Previewing helps students activate prior knowledge so that they might make connections with new knowledge. Figure 6.1 (page 90) depicts the self-rating scale for previewing strategies.

Score	Description
4: Innovating	I engage in all behaviors at the Applying level. In addition, I identify those students who are not making connections between new content and what they have learned previously and design alternate activities and strategies to meet their specific needs.
3: Applying	Along with adequate guidance and support, I engage students in activities that help them preview upcoming content and monitor students to ensure that they are making connections between new content and what they have learned previously.
2: Developing	I engage students in activities that help them preview upcoming content and provide adequate guidance and support.
1: Beginning	I engage students in activities that help them preview upcoming content but do not provide adequate guidance and support, such as demonstrating the purpose for previewing and providing adequate time for students to preview content.
0: Not Using	I do not engage students in activities that help them preview upcoming content.

Figure 6.1: Self-rating scale for element 15—Previewing strategies.

We associate the following strategies with this element.

- Bell ringers
- What do you think you know?
- K-W-L strategies
- Preassessments

Bell Ringers

Also called sponge activities, teachers can issue bell ringers at the start of class to draw a link between a previous and an upcoming lesson or engage students in new material. Additionally, this strategy helps support classroom management as it readily occupies students' attention.

Teachers explicitly explain this classroom routine so that students know to consistently enter a class period or begin a new transition by immediately responding to the bell-ringer prompt. Students read what the teacher posts on an interactive whiteboard, whiteboard, or electronic device, or—for primary students—the teacher can read the prompt aloud. It is a brief exercise within the first several minutes of class. Afterward, teachers connect students' responses and the day's lesson, then commence with planned instruction.

When learning about describing words, teachers might ask elementary students to label a picture with adjectives, make a list of descriptive words for items they see around the classroom, or turn to an elbow partner and describe in detail what he or she is wearing. Secondary students can locate descriptions in a text, rewrite a brief passage from a text that lacks description, or succinctly explain how imagery can enhance a text.

If targeting similarities and differences, teachers can ask elementary students to turn to a partner and say what is the same and different about objects like a lamp and a flashlight, a clock and a watch, or an electric car and a truck. Once they articulate what is alike and different about these common objects, teachers can introduce a comparison-and-contrast graphic organizer and transition to classroom content, such as attributes of a fable and fairy tale or the protagonist and antagonist. For secondary students, teachers can ask them to write or type how tone and mood, persuasive and argumentative writing, two civilizations, or similar words (such as *ambitious* and *determined*) are similar and dissimilar.

When focusing on causes and effects, teachers can provide the effects *(The Patriots revolted. The window is foggy. The writing is choppy.)* and ask students to record logical causes or vice versa as a springboard to the day's lesson. To promote vocabulary instruction, teachers can write a word and ask students to list all different forms of it, such as *constitute, constitution, constitutional,* and *unconstitutional* or for elementary students, forms of a verb—*hop, hopping, hopped, hops.* Or, they might list all words using a specific affix and identify the meanings of each variation.

Endless possibilities for bell ringers abound—form a sentence using scrambled words, write a compound sentence, begin a sentence with a dependent clause and label its parts, justify a mathematics answer, write a definition and provide an example, draw a simple diagram, identify the thesis from a featured sample paragraph, and so forth.

What Do You Think You Know?

To optimize student success, teachers clearly articulate learning goals (see element 1, chapter 1, page 11). In this regard, they can introduce students to the criteria for an upcoming writing assignment by conducting a roundtable activity. This serves as an opportunity to share expectations for a culminating writing piece and to uncover what students think they know at a nascent point in the unit to check their understanding.

To begin the roundtable activity, each student has a writing tool and students each in turn contribute a line item on a group sheet of paper in response to a prompt. Alternatively, students can pass around an electronic device. Here is a five-step process for how it can go.

1. Teachers pose a prompt such as, "What does a strong opinion piece include?" (or, a mystery, fairy tale, realistic fiction, personal narrative, or other).
2. Students pass one paper (or a single device) clockwise in their groups. Each student adds a line item different from what is already listed. Teachers emphasize to students to record a bulleted or numbered list of one- to three-word items rather than sentences. For an opinion paper, they might record *reasons, facts, examples, opinion statements* (or a *thesis*), and so on. Teachers should remind students to also enter what makes for a strong paper in general, for example, *transitions, sentence structure, punctuation,* and *indenting.*
3. After students exhaust possibilities on their group sheets, each group shares an item to compile a class-generated list of what students think contributes to a strong opinion piece. Teachers record these collective entries.
4. Students discuss the master list of items to add to it, or edit and revise, such as delete unnecessary entries or merge others. Teachers guide them in categorizing the items.
5. Teachers then distribute a prepared checklist or analytic rubric that reveals the expectations for an eventual culminating writing task. Students compare their compiled list with the teacher's criteria sheet. They discuss items on the checklist or rubric that do not appear on the class list (or vice versa) to determine whether or not they should add them.

The dual purpose of this exercise—to reveal criteria for a writing task and to check what students think they know—sets the stage for an upcoming writing unit and informs teachers' instruction moving forward.

K-W-L Strategies

K-W-L is a popular strategy in which the K represents what students already know about an upcoming curricular topic, the W prompts them to answer what they want to learn about it, and the L comes later when students have gleaned information and knowledge (see figure 6.2, page 92).

After learning the material, teachers instruct students to return to and focus on the items in their K column. They circle any entries related to prior knowledge that are correct or cross out inaccurate ones. Then

K-W-L Chart		
Directions:		
• In the **K column**, write down what you **know** about _____. Complete sentences are not necessary; enter words and short phrases.		
• In the **W column**, write down what you **want** to know about _____. You can write sentences, questions, words, or phrases.		
• Leave the **L column** blank for now. Later you will record what you have **learned**.		
K What do I know?	W What do I want to know?	L What have I learned?

Figure 6.2: K-W-L chart.

*Visit **go.SolutionTree.com/instruction** for a free reproducible version of this figure.*

they use the last column—the L—to rewrite and revise any K items and make necessary contributions of new information. Additionally, students review the W column to determine which questions remain unanswered after instruction or research they conduct. Teachers might help students address them by discussing what resources students might use to find answers.

Students can add other columns to the basic K-W-L chart to percolate ideas and for practicing skills. For example, students can include an H column—How do I find out what I don't know?—or a Q column to answer the question, What new questions do I now have? As students work on an informational report or learn more about their stance in opinion or argument papers, this strategy can serve as a precursor for more in-depth research. Later, they use graphic organizers and other note-taking strategies to accumulate and organize their research.

Preassessments

Teachers can conduct myriad preassessment tasks to inform them about students' current knowledge pertaining to writing. Preassessments can also function as introductory activities to launch a unit of instruction. Here are some of the many options.

- **Issue an on-demand writing prompt and ask students to respond:** Teachers can assess students' writing by taking note of strengths and weaknesses to plan for future instruction. Although they can devise their own, teachers can use the Achieve the Core prompts in K–5 and 6–12 grade clusters with accompanying student samples for the following text types.
  - *Opinion or argument*—The prompt kindergarten to grade five students respond to is "Which kind of pet is best, a cat or a dog?" Downloadable materials for teacher and student directions, plus student work samples, are available at Achieve the Core (https://bit.ly/2yiuCHC). In grades 6–12, the prompt is "Should your school participate in 'Shut Down Your Screen Week'?" (https://bit.ly/2tf9goF). In all grades, students are expected to read and cite a provided complex text as the basis for formulating their written responses.

- *Informational*—Students in kindergarten through grade 5 respond to this focusing question: "What can you do to save water?" They watch a short video and listen to a reader's theatre or article and use what they learn from these texts within their responses. Teacher and student directions, along with student work samples, are available from Achieve the Core (https:// bit.ly/2hdipdv). The question students in grades 6–12 address is "What effect did the Great Depression have on people who lived through it?" As the basis for their responses, they read the furnished memoir, poem, and informational article (https://bit.ly/2LDBD8i).

- *Narrative*—In the K–5 assessment, students write a realistic or imaginary story based on a painting about three dogs and a cat. Visit Achieve the Core (https://bit.ly/2J7fSPW) for K–5 materials. Students in grades 6–12 read text pertaining to the Dust Bowl and view accompanying iconic photographs of this historical period as the stimulus for writing. They write a narrative showing how a specific small moment during this experience affected one person (https://bit.ly/2GQvEt3).

- **Review writing samples to identify purpose and characteristic elements:** Teachers give an exemplary writing sample to each student in a genre that is the focus for a unit of study. They ask students to indicate the purpose for writing, identify the elements of the genre (such as setting or character for narrative) in the margins, and name any literary devices (for example, allusion, symbolism, irony, and dialect). They also identify the text structure.

- **Compare and contrast writing samples:** Teachers distribute a strong and weak writing sample from the same genre to each student. They instruct them to write about the differences between the two, including support for their reasoning, using evidence from both texts. Teachers can also ask students to rewrite the weaker version in its entirety or focus on an area needing improvement and rewrite that section only.

- **Organize characteristic elements:** Teachers instruct students to organize a list of provided terms of a genre in an outline, web, or other structure. Additionally, students write an explanation or rationale for how they group these items. Figure 6.3 (page 94) features an example of this type of preassessment for a narrative; teachers can adapt this exercise to pertain to other writing genres. Figure 6.4 (page 94) is a completed web that teachers can use to introduce a narrative unit after students finish the preassessment. Students can make a sketch of this figure in their academic notebooks, or teachers provide a copy of it.

  For elementary students, teachers can provide cards of words and pictures associated with narrative and ask students to sort them in a way that makes sense and explain their thinking. For example, prepare pictures of possible characters—dog, princess, boy, adult—and a word label *character*; picture cards of settings like lake, house, castle, forest, and park with the label *setting*; pictures of tenuous situations to reflect a story problem, such as a girl climbing an unsteady ladder, with *problem* as the word label; and so forth.

- **Recall familiar text within a genre:** To ascertain students' familiarity with texts within a genre, teachers can provide hints to elicit what they know. Figure 6.5 (page 95) features an elementary example that students complete with the aid of an adult reading the prompts aloud and recording their responses. Additionally, teachers can solicit more preassessment information. For example, ask students to name what fairy tales have in common—evil and good characters, magical events and characters, consistent beginnings and endings, and so forth.

Make a Web Preassessment
1. On a separate sheet of paper, create an outline, web, or other graphic organizer of your choice that uses the following words and phrases in a way that you think makes sense. If you want to add your own words or phrases to your organizer, please do.

- Third person
- When
- First person
- Where
- Point of view
- Central message
- Setting

- Plot
- Character
- Rising action
- Theme
- Falling action
- Antagonist
- Resolution

- Central conflict
- Introduction
- Time
- Place
- Elements
- Climax
- Protagonist

2. Write a paragraph that explains your graphic organizer.

Source: Glass, 2018, p. 47.

Figure 6.3: Narrative preassessment.

*Visit **go.SolutionTree.com/instruction** for a free reproducible version of this figure.*

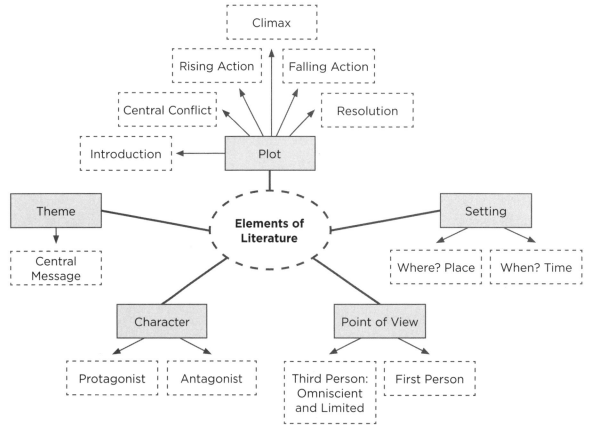

Source: Glass, 2018, p. 48.

Figure 6.4: Elements of literature web.

*Visit **go.SolutionTree.com/instruction** for a free reproducible version of this figure.*

Who Is Speaking?

Directions: Write the name of the character who says each quote. Write the name of the fairy tale if you know it.

RUN, RUN, fast as you can! You can't catch me . . .

Name of character:

Name of fairy tale:

The sky is falling! The sky is falling!

Name of character:

Name of fairy tale:

Mirror, mirror, on the wall, Who's the fairest of them all?

Name of character:

Name of fairy tale:

FE-FI-FO-FUM! I smell the blood of an Englishman!

Name of character:

Name of fairy tale:

I'll HUFF and I'll PUFF and I'll blow your house down!

Name of character:

Name of fairy tale:

No, no! Not by the hair of my chinny chin, chin!

Name of character:

Name of fairy tale:

Oh, grandmother! What big ears you have!

Name of character:

Name of fairy tale:

Who's been sitting in MY chair?

Name of character:

Name of fairy tale:

Figure 6.5: Fairy-tale preassessment.

*Visit **go.SolutionTree.com/instruction** for a free reproducible version of this figure.*

Element 16: Highlighting Critical Information

Figure 6.6 depicts the self-rating scale for highlighting critical information, which helps students focus on the content that is the most important relative to their learning.

Score	Description
4: Innovating	I engage in all behaviors at the Applying level. In addition, I identify those students who are not aware of critical information and how its pieces fit together and design alternate activities and strategies to meet their specific needs.
3: Applying	I engage in activities to highlight critical information for students without significant errors or omissions and monitor the extent to which students are aware of critical information and how its pieces fit together.
2: Developing	I engage in activities to highlight critical information for students without significant errors or omissions.
1: Beginning	I engage in activities to highlight critical information for students but do so with errors or omissions, such as highlighting information that is not critically important and not putting adequate emphasis on critical information.
0: Not Using	I do not engage in activities to highlight critical information for students.

Figure 6.6: Self-rating scale for element 16—Highlighting critical information.

These strategies align to the element of highlighting what is most important which is the focus of this section.

- Using visual activities
- Providing advance organizers to cue critical content

Using Visual Activities

Designing and conducting activities that incorporate visual aids serve to highlight important information and support students in creating mental images that promote comprehension and recall. Graphic organizers and webs function as this kind of tool in writing, too, as they help students remember the characteristics and structure of a specific text type or genre. For example, the visual of a hamburger reveals a body paragraph format with a topic sentence (top bun), supporting details (meat), and an ending sentence (bottom bun); figure 6.4 (page 94) shows the elements of literature for narrative reading and writing.

Symbols and pictures signify visual aid tools as well. For instance, teachers can make a poster and handout of the four Ts—*topic, time, territory, talker*—to explain paragraphing (figure 6.7). During the lesson, they prepare laminated bookmarks of the four Ts (figure 6.8), and distribute a set to each student. As they read independent books, students insert the appropriate bookmark in a page that demonstrates their understanding of a type of indenting rule. The teacher circulates around the room and verifies correctness or reminds them of the rule and to try again. Additionally, the bookmarks can double as mini-signs that students hold up as teachers read a text aloud.

Teachers can adapt this strategy to create bookmarks and posters for learning other reading and writing skills, such as methods of characterization (what a character says, does, looks like, feels, and what others say about a character), types of dialogue tags (beginning, ending, and middle), ways to begin sentences (dependent clause, subject, and prepositional phrase), and so forth.

When do I begin a new paragraph?	
Topic	Indent when you begin a new topic or idea.
Time	Start a new paragraph when you change the time. For example, if you switch from one day to the next, then each day needs its own paragraph.
Territory	Start a new paragraph when you change the setting or place. If you write about being at home then in the forest, home and the forest are each in separate paragraphs.
Talker	Start a new paragraph each time a character speaks even if it is just one word or sentence of dialogue. For example: "Lucy, can you come over to my house on Saturday?" Alex inquired. "I'd love to," Lucy replied, "but I need to check with my mom first." "Okay, call me tonight to let me know, please." "For sure!"

Figure 6.7: Paragraphing poster.

*Visit **go.SolutionTree.com/instruction** for a free reproducible version of this figure.*

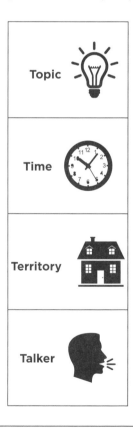

Figure 6.8: Paragraphing bookmark.

*Visit **go.SolutionTree.com/instruction** for a free reproducible version of this figure.*

Providing Advance Organizers to Cue Critical Content

When teachers preview content for students, they can display an advance organizer to show the structure and organization of new information and its connection to what was previously learned. The K-W-L chart (figure 6.2, page 92) and elements of literature web (figure 6.4, page 94) are both examples. An advance organizer can also be used when highlighting critical information, which is this element's focus. For this purpose, teachers employ the strategy to emphasize content that is particularly noteworthy and deserves more attention. Aside from graphic organizers and visual representations used to focus students' attention on salient information, advance organizers can include a verbal cue to remind student writers to connect reasons to a thesis or supporting details to a topic sentence, a classroom chart of sentence types, an anecdote of a real-world experience for how an argumentation speech fueled change, or a descriptive metaphor comparing memoir to personal narrative.

Element 17: Reviewing Content

Reviewing content provides students with the opportunity to recall material that they previously learned and perhaps alter their thinking about it. Figure 6.9 depicts the self-rating scale for reviewing content.

Score	Description
4: Innovating	I engage in all behaviors at the Applying level. In addition, I identify those students who do not have correct and complete understanding of the previously learned content and design alternate activities and strategies to meet their specific needs.
3: Applying	I engage in activities to review content without significant errors or omissions and monitor the extent to which students have a correct and complete understanding of the previously learned content.
2: Developing	I engage in activities to review content with students without significant errors or omissions.
1: Beginning	I engage in activities to review content with students but do so with errors or omissions, such as not reviewing content that is important to the upcoming lessons and not making connections to broader concepts and generalizations.
0: Not Using	I do not engage in activities to review content with students.

Figure 6.9: Self-rating scale for element 17—Reviewing content.

We highlight the following strategies aligned to this element within this section.

- Cloze activities
- Demonstration
- Give one, get one

Cloze Activities

Conducting a cloze activity helps students with comprehension of new information. Once students have experienced the content, teachers can create a paragraph with key words removed and ask students to fill them in to show understanding. Figure 6.10 features two examples—one for plot and the other for a sentence. Some students benefit from a word bank to help them complete the cloze activity. Teachers can ask students to create their own cloze paragraphs to share with classmates as a formative assessment.

Cloze Activity Examples
There are six basic elements in a _____. The introduction usually includes information about the _____ and characters. What sets the story in motion is the _____ conflict. Once this is presented, writers create a _____ that includes a series of _____. Strong writers add _____ to create tension and excitement leading to the highest point in the story called the _____. Once this is over, the _____ ties up loose ends and begins to address any questions readers might have. Lastly, the _____ ends the story and resolves the _____.
Answer:
There are six basic elements in a **plot**. The introduction usually includes information about the **setting** and characters. What sets the story in motion is the **central** conflict. Once this is presented, writers create a **rising action** that includes a series of **events**. Strong writers add **suspense** to create tension and excitement leading to the highest point in the story called the **climax**. Once this is over, the **falling action** ties up loose ends and begins to address any questions readers might have. Lastly, the **resolution** ends the story and resolves the **central conflict**.
A _____ is a group of words with a complete idea. All sentences have these two parts: a _____ and a _____. The subject names _____ or _____ the sentence is about. The _____ tells what the subject is doing.
Answer:
A **sentence** is a group of words with a complete idea. All sentences have these two parts: a **subject** and a **verb**. The subject names **who** or **what** the sentence is about. The **verb** tells what the subject is doing.

Figure 6.10: Cloze activity examples.

Teachers can also target vocabulary skills using the cloze procedure by using an excerpt from a published author's text like the one featured in figure 6.Students read the cloze excerpt first, then insert words they feel are appropriate. After reading the author's work, they discuss the comparison between words they insert and the original ones. Teachers record a class-generated list of words based on the author's and students' contributions. They can ask students to sort them by part of speech and include favorite words in their academic notebooks to use, as needed. (See the academic notebook discussion for element 8 in chapter 3, page 46, and in this chapter on page 101.)

I leaned over and looked inside. I saw a woman with _____ cheekbones and a _____ smile with one _____ front tooth, just like mine. She had _____ blue eyes and _____ brown hair that fell to her shoulders. I felt her eyes _____ in. We _____ together for a moment.
Author's Excerpt:
I leaned over and looked inside. I saw a woman with **high** cheekbones and a **broad** smile with one **overlapping** front tooth, just like mine. She had **glistening** blue eyes and **tousled** brown hair that fell to her shoulders. I felt her eyes **drink me** in. We **breathed** together for a moment.

Source: Polacco, 1998a, p. 8.

Figure 6.11: Cloze activity with author's excerpt.

Demonstration

By demonstrating a skill or process using information or a procedure they previously learned, students review the content and deepen their understanding. For example, teachers invite students to draft a paragraph about the protagonist for their own story by applying what they learned about how authors use methods of characterization to develop characters. Or students write a thesis statement containing a subordinate clause for an argumentation essay after they have studied the construction of this kind of clause and examples for how it sets up an argument. For the elementary level, teachers instruct students to apply what they learned about elaboration by adding prepositional phrases and modifiers to add details to simple sentences. Demonstrating a skill or process requires students to use and apply information as evidence of their learning.

Give One, Get One

As the strategy's name denotes, with give one, get one, students literally give a classmate an idea or example and receive one in return to add to their inventory. Sharing with one another can further cement what students have learned, so this strategy is a strong review technique. After one partnership exchanges with each other, two others share ideas. Then students can return to their seats and add to or revise what they might have recorded in their academic notebook (see element 18, that follows). Alternatively, they can have their academic notebooks in hand when meeting with peers to record the contributions they receive from others. Refer to the following list for an example of directions a teacher might say to students to conduct this activity.

1. **Review** the different ways that an informational paper can begin to engage readers from the notes in your academic notebook (or on the handout). In a few minutes, you will share these engagement strategies with others, so be prepared.

2. Everyone stand up. **Find a partner** who is nearby. Choose one of you to be partner A; the other will be partner B.

3. **When I say "give," Partner A** will share one way that writers can begin an informational paper that can engage a reader along with an example.

4. **When I say "get," Partner B** will share a different engagement strategy plus an example.

5. **When I say "switch,"** find another partner, and we will repeat this exercise.

At the primary level, students can exchange sensory words, single-syllable words with a short vowel sound, or a pair of rhyming words. Elementary students can share examples of topics they could personify, alternatives to the words *said* that they can use in their writing, or unvarying elements of a fairy tale (such as magical events, similar beginnings, and types of characters). At the secondary level, students can exchange examples of oxymoron or euphemism, or share types of evidence and examples of each that they plan to use in their papers.

Element 18: Revising Knowledge

Revising knowledge is the overt act of creating opportunities for students to make changes or add to what they thought they understood. Figure 6.12 depicts the self-rating scale for this element.

The following strategies provide teachers with ways to facilitate students' intentional revision of their knowledge.

- Academic notebook entries
- Academic notebook review
- Peer feedback
- Assignment revision
- Visual symbols
- Writing tools

Score	Description
4: Innovating	I engage in all behaviors at the Applying level. In addition, I identify those students who are not making changes to their knowledge that enhance their understanding and design alternate activities and strategies to meet their specific needs.
3: Applying	Along with adequate guidance and support, I engage students in activities that help them revise their knowledge and monitor the extent to which students are making changes to their knowledge base that enhance their understanding of context.
2: Developing	I engage students in activities that help them revise their knowledge and provide adequate guidance and support.
1: Beginning	I engage students in activities that help them revise their knowledge but do not provide adequate guidance and support, such as reminding them to look for and correct mistakes, identify and fill in gaps in understanding, and examine the reasons behind the changes they are making.
0: Not Using	I do not engage students in activities that help them revise their knowledge .

Figure 6.12: Self-rating scale for element 18—Revising knowledge.

Academic Notebook Entries and Academic Notebook Review

Students expand their writing capabilities in a wide variety of ways as they acquire new skills, processes, strategies, vocabulary, and so forth. They catalog what they learn in academic notebooks through linguistic and nonlinguistic methods as detailed in element 7 in chapter 3, page And now, in this element, the strategy around academic notebooks involves students returning to their hard copy or electronic notebooks during or at the close of a lesson to add information or review and revise existing entries. For example, they consistently augment vocabulary lists and review previous entries to reinforce and build their inventory of words for oral and written discourse. Or, as students progressively boost their expertise with grammar rules and conventions, they add resources to support them in error-free writing, which also includes more sophisticated grammatical construction.

Peer Feedback

Peers play a significant role in student writing projects in various ways, such as collaborating to share resources for a research project, acting as thought partners to brainstorm ideas for a writing topic, helping to generate figurative language examples, or reviewing each other's papers for revision suggestions. For this element— *revising knowledge*—feedback among peers involves trading academic notebooks to respond in writing to each other's entries. For example, students include definitions and examples of sentence constructions like complex sentences or parallelism along with examples or a list of words organized by parts of speech. They rely on peer feedback to check their examples and make corrections or verify accuracy, as needed. See Peer-Response Groups in element 22 in this chapter (page 114) for many additional ways to capitalize on student interaction to improve their written work.

Assignment Revision

To learn many targeted skills, students generate writing products of different lengths and forms for short- and long-term assignments for a variety of purposes. They might practice crafting a thesis statement, using various sentence structures, or sketching a character description. They might be learning how to add transitions, avoid extraneous dialogue, include reasons for an opinion, use concrete nouns and their synonyms, draw using details, include text features to help organize ideas, and so forth. These more discrete skills coalesce as students produce a comprehensive writing piece that demonstrates the collective application of what they have learned. When students participate in learning these skills, teachers and peers provide feedback. As well, students self-assess to determine areas of strength and weakness. With this input, they encourage students to revise their assignments to improve their craft as writers and to obtain a higher score. Doing so engenders an ongoing sense of growth and commitment to learning. (See the "Writing Tools" section that follows for more suggestions.)

Visual Symbols

During the editing stage of the writing process, teachers introduce students to the standard proofreading marks featured in table 6.1. Teachers can make a copy of this table and instruct students to store it in their academic notebooks for reference. For elementary students, teachers can conduct an internet search and find a modified version, or they can create their own poster using selected age-appropriate items from the provided table. Using a student sample, they model how to edit for specific purposes and how to insert these symbols. Students should also be equipped with proofreading supplies for editing their work, such as sticky notes, colored pencils, highlighter tape, and so forth.

Writing Tools

Teachers can use writing as a tool for students to revise their knowledge by asking them, for example, to summarize, respond to a quick-write, or complete sentence stems. Another revision strategy involves giving students the opportunity to examine their own work. As well as collecting input from others, critically reviewing one's own writing through self-assessment leads to improvement. Teachers can prepare and distribute a revision sheet for this purpose. It compels students to generate a clear assessment of their writing to direct revisionary efforts. Figure 6.13 (page 104) features such a tool for narrative writing for secondary students; figures 6.14 (page 107) and 6.15 (page 108) are elementary versions. Teachers can download any pertinent figure and adapt, if necessary.

To use figures 6.13 or 6.14, students read their papers and enter information guided by the revision sheet prompts. (Figure 6.15 is more simplistic and can be used to guide a discussion between the teacher and elementary writers or for dictated writing among early elementary students.) Some items, though, may not appear in their papers. For example, if students cannot provide evidence for the line item in figure 6.13, "Write an important dialogue exchange showing plot movement or character interaction," because they neglect to write dialogue or the dialogue doesn't reflect purpose, students must leave that line item blank. Other times, students might address an item, but weakly represent it. If this is the case, they can include it on the revision sheet and enclose the excerpt in parentheses to indicate that during revision they will endeavor to do a better job of addressing it. For instance, students can record on the revision sheet a sentence or two where they attempted to write the story's climax but place parentheses around the entry to remind them to revisit this part of their paper. When they write strong examples in response to a line item, they record the excerpt with an asterisk.

Once students complete the revision sheets as a self-assessment, they review them to see where they have blank lines or entries in parentheses and use this information to revise their papers. When they produce a subsequent draft, teachers can distribute clean copies and use them for peer review as well as for parents or guardians to complete outside of class. Collecting feedback from all invested parties can support students in making strategic, intentional revisions.

Table 6.1: Proofreading Marks

Mark	What It Means	How to Use It
ℐ	Delete a letter, word, or phrase.	Harry Potter was was sorted into Gryffindor.
∧	Insert a letter, word, or phrase.	Ron Wesley was also in Gryffindor.
⊙	Insert a period.	Professor Snape didn't like Harry He gave him lots of homework.
⌄	Insert a comma.	King's Cross Station is in London England.
|#	Insert a space.	Hermione had very bushy hair.
⌵	Insert a quotation mark or an apostrophe.	"Happy Christmas, Harry, said Ron.
⌣	Delete space; close up the gap.	Harry a nd Ron were mad about Quidditch.
ℐ	Delete and close the gap.	Ron had a pet rat named Scabbers.
¶	Begin a new paragraph.	"He's not Fred. I am," said George. "Just kidding," said Fred.
⌐	Run up; keep sentences in the same paragraph.	Ron couldn't wait to get to dinner. He was positively starving.
∿	Transpose; switch words or phrases around.	Ron and Harry both were thrilled to be back at Hogwarts.
≡	Capitalize a letter, word, or phrase.	Hermione granger was the smartest girl in the class.
/	Make this lowercase.	Harry's Uncle despised magic.
◯	Spell this out.	His 2 favorite teachers were Professor Dumbledore and Professor McGonagall.
(Stet)	Let it stand; do not change.	Use when a proofreading mark is incorrect.

Source: Glass, 2017a, p. 29.

*Visit **go.SolutionTree.com/instruction** for a free reproducible version of this table.*

Realistic Fiction Revision Sheet		
General Descriptors	**Circle**	
	Yes or No	
The writing genre is a **realistic short story**.	Yes	No
There are **no grammar or convention errors**; the paper is properly **formatted**.	Yes	No
Paragraphs are used where they should be and are indented properly.	Yes	No
There is an original or creative **title**.	Yes	No
The paper maintains a consistent and appropriate **point of view** or is written from multiple viewpoints that readers can easily follow.	Yes	No

Descriptors	Story Elements
An engaging **beginning** draws in readers.	Write a sentence that draws in readers.
A **setting** and **characters** are established and provide context.	Who are the characters?
	What is the setting?
The beginning includes a **central conflict** to set the story in motion.	Briefly identify the central conflict.
The rising action creates **suspense**.	Include three major events that build suspense toward the climax. 1.
	2.
	3.
The **story's climax** presents the highest point of tension.	Identify the moment of climax in the story.
The **resolution** addresses the central conflict.	What satisfying ending resolves the central conflict?

Descriptors	Literary Devices
Literary devices involving the **plot** create interest, but do not distract or confuse readers.	Which device does the student use, such as flashback, flash forward, multiple plotlines, and suspense?
	Provide proof (evidence) of its effectiveness.
Meaningful and intentional **dialogue** enhances the storyline.	Write an important dialogue exchange showing plot movement or character interaction. (Or indicate this section on the actual paper.)
Dialect reflects characters' geographical region, social status, era, bias, or other.	Write two excerpts of dialogue in which the student effectively uses dialect. 1.
	2.

Descriptors	Description
Vocabulary and **figurative language** enhance setting, characters, or events.	Provide two examples of figurative language—simile, metaphor, personification, hyperbole, or imagery. Underline precise words. 1.
	2.
The writing elicits emotion through **mood**.	Write two phrases that show mood. Indicate the emotion in parentheses. 1.
	2.
Strong verbs in the dialogue tags accentuate a character's words.	List at least four strong verbs used in dialogue tags.

Figure 6.13: Narrative revision sheet, secondary level.   continued →

Descriptors	Sentence Structure and Transitions
Sentences **begin in different ways**.	Write two sentences that each begin in a different way. 1. 2.
Sentence structures vary.	Write two sentences that each have a different sentence structure. 1. 2.
The writing includes **parallel** construction.	Write two sentences that use parallelism. 1. 2.
Appropriate **transitions** show event sequence and a shift in time and place.	Write two examples of transitional usage. 1. 2.

Source: Glass, 2018, pp. 103–105.

*Visit **go.SolutionTree.com/instruction** for a free reproducible version of this figure.*

Personal Narrative Revision Sheet 1	
Ideas, Content, and Organization	
There is an **original title**.	Write the original title.
This is a **personal narrative** about something **true** that happened to me.	Write the event.
There is a description of a **setting**.	Write the setting including one adjective to describe it.
There is a description of a **character**.	Write one character including an adjective to describe him or her.
There is a **logical order** to explain **what happened**.	Write what happened in a logical order.
The writer tells why the event or experience **is important** or how the writer **feels** about what happened.	Write why the event or experience is important or how the writer feels about it.
Sentence Fluency	
Sentences begin in **different ways**.	Write a sentence:
	Write another sentence that begins in a different way:
There are **order words** to connect sentences.	Write the order words that connect different sentences:
Word Choice	
There are interesting **adjectives**.	Write interesting adjectives:
There are interesting **verbs**.	Write interesting verbs:

Source: Adapted from Glass, 2012, p. 212.

Figure 6.14: Personal narrative revision sheet 1, elementary level.

*Visit **go.SolutionTree.com/instruction** for a free reproducible version of this figure.*

Personal Narrative Revision Sheet 2		
	| Circle	
Ideas, Content, and Organization		
This is a personal narrative about **something true** that happened to the writer.	Yes	No
There is a **title**.	Yes	No
The writing **begins** with a description of a **setting**.	Yes	No
The writing **begins** with a description of a **character**.	Yes	No
The writing **begins** with a **telling sentence about what happened**.	Yes	No
In the **middle**, the writer explains **what happens in a logical order**.	Yes	No
The **ending** tells why the event is **important** or how the writer **feels** about what happened.	Yes	No
Voice		
The writer uses first-person point of view using the **pronoun** I because I write what happened to me.	Yes	No
Sentence Fluency		
All **sentences** are **complete**.	Yes	No
There are **no run-on sentences**.	Yes	No
Sentences **begin with different words**.	Yes	No
Order words connect sentences.	Yes	No
Word Choice		
Sensory details help readers picture the writing.	Yes	No
The writer uses interesting **adjectives and verbs**.	Yes	No
Conventions		
Words are **spelled** correctly.	Yes	No
There are correct **end marks** at the end of each sentence.	Yes	No
Letters at the beginning of sentences, names of people, and the word I are **capitalized.**	Yes	No
When the paper is read aloud, it **makes sense**.	Yes	No
The **handwriting is easy to read**, and the paper is **neat**.	Yes	No
The writer leaves **space** between words and sentences.	Yes	No

Figure 6.15: Personal narrative revision sheet 2, elementary level.

Visit **go.SolutionTree.com/instruction** *for a free reproducible version of this table.*

Element 19: Reflecting on Learning

Reflecting on learning involves students analyzing the extent to which they are behaving as effective learners. Figure 6.16 depicts the self-rating scale for this element.

Score	Description
4: Innovating	I engage in all behaviors at the Applying level. In addition, I identify those students who are not aware of their major impediments to learning and design alternate activities and strategies to meet their specific needs.
3: Applying	Along with adequate guidance and support, I engage students in activities that help them reflect on their own learning and monitor the extent to which students are aware of their major impediments to learning.
2: Developing	I engage students in activities that help them reflect on their own learning and provide adequate guidance and support.
1: Beginning	I engage students in activities that help them reflect on their own learning but do not provide adequate guidance and support, such as reminding them to continually monitor their level of understanding as well as their levels of effort and attention.
0: Not Using	I do not engage students in activities that help them reflect on their own learning.

Figure 6.16: Self-rating scale for element 19—Reflecting on learning.

The following strategies are associated with this element.

- Reflective journals
- Exit slips

Reflective Journals

After a class lesson or at the end of a unit, teachers can pose questions that students respond to in their academic notebooks, prompting self-assessment and awareness. For example, students ascertain whether a skill is easy or difficult to master, how well they understand the difference between genres, how they feel they participate in critiquing a writing sample, or ways they might contribute more during a peer review session.

After students produce the culminating written product, teachers provide them with multiple opportunities to respond to reflective questions or prompts about themselves as writers, the writing process, and what they glean from the unit. These questions are some of the many options teachers can pose to students.

- **Writing process:** Did the steps in the writing process help me produce my best work? How so? Did I miss or abbreviate any steps? How did that impact my writing? Could I have used the steps differently?
- **Writing topic:** What was the most significant takeaway about this topic? What would I want others to know about it? What surprised me? What do I want to know more about with this topic? Have I matured in my thinking as a result of this writing piece? How so?
- **Research:** Was I an effective researcher? What did I learn about researching that I will use next time I conduct research? What did I find difficult when researching? How did I address this problem, or what could I have done differently?
- **Writing skills:** What new writing skill did I learn and apply during this unit? Did I feel I used it well? What is an example of how I used it? What additional practice or knowledge do I need help with to use it better? What other skill do I want to learn to help me be a better writer?

Exit Slips

Teachers can take a quick pulse of students' mastery of learning goals by issuing a prompt or question for students to address during the last three to five minutes of class (or before transitioning to another subject). For example, at the primary level, teachers might ask students to write words or draw pictures that describe how they are feeling, words beginning with a particular sound, or words that rhyme. Elementary students can write a compound sentence and underline the coordinating conjunction, a simile, or an opinion statement. Secondary students can write a piece of evidence to support a position, questions to drive research they will conduct, or parts of a lab report. Some teachers use a 3-2-1 format for exit cards. For instance, write three ways to begin a sentence, two subordinating conjunctions, and one dependent clause. Or, write three adverbs, two action verbs, and one pronoun.

Teachers can also ask generic questions, such as, "What did you find challenging today?" "What questions do you have about today's lesson?" "How well do you think you participated today?" "On a scale of 1–5, how successful do you feel in reaching your goals today?" Students record their responses on recycled paper or index cards, which teachers collect and review. If the teacher has centered the exit card on a skill, process, or strategy, the responses determine which students need additional support and which are ready to move ahead so that teachers can act accordingly. Some teachers separate cards into three piles—(1) those who "get it" and can proceed to the next lesson, (2) students who are somewhat murky in their knowledge, and (3) those who clearly missed the mark. As an alternative to collecting paper exit cards, students can electronically respond to prompts on Google Forms—where the information populates onto a spreadsheet for teachers to review—or a similar platform.

Element 20: Assigning Purposeful Homework

Teachers frequently use homework, but not always in ways that enhance student learning. Figure 6.17 represents the self-rating scale for this element.

Score	Description
4: Innovating	I engage in all behaviors at the Applying level. In addition, I identify those students for whom the assigned homework does not enhance learning and design alternate activities and strategies to meet their specific needs.
3: Applying	I engage in activities to assign purposeful homework without significant errors or omissions and monitor the extent to which the homework enhances student learning.
2: Developing	I engage in activities to assign purposeful homework without significant errors or omissions.
1: Beginning	I engage in activities to assign purposeful homework but do so with errors or omissions, such as assigning homework not directly related to the critical content addressed in class and assigning homework for which students are not adequately prepared.
0: Not Using	I do not engage in activities to assign purposeful homework.

Figure 6.17: Self-rating scale for element 20—Assigning purposeful homework.

In this element, we focus on the strategy of parent-assessed homework.

To foster a home-school connection and give parents or guardians guidance in helping students improve their writing skills, teachers send figure 6.18 home with a student's writing draft. It serves to focus parents in offering constructive feedback. Alternatively, as mentioned earlier, parents can complete one of the revision sheets in the Writing Tools section (see element 18; figures 6.13, 6.14, or 6.15, pages 104–108). Armed with parents' or guardians' comments, students incorporate salient input into a subsequent draft. This support

Dear Parent or Guardian,

I am invested in helping students become better writers. To this end, I gauge each student's writing ability and build on his or her strengths and address weaknesses. Many parents choose to partner with teachers to help in this endeavor. Following are suggestions to assist with improving your child's writing skills. Please refrain from writing on your child's paper; instead, offer feedback using these pointers as a guide. In doing so, you empower your student writer to find ideas for revision, which contributes to achievement. Feel free to attach a note with any specific comments or questions that your child can address in class during peer or teacher conferences.

Focus on the assignment task and expectations. Ask to see the assignment sheet, checklist, or rubric. Review the task and criteria with your child to clarify a particular assignment's expectations. Encourage him or her to ensure the paper addresses all parts of the writing assignment and criteria.

Recognize proper organization. Ask for evidence of proper organization of the whole paper and within paragraphs based on the genre of the piece. Look at the checklist or rubric to guide this discussion, and ask questions such as the following.

- "Are you writing a story? If so, is there a logical sequence? Have you included plot elements, such as a central conflict, rising action, a climax, and so forth?"
- "Is this an argumentation essay? If so, can you show me your thesis statement that stakes a claim? Are your reasons in a logical order? Do your reasons and evidence support your thesis? Are there counterarguments? If so, are they well placed to support your argument?"
- "Are your paragraphs for expository text structured appropriately? Is there a topic sentence, supporting details or evidence, and an ending? Do the details connect to the topic sentence?"
- "Do you include text features—such as charts, graphs, a table of contents, subheadings, a glossary, and so on? Let's reread the paper to be sure that these text features help organize the piece."

Consider the development. Is the paper complete? If it's a story, are characters, setting, and events fully developed? Are narrative techniques included to enhance it (like dialogue and description)? If it is an argument, are there enough reasons, and is there sufficient evidence and elaboration to support each reason? Are counterarguments acknowledged and addressed? Refer to the checklist and rubric to ensure all items have been thoroughly met.

Look at word choice. Ask your child to do the following. Review the paper and circle words that he or she feels are strong and reflect the best choice. Reread the paper and assist your child to replace any words that could be more precise or descriptive using a print or digital resource (www.merriam-webster.com, www.vocabulary.com, www.collinsdictionary.com, or www.thesaurus.com), classroom textbook, or other resource, as needed.

- Ensure that the word choice or language is appropriate for the audience.
- Make sure your child uses words accurately, including subject-matter terms related to topics or content areas. If he or she does not, refer your child to an appropriate resource.

Examine sentence beginnings and structure. Ask your child to read the first three words of each sentence. Ask these questions: "What do you notice about the beginnings of sentences? Are the words and parts of speech different? Do they sound too repetitive?" Ask him or her to revise sentence beginnings, as appropriate, so there is variety. Additionally, discuss sentence structure, and ask if he or she has varied the types of sentences (for example, simple, compound, and complex sentences) so there is a natural rhythm to the writing.

Conduct oral reading to detect convention errors. Ask your child to read the paper aloud and self-assess by doing the following.

- Listen for clarity—If a sentence is hard to read, it could reflect a grammatical error. Ask him or her to find and correct any grammatical errors.
- Listen for natural stops or pauses—When there is a natural stop, ask if there is proper end punctuation (a period, exclamation mark, or question mark). This will also help to detect run-on sentences or fragments that need fixing. If there is a pause, inquire whether a comma or end punctuation mark is needed and what rule might apply.

Source: Glass, 2017a, p. 26.

Figure 6.18: Suggestions for parents or guardians in assisting student writers.

*Visit **go.SolutionTree.com/instruction** for a free reproducible version of this figure.*

helps with those parents who might feel compelled to obtrusively interfere with their child's paper and for those who want to comment but aren't sure how to go about it.

Element 21: Elaborating on Information

Elaboration is an inferential act that results in the creation of new awareness when students engage in it effectively. Figure 6.19 depicts the self-rating scale for this element.

Score	Description
4: Innovating	I engage in all behaviors at the Applying level. In addition, I identify those students who are not making substantive additions to their knowledge base and design alternate activities and strategies to meet their specific needs.
3: Applying	Along with adequate guidance and support, I engage students in activities that help them elaborate on information and monitor the extent to which students are making substantive additions to their knowledge base.
2: Developing	I engage students in activities that help them elaborate on information and provide adequate guidance and support.
1: Beginning	I engage students in activities that help them elaborate on information but do not provide adequate guidance and support, such as not sequencing questions in such a way as to gradually increase the rigor of students' responses and not pushing students to expand on their answers.
0: Not Using	I do not engage students in activities that help them elaborate on information.

Figure 6.19: Self-rating scale for element 21—Elaborating on information.

For this element, we focus on the strategy of elaborative interrogation.

As discussed, when students progress through the writing process, they benefit from input across the board, including critically self-assessing their own papers. Additionally, they solicit feedback from classmates and perhaps others outside the classroom (for example, parents, guardians, or those in an electronic writing community). Teachers also play a vital and active role to support students in producing optimal results. To do so, they connect with each student and conduct short conferences in which they artfully ask questions to probe student thinking and stimulate new ideas. They can pose general questions such as, "How is your writing going?" "Is there a part that confuses you that you might want me to read?" "Can I help you strengthen some area of your paper?" Or ask other sorts of questions, such as the following (Glass, 2017a, p. 25):

- What impression do you want to leave on readers? Do you feel your conclusion does this?
- Which reason is the most convincing in your argument? Do you have enough evidence to support it properly?
- Is all this dialogue meaningful to the story, and does it move the plot forward? Where do you feel you might delete some of it?

In elaborative interrogations (Marzano, 2007), teachers compel students to reflect on their thinking and justify a response as if answering the question: "Why do you believe that to be true?" Or, teachers can use the frame "What would happen if you . . . ?" tailored to the writing task, for example:

- What would happen if you introduce the central conflict earlier?
- . . . add more figurative language?
- . . . add more detail to your pictures?
- . . . include text features?
- . . . change the point of view?

- ... rearrange sections of your paper?
- ... research to find more evidence?
- ... provide more elaboration?

Probing further, the teacher then asks, "Why do you think this is so?" After discussion with the student, the teacher restates the student's thinking using the stem, "It seems to me that you are saying. . . ." This becomes an *if/then* construct that helps students critically reexamine what they wrote and articulate their next writing moves. For example, "It seems to me that you are saying *if* you shave off some of the beginning of your story, *then* you would get to the central conflict earlier and engage readers more effectively." "It seems to me that you are saying *if* you research to find more evidence, *then* you could make a stronger argument since you'd have more ammunition to make your point." This sequence of elaborative interrogations prompts students to review and reconsider their logic so they can make more thoughtful and intentional revisions.

Since teachers have limited time with students during the day, they can collect students' papers or access them electronically, read them, and generate questions in preparation for each student conference. As well, they can share these questions with students in advance of the conference to give students valuable time to think about how they might respond to improve their papers. Teachers can still ask additional questions that surface during the conference, but it gives a good starting point for a more fruitful discussion when students—as well as teachers—have had a chance to carefully review papers in advance.

Element 22: Organizing Students to Interact

Teachers must organize students into groups thoughtfully to ensure that students collaborate to effectively enhance their learning. Figure 6.20 depicts the self-rating scale for this element.

Score	Description
4: Innovating	I engage in all behaviors at the Applying level. In addition, I identify those students who are not actively involved and interacting deeply about the content and design alternate activities and strategies to meet their specific needs.
3: Applying	I engage in activities that organize students to interact without significant errors or omissions and monitor the extent to which students are actively involved and interacting deeply about the content.
2: Developing	I engage in activities that organize students to interact without significant errors or omissions.
1: Beginning	I engage in activities that organize students to interact but do so with errors or omissions, such as failing to establish protocols for interaction and a clear purpose and goals for interacting.
0: Not Using	I do not engage in activities that organize students to interact.

Figure 6.20: Self-rating scale for element 22—Organizing students to interact.

For this final element pertaining to all types of lessons, we focus on the following strategies relative to writing instruction.

- Fishbowl demonstration
- Think-pair-share and think-pair-square
- Peer-response groups

Fishbowl Demonstration

In a fishbowl demonstration, the teacher invites a student group to the front of the class to model how to do something. Those participating in the fishbowl can switch roles with observers at some point so others get a turn at modeling. For example, students watch group-work skills in action, like how to solicit input from reluctant peers in a collaborative discussion or maintain eye contact with the whole group to include everyone. Fishbowl also serves to demonstrate ways students can contribute to a fruitful discussion, such as asking and answering questions, transitioning between comments, and respectfully disagreeing with others.

For teaching writing in particular, teachers can implement this strategy to show students how to provide feedback for peers' drafts. This can be a discussion either between a pair of students or within a small group in which one student reads a portion of his or her paper aloud and the others provide feedback based on the student writer's direction. Teachers feature the steps in a peer-feedback session so participants and observers can learn from the sequence that they will emulate. For example, the student writer asks for specific feedback in an area and poses questions he or she wants others to answer, the student writer reads the targeted portion of the paper aloud, reviewers make suggestions orally that the student writer records, and the student writer accepts feedback graciously. The student writers do not necessarily incorporate all feedback into their drafts; however, they should show appreciation nevertheless for the comments.

Think-Pair-Share and Think-Pair-Square

Teachers can distribute the same or different writing samples to students and ask them to determine the problem with the paper, such as "lacks figurative language," "faulty sentence construction," or "topic sentences disconnected from thesis." Students work individually to discover the issue (*think*), and then work in pairs to discuss it. Together they agree on the issue and suggest revisions to improve the paper (*pair*). Finally, students can share with another partnership (*square*), or teachers lead a class discussion in which pairs or foursomes report the highlights of their findings (*share*). For links of student and published work samples to use for this exercise, see element 9 in chapter 4 (page 55). This strategy also works well for reluctant learners in that it provides students time to rehearse and correct their answers before sharing them with the whole class.

Peer-Response Groups

One hallmark of teaching writing is peer feedback. Teachers explicitly teach how to effectively solicit and receive input that students use to revise their work and produce a subsequent draft. Students can provide and receive feedback in a face-to-face partnership situation, a small-group setting, or electronically with peers or others outside the classroom community.

Before students review each other's work, teachers communicate the following guidelines and can use the fishbowl demonstration (detailed in the previous section) to demonstrate these points. Student writers need to know that teachers will not require them to take all reviewers' comments and incorporate them into the next draft. They collect the feedback and ultimately make their own decisions.

- **Be respectful:** When giving (and receiving) feedback, students should be tactful and courteous.
- **Focus feedback:** Before comments, reviewers ask the student writer what he or she wants feedback on so they can focus their attention. They use the writing task and rubric (or checklist) to pinpoint these areas. Student writers can also use a revision sheet like those in chapter 5 (figures 5.5 and 5.6, pages 79–81) to direct peer reviewers to concentrate on specific areas. In turn, reviewers comment on this same sheet (see element 13, chapter 5, offering feedback, on page 77).

- **Emphasize strengths:** Begin with what works well in the paper. For instance, students can state their overall impression, phrases that are particularly vivid, or something they learned.
- **Be constructive:** Reviewers offer feedback that is tangible and directs revision, such as the following examples.
  - "The rising action is exciting and got me into the story. I was waiting for the climax and didn't notice where it was. My suggestion is to work on that part of your story."
  - "You write details about the protagonist so readers can picture him in our heads. You might do the same for the antagonist so we get a better idea of what she looks like and her personality."
  - "This paragraph has a solid topic sentence and strong details for support. It is missing an ending to wrap it up."
  - Suggest this sentence starter: "This part confuses me because _____." "Your paper is missing _____." "The strongest part of your paper is when _____. Try this technique when _____ (identify another area to apply this strength)."
- **Recommend resources:** Reviewers can offer student writers resources that might be helpful for revision, such as a handout the teacher provided, a bookmarked internet page, or a section in a classroom textbook. The reviewer might say, "I recommend using the resource _____ (name the resource) for _____ (identify the purpose for the resource and how the student can use it)."

GUIDING QUESTIONS FOR CURRICULUM DESIGN

For using strategies that appear in all types of lessons—direct instruction, practicing and deepening, and knowledge application lessons—this is the design question: *Throughout all types of lessons, what strategies will I use to help students continually integrate new knowledge with old knowledge and revise their understanding accordingly?* The following specific questions align to each of the eight elements in this chapter and serve to guide teachers in planning instruction.

- **Element 15:** How will I help students preview strategies?

_____
_____
_____
_____

- **Element 16:** How will I highlight critical information?

_____
_____
_____
_____

- **Element 17:** How will I help students review content?

_____
_____
_____
_____

- **Element 18:** How will I help students revise knowledge?

  _____

  _____

  _____

  _____

  _____

- **Element 19:** How will I help students reflect on their learning?

  _____

  _____

  _____

  _____

  _____

- **Element 20:** How will I use purposeful homework?

  _____

  _____

  _____

  _____

  _____

- **Element 21:** How will I help students elaborate on information?

  _____

  _____

  _____

  _____

  _____

- **Element 22:** How will I organize students to interact?

  _____

  _____

  _____

  _____

  _____

Conclusion

Although theoretically teachers could incorporate all elements in every kind of lesson, this would not necessarily be wise practice. Rather, teachers should use their professional judgment to judiciously balance the use of these elements to help students continually integrate new knowledge with old. In the next chapter, we begin the category of _context_ and discuss using engagement strategies.

PART III
Context

CHAPTER 7

Using Engagement Strategies

As stated in the introduction, *context*—the third of the overarching three categories—refers to students' mental readiness during the teaching-learning process. For students to be ready, their needs relative to engagement, order, a sense of belonging, and high expectations must be met.

Many people use the term *engagement*; however, it is a term that does not always have a clear definition. In fact, educators ascribe a wide variety of meanings to the term. For example, some educators might use the term to mean the simple behavior of paying attention to what the teacher is doing in class, while others might use it to mean students being intrinsically motivated by what occurs in class. *The New Art and Science of Teaching* (Marzano, 2017) addresses engagement from four perspectives. One is the traditional notion of attention. That is, some of the elements are designed to ensure that students attend to what occurs in the classroom. Another perspective is energy level. Some elements involve strategies designed to increase students' energy levels, particularly when those levels are getting low. A third perspective is intrigue. Some of the elements address techniques that help stimulate high levels of student interest in such a way that students seek further information about the content on their own. The fourth perspective is motivation and inspiration. As the name implies, these elements include strategies that spark students' desire for self-agency and propel them to engage in tasks of their own design and control.

The following elements focus on engagement.

- **Element 23:** Noticing and reacting when students are not engaged
- **Element 24:** Increasing response rates
- **Element 25:** Using physical movement
- **Element 26:** Maintaining a lively pace
- **Element 27:** Demonstrating intensity and enthusiasm
- **Element 28:** Presenting unusual information
- **Element 29:** Using friendly controversy
- **Element 30:** Using academic games
- **Element 31:** Providing opportunities for students to talk about themselves
- **Element 32:** Motivating and inspiring students

Element 23: Noticing and Reacting When Students Are Not Engaged

The first step in addressing student engagement is for the teacher to recognize when students are not engaged and react accordingly. Figure 7.1 depicts the self-rating scale for this element about attending to students when they are disengaged.

Score	Description
4: Innovating	I engage in all behaviors at the Applying level. In addition, I identify those students who are not re-engaging and design alternate activities and strategies to meet their specific needs.
3: Applying	I engage in activities to notice and react when students are not engaged without significant errors or omissions and monitor the extent to which students re-engage based on their actions.
2: Developing	I engage in activities to notice and react when students are not engaged without significant errors or omissions.
1: Beginning	I engage in activities to notice and react when students are not engaged but do so with errors or omissions, such as focusing on only a few students when checking on student engagement and not reacting in a timely manner when students are disengaged.
0: Not Using	I do not engage in activities to notice and react when students are not engaged.

Figure 7.1: Self-rating scale for element 23—Noticing and reacting when students are not engaged.

For this element, our focus is on the strategy of re-engaging individual students.

When teachers notice disengagement, they should approach students to determine the cause of their disenfranchisement. Taking the time to acknowledge when something is not working well for students shows respect and contributes to relationship building.

When students tackle a writing assignment, their interests might wane or they encounter a slump—perhaps writer's block—so teachers need to reignite or provoke interest to re-energize and engage them. For example, they can suggest a different topic for a research report, allow students to choose another historical era as the basis for a historical fiction piece rather than their original selection, change argumentation topics for an essay or speech that they are more passionate about, or begin writing a narrative again if the original one started off in the wrong direction. Teachers can offer these and other suggestions, as well as ask students what they might want to do to foster their own engagement. Giving them the license to redirect or amend an initial course can help to revitalize and invest them in the work ahead.

Element 24: Increasing Response Rates

Increasing the number of students who respond to a single question can greatly enhance the engagement level of the class as a whole. Figure 7.2 depicts the self-rating scale for this element.

Score	Description
4: Innovating	I engage in all behaviors at the Applying level. In addition, I identify those students who are not generating thoughtful and accurate responses and design alternate activities and strategies to meet their specific needs.
3: Applying	I engage in activities to increase response rates of students without significant errors or omissions and monitor the extent to which students are generating thoughtful and accurate responses.

Score	Description
2: Developing	I engage in activities to increase the response rates of students without significant errors or omissions.
1: Beginning	I engage in activities to increase the response rates of students but do so with errors or omissions, such as not providing adequate time for students to respond to the activity and not acknowledging that students have responded.
0: Not Using	I do not engage in activities to increase the response rates of students.

Figure 7.2: Self-rating scale for element 24—Increasing response rates.

The following strategies relate to increasing students' response rates.

- Hand signals
- Response cards

Hand Signals

Using hand signals—either thumbs or fingers—to respond to prompts provides an informal means of gathering information about students' understanding. For thumb signals, teachers present a prompt and students respond with thumbs up to indicate *yes* or *true*, or down for *no* or *false*. For finger signals, teachers provide a key to show what each number—one, two, three, or even four fingers—means, and students respond accordingly. Students show a fist for either type of response to signify "I am unsure" or "I don't know." See figure 7.3 (page 122) for ways to use this strategy. Notice the versatility in this strategy: prompts can appeal to the subject-matter content that serves as the basis for writing or to specific writing skills.

Before initiating the prompts involving hand signals, teachers communicate the following points to students.

- I'll ask you to participate in an exercise to help me gauge what you know, don't know, or are unsure about so that I can target my teaching better.

- I will read a series of prompts and ask you to respond to each one at a time using your thumb or fingers.

- I will read each prompt two times. After the second time, I will say "Wait" then "Show" (or "Signal"). At that time, show your response by using a thumb or fingers. Anytime you are unsure of an answer, please show a fist.

- Signal at chest level so that you communicate with me directly. If you hold your arm up in the air to signal, others are influenced by your response. I want to know what you think.

Teachers determine the number of prompts to issue based on the information they need to collect. Once they pose a prompt and all students signal, they pan the room to collect informal data. After each response, they merely report out the correct answer, such as "Thumbs up is the correct answer." Or, "Number 2—simile—is the correct answer." Sometimes teachers can pause after each prompt and solicit volunteers to explain the correct answer. Other times they can promote self-discovery by asking students to pay attention to their responses, compare them to the right answers, then self-correct along the way, as needed. Based on responses, teachers can determine how to proceed with individuals or groups of students, such as reteaching or proceeding with planned instruction.

THE NEW ART AND SCIENCE OF TEACHING WRITING — page 122

Hand Signal Examples

Thumbs Up = True / **Thumbs Down** = False / **Fist** = I am not sure.	**Thumbs Up** = True / **Thumbs Down** = False / **Fist** = I am not sure.	**Thumbs Up** = Sentence begins with a dependent clause. / **Thumbs Down** = Sentence doesn't begin with a dependent clause. / **Fist** = I am not sure.	**Thumbs Up** = Correct sentence mechanics / **Thumbs Down** = Incorrect sentence mechanics / **Fist** = I am not sure.
1. An element is a substance that contains only one kind of atom. 2. All substances are made up of tiny particles called atoms. 3. Most elements are found together as combined substances called compounds. 4. H_2O is a chemical symbol for a single molecule of water. It's composed of one hydrogen and one oxygen atom. 5. Scientists believe that 50 percent of the universe comprises hydrogen and helium.	1. Bats are dirty. 2. Bats are very good fliers. 3. Bats are blind. 4. Some bats hunt using only their sense of sight. 5. Vampire bats turn into human vampires.	1. While I was walking, I spotted a leopard staring at me. 2. As she glanced at him, he blushed. 3. By the way, I think she is a very good teacher. 4. Skydiving is something I can't wait to do. 5. Even though he loves books, he sometimes doesn't finish them. 6. If I were to travel to Florida, I'd bring my bathing suit. 7. In the morning, I called my sister.	1. sally is my sister 2. "Will you help me?" the Boy asked. 3. Tim said, "I will help you." 4. The dog ran away from the house. 5. dont ring the doorbell late at nite

1 Finger = Noun / **2 Fingers** = Adjective / **3 Fingers** = Verb / **Fist** = I am not sure.	**1 Finger** = Simile / **2 Fingers** = Personification / **3 Fingers** = Metaphor / **Fist** = I am not sure.	**1 Finger** = Continent / **2 Fingers** = State / **3 Fingers** = Water / **Fist** = I am not sure.	**1 Finger** = Beginning speaker tag / **2 Fingers** = End speaker tag / **3 Fingers** = Middle speaker tag / **Fist** = I am not sure.
1. Mrs. Kaplan 2. Teacher 3. Hop 4. Lonely 5. Skip 6. Dancer 7. Pretty 8. Mad 9. President Truman 10. Is 11. January 12. Thin	1. Hunger sat shivering on the road. 2. Kimberly's teeth are as straight as rows of cans neatly lined up on a grocery shelf. 3. Her nose is a pointed hat stuck on her inflated face. 4. The leaves are a carpet covering the ill-kept lawn. 5. Flowers danced about the meadow in unison.	1. Asia 2. North America 3. Atlantic Ocean 4. California 5. Pacific Ocean 6. Mississippi River 7. Europe 8. The Nile 9. Alaska	1. "Careful," his mom scolded, "or you might spill your drink." 2. "What time is the movie?" Leo asked his friend James. 3. Pedro smiled widely and said, "That was the best party ever!" 4. "Please," the mermaid pleaded, "don't tell anyone you saw me." 5. "Yes, indeed!" she exclaimed.

Figure 7.3: Hand signal examples.

Visit go.SolutionTree.com/instruction for a free reproducible version of this figure.

Once students are aware of how this active participation exercise works, they can make prompts using varied resources. Then they lead their peers in a small group or as a whole class in a hand signal activity. Creating the prompts presents a critical-thinking opportunity that supports student learning.

Response Cards

This is the same strategy as in element 4 in chapter 2 (page 29), response boards, where the focus is on gathering assessment data of the whole class. Teachers can take note of student responses and plan the next instructional moves accordingly. In addition to using this strategy to collect informal data, here the purpose is to heighten students' attention level. Teachers elect to incorporate this strategy in their arsenal when they feel a need to solicit responses from the entire class simultaneously to increase response rates.

Element 25: Using Physical Movement

Energy is essential to engagement; physical movement is a straightforward approach to raising energy. Figure 7.4 depicts the self-rating scale for this element about incorporating physical movement into the classroom.

Score	Description
4: Innovating	I engage in all behaviors at the Applying level. In addition, I identify those students who do not exhibit increased energy levels and design alternate activities and strategies to meet their specific needs.
3: Applying	I engage in activities to increase the physical movement of students without significant errors or omissions and monitor the extent to which students exhibit increased energy levels.
2: Developing	I engage in activities to increase the physical movement of students without significant errors or omissions.
1: Beginning	I engage in activities to increase the physical movement of students but do so with errors or omissions, such as not using physical movement at times when students need an energy boost and not providing an appropriate amount of time for the physical activities.
0: Not Using	I do not engage in activities to increase the physical movement of students.

Figure 7.4: Self-rating scale for element 25—Using physical movement.

We explore the strategy of body representations and drama-related activities for this element.

To assist with comprehension of complex text, students can select and act out a critical scene in a realistic fiction book or an autobiography they are reading. Or they can determine which event in a historical period precipitated a series of actions and act out either the causes or effects. They can also create human graphic organizers to show relationships among characters or the sequence of events. For example, they can sit, crouch, or stand to represent a hierarchical struggle among characters or to reflect parent and offspring relationships. As well, movement can augment their physical positions as they might show interaction of causes and effects with a push and pull of their bodies. Any of these ideas can precede an electronic or handcrafted graphic organizer that serves as a prewriting exercise. Teachers can also ask audiences to give their impressions.

Teachers can ask groups to invent and perform a tableau in which students freeze in a particular pose based on selected episodes in a text that they deem pivotal. The teacher could incorporate writing by having students brainstorm the basis for their "living picture"; after groups present their tableaus, students submit a written response of their impressions.

More specifically, a tableau calls on students to read for deep meaning, isolate a noteworthy situation, imagine themselves in the situation the characters or individuals face, and determine their reactions. Students pretend that someone takes a snapshot that requires them to freeze in place with intentional bodily stances, facial expressions, and positions intact to reflect the highlighted scene. They are silent and motionless, but their poses, gestures, and expressions replace words to communicate meaning. Each pair, trio, or small group can create a different tableau, such as plot elements, episodes in an autobiography, or events in history. Figure 7.5 is a tableau assignment sheet that teachers can use as is or adapt for their students.

Tableau Assignment

Arrange students in trios for this assignment. Choose a student who will videotape the tableaus to use for audience reactions or students can conduct live tableaus.

Planning and Presenting

Ask students the following questions and instruct them on their planning and presenting.

1. What particular scene in *Romeo and Juliet* in Act 3 is most pivotal? Justify your response to support why you think it is most pivotal.

   - Note: Students might choose one of these scenes—
     - Death of Mercutio
     - Romeo kills Tybalt
     - Juliet decides if she stays by Romeo's side or leaves him because he kills Tybalt
     - Romeo gets banished from Verona

2. You will create a tableau based on this scene. In a tableau, you will freeze in place to capture it. Pay particular attention to the following when you plan and present your tableau:
   - What characters are featured in your tableau?
   - How are the characters positioned? For example, are they standing, sitting, or crouching?
   - What facial expressions do the characters show? What do you want the audience to feel? How can each of you capture their emotion through facial features?
   - What gestures will the characters use? How will you position your hands to convey this scene?

Audience Reaction

Lead a discussion after each group appears on the video or performs in person using the questions from this section. Then ask the tableau group if the audience response matched their intentions. Also ask them if they would change their tableau in any way.

3. As you watch each tableau, answer these questions:
   - Which scene is this? Do you think it is one of the pivotal scenes and why? Show your understanding of the text when responding.
   - What particular aspect of this tableau best reflects the scene and why?

Figure 7.5: Tableau assignment sheet with teacher directions and potential student responses.
*Visit **go.SolutionTree.com/instruction** for a free reproducible version of this figure.*

Element 26: Maintaining a Lively Pace

When teachers maintain a lively pace, they generate heightened energy levels in students. Figure 7.6 depicts the self-rating scale for maintaining a lively pace.

The following strategies illuminate this element.

- Instructional segments
- Motivational hooks

Score	Description
4: Innovating	I engage in all behaviors at the Applying level. In addition, I identify those students who do not exhibit increased energy levels and design alternate activities and strategies to meet their specific needs.
3: Applying	I engage in activities to maintain a lively pace without significant errors or omissions and monitor the extent to which students exhibit increased energy levels.
2: Developing	I engage in activities to maintain a lively pace without significant errors or omissions.
1: Beginning	I engage in activities to maintain a lively pace but do so with errors or omissions, such as not slowing down when students are confused and not varying the pace when it is clear that a change of pace would be useful.
0: Not Using	I do not engage in activities to maintain a lively pace.

Figure 7.6: Self-rating scale for element 26—Maintaining a lively pace.

Instructional Segments

Running a classroom effectively takes preparation and planning. Therefore, teachers proactively think about and choreograph the management details for each lesson to ensure smooth pacing and prioritize learning. To effectively manage literacy centers in a primary classroom, for example, teachers plan for and explain to students how to use the work board to determine which center is next in the rotation. Teachers anticipate transition times and explain how to smoothly move from perhaps listening to a minilesson to sitting down independently and practicing the featured writing skill. For elementary and secondary students, teachers can orchestrate a peer review system so students know which of their classmates they will confer with and at what point in the writing process they solicit this support.

Motivational Hooks

To entice students, teachers can use myriad devices, such as telling a story, playing an audio clip, showing a short video, sharing a commercial, or reading interesting headlines. These kinds of motivational techniques pique students' interest in a learning goal, energize them, and help to maintain a dynamic pace.

Storyline Online (www.storylineonline.net/library), a program that the SAG-AFTRA Foundation produces, features different actors reading stories, such as *Wilfrid Gordon McDonald Partridge* by Mem Fox (1984); *The Rainbow Fish* by Marcus Pfister (1992); and *Thank You, Mr. Falker* by Patricia Polacco (1998b). Participating actors include Viola Davis, Jane Kaczmarek, and Elijah Wood, among others. These stories not only entertain elementary students and introduce them to rich content, but also serve as models for students to retell stories through dictation, drawing, and writing.

Another idea for this strategy is to prepare paper bags with different multisensory objects in them for an imagery lesson. For example, prepare fine sugar or coarse sand in individual baggies, cut out sandpaper strips, get bottles of spices and extracts, find bells, and collect various textures of fabric swatches and ribbon. Students experience the different senses associated with the objects then generate descriptive words.

YouTube videos can also aptly grab students' attention. For instance, when teaching figurative language, such as metaphor, simile, and personification, teachers can use engaging and even interactive videos to determine which types of figurative language students can name and identify. One video that works for this purpose is by Jedd Bloom (2012); visit http://bit.ly/2F8jmQg to access the video. Teachers can search YouTube and similar libraries to access videos aligned to various learning targets and grade levels.

Element 27: Demonstrating Intensity and Enthusiasm

Teacher intensity and enthusiasm about content can be contagious. Figure 7.7 depicts the self-rating scale for this element.

Score	Description
4: Innovating	I engage in all behaviors at the Applying level. In addition, I identify those students who do not exhibit increased energy levels and design alternate activities and strategies to meet their specific needs.
3: Applying	I engage in activities to demonstrate intensity and enthusiasm without significant errors or omissions and monitor the extent to which students exhibit increased energy levels.
2: Developing	I engage in activities to demonstrate intensity and enthusiasm without significant errors or omissions.
1: Beginning	I engage in activities to demonstrate intensity and enthusiasm but do so with errors or omissions, such as not demonstrating intensity and enthusiasm at times when it is clear students need a boost of energy and demonstrating intensity and enthusiasm so frequently that it lessens its effect.
0: Not Using	I do not engage in activities to demonstrate intensity and enthusiasm.

Figure 7.7: Self-rating scale for element 27—Demonstrating intensity and enthusiasm.

Out of the strategies we list in figure A.1 in appendix A (page 156) for teaching with intensity and enthusiasm, we focus on the following here.

- Personal stories
- Video clips (such as movie and film clips)

Personal Stories

Teachers can present stories that reflect how a particular writing piece serves as an effective communications device—either something they read that is useful or a piece of writing they compose. Perhaps a detailed review lures them to an outstanding movie or restaurant, or else it could deter them from going. They can tell anecdotes about how their cover letter helped a potential employer read their resume with more interest and landed them a position. Or share how a letter of complaint yielded positive results in a situation that might have otherwise gone unnoticed: for example, a letter to a grocery manager concerning an ill-positioned display that made maneuvering a cart difficult, or how tight aisles in a clothing store made baby strollers impossible to pass.

Kathy once began a school day with students all abuzz about her hair color. She proceeded to tell the true story of how the picture of the color on the product's label was a misrepresentation of the actual color in the bottle; what she thought was dark brown turned out to be an intense black. As an activity, the class composed a complaint letter and waited anxiously for a response. After a few weeks passed, Kathy received a letter with an apology, a gift card for more products encouraging her to try again, and a check to cover a hairdresser appointment to rectify the situation. Kathy then took suggestions from students about what to include in a thank you note! The real-life power of writing can make a deep impression on students.

Video Clips

Video clips of movies, documentaries, speeches, and news stories can effectively generate intrigue, intensity, and enthusiasm. For example, TED Talks bring content to life, enticing students. When teaching about the imperative of finding evidence from credible sources, teachers can share this six-minute video about the danger of spreading fake news and how it hindered the rescue of victims (Busari, 2017; http://bit.ly/2BQjjXc). It is suitable for high school students as the subject is the Boko Haram kidnapping of girls in Nigeria.

Teachers can also provoke a visceral reaction in students by connecting them to emotionally charged content, then ask students to write a response. For instance, they can show the video clip of Kunta Kinte being ripped from his village to become a slave in Alex Haley's (1977) miniseries production of *Roots*.

For primary grades through high school, National Geographic captures real life in pictures and videos typically inaccessible to most students. The Google Cultural Institute provides tools and technologies to bring the world's cultural heritage online, such as virtual tours of museums around the world, up-close vantage points of famous art pieces, or news bits of noteworthy cultural icons. Teachers can use any of these and similar sources to foster and promote writing; they can also make such resources available to students when they conduct research for their own projects.

In addition to showing the intensity of a situation aligned to content, teachers can also play uplifting clips that connect to their world. Visit http://bit.ly/2oseRGw to view a compilation of videos and songs on YouTube (ndonnenwerth1, 2015) that features examples of various pop culture artists (Taylor Swift, Lady Gaga, Macklemore, Katy Perry, Bruno Mars, and others), plus popular movie excerpts and other clips students likely find interesting that incorporate figurative language. It is interactive as it asks students to identify which type of figurative language each clip uses.

Here are just a few more of many available resources.

- **PBS LearningMedia (http://ca.pbslearningmedia.org/standards/0):** This site offers more than 100,000 videos, images, interactives, lesson plans, and articles drawn from PBS programs and expert content contributors.
- **USC Shoah Foundation (http://sfi.usc.edu/vha/vha_program):** The Visual History Archive includes a digital collection of audiovisual interviews, with 53,000 testimonies of survivors and witnesses of the Holocaust as well as other genocides, providing a compelling voice for education and action.
- **"Lives" section of the *New York Times Magazine* (http://goo.gl/vM9R3P):** This section of the magazine's website features stories about meaningful personal experiences.

Element 28: Presenting Unusual Information

Unusual information generally stimulates students' interest and intrigue and is an excellent way to provoke engagement. Figure 7.8 depicts the self-rating scale for element 28.

Score	Description
4: Innovating	I engage in all behaviors at the Applying level. In addition, I identify those students who do not exhibit increased interest and intrigue in the content I present in class and design alternate activities and strategies to meet their specific needs.
3: Applying	I engage in activities to present unusual information without significant errors or omissions and monitor the extent to which students exhibit increased interest and intrigue in the content I present in class.
2: Developing	I engage in activities to present unusual information without significant errors or omissions.
1: Beginning	I engage in activities to present unusual information but do so with errors or omissions, such as presenting unusual information that has little or no relationship to content I present in class and not allowing adequate time for students to discuss and react to the unusual information.
0: Not Using	I do not engage in activities to present unusual information.

Figure 7.8: Self-rating scale for element 28—Presenting unusual information.

The following strategies apply to this element.

- Teacher-presented information
- Fast facts
- Guest speakers

Teacher-Presented Information

To capture students' attention, teachers can present unusual or intriguing information—preferably facts or information related to content. In the realm of writing, teachers can illustrate the perseverance it takes to get written work published and a passion for this form of communication by sharing rejection letters publishers wrote to famous authors. For example, these authors submitted manuscripts and received denials from various publishing houses: J. R. R. Tolkien for *Lord of the Rings*, John Steinbeck for *Grapes of Wrath*, Alice Walker for *The Color Purple*, and J. K. Rowling for *Harry Potter and the Philosopher's Stone*.

Teachers can share with students how many times certain authors received rejections for published works or their reminiscences about launching their careers. For example, publishers denied twenty-seven of Dr. Seuss's manuscripts (Andrews, n.d.), William Golding received twenty rejections for *Lord of the Flies* before it was finally published (Arbeiter, 2017), and Judy Blume (n.d.) endured two years of rejections before finally getting accepted into the literary world. She writes on her website:

> I would go to sleep at night feeling that I'd never be published. But I'd wake up in the morning convinced I would be. Each time I sent a story or book off to a publisher, I would sit down and begin something new. I was learning more with each effort. I was determined. Determination and hard work are as important as talent.

Such sentiments are powerful for students to read and hear.

For the secondary level, teachers can share excerpts from Anne Lamott's (1995) book *Bird by Bird: Some Instructions on Writing and Life*. In it, she has a chapter about first drafts in which she shares this about the reality of writing bad first drafts:

> All good writers write them. This is how they end up with good second drafts and terrific third drafts. People tend to look at successful writers, writers who are getting their books published and maybe even doing well financially, and think that they sit down at their desks every morning feeling like a million dollars, feeling great about who they are and how much talent they have and what a great story they have to tell; that they take in a few deep breaths, push back their sleeves, roll their necks a few times to get all the cricks out, and dive in, typing fully formed passages as fast as a court reporter. But this is just the fantasy of the uninitiated. (pp. 21–22)

Fast Facts

When students research to write papers such as biographies or research reports, they can share unusual facts about their subjects or topics. At the primary and elementary levels, students might write an *All About Animals* book. In doing so, they can research fun facts they uncover that are atypical and interesting. For example, on the topic of owls, students might find these facts intriguing and feel compelled to tell others about their research: "Scientists believe owls have been around for about 65 million years. . . . A large owl in the wild can live to be 30 years old. In a zoo, where it is protected, an owl can live to be 60 years old" (Gibbons, 2005, p. 32).

Guest Speakers

Teachers can invite guests to share their experiences related to writing, which is a pervasive skill pertaining to myriad occupations. Journalists write newspaper and magazine articles; some people write for blogs or public relations companies. Authors can write children's books, autobiographies, novels, and mysteries. Some people write industry manuals, directions for operating a tool or playing a game, and scripts for a radio production; the list goes on. Teachers can invite professionals in any field of writing to share their experiences about how they generate ideas, use the writing process, approach a writing task, or publish their work. Students can prepare questions in advance to pose when they speak to the class. Afterward, students can write the guests a thank you letter detailing what impressed them the most, insights they had, or future plans they outline as a result of the visit.

Element 29: Using Friendly Controversy

To help stimulate intrigue and enhance subject-matter knowledge, teachers can employ strategies that foster controversy (or disagreement) in a civil manner. When executed well, friendly controversy helps students analyze content with a critical eye. Figure 7.9 depicts the self-rating scale for this element.

Score	Description
4: Innovating	I engage in all behaviors at the Applying level. In addition, I identify those students who do not exhibit increased interest and intrigue in the content I present in class and design alternate activities and strategies to meet their specific needs.
3: Applying	Along with adequate guidance and support, I engage students in activities that involve friendly controversy without significant errors or omissions and monitor the extent to which students exhibit increased interest and intrigue in the content I present in class.
2: Developing	I engage students in activities that involve friendly controversy and provide adequate guidance and support.
1: Beginning	I engage students in activities that involve friendly controversy but do not provide adequate guidance and support, such as structuring the activity so students have clear roles and responsibilities and not allowing the controversy to become emotionally charged.
0: Not Using	I do not engage students in activities that involve friendly controversy.

Figure 7.9: Self-rating scale for element 29—Using friendly controversy.

We recommend the following strategies for using friendly controversy.

- Expert opinions
- Diagrams comparing perspectives

Expert Opinions

When students in upper grades prepare their argumentation pieces, it is incumbent upon them to acknowledge and address an opposing point of view to their position. This part of the paper includes qualifiers and answers the question, *What are exceptions to your claim?* In doing so, they display credibility since they bring counterclaims to the forefront and address the weaknesses in them to support their overarching claim; readers highly value these aspects of a piece of writing.

To prepare them, teachers ask students to research opinions from experts who have points of view that are contrary to theirs. Students can present their position and the researched evidence they accumulate pertaining to the opposition to small groups or a partner. They lead a discussion about the merits of the different perspectives that are counter to theirs and solicit ideas about how they would address the limitations or lack of validity when they write their arguments. Then they use what they glean from discussion to help them draft counterarguments. Review element 14 in chapter 5 (page 82), generating and defending claims, for additional information about teaching this skill, including sentence frames students can use in their writing (see figure 5.12, page 86).

Diagrams Comparing Perspectives

With elementary students, teachers can introduce or review how to use a Venn diagram to identify what is the same and different about two points of view. This exercise prepares students to recognize that for every opinion there is an opposite viewpoint. For example, one student might prefer summer, and another enjoys winter more. In elementary grades, the Venn diagram helps students elucidate their thoughts and arrive at a position they will support for an opinion paper.

As students advance in the grades, teachers can show a Venn diagram with three intersecting circles or another graphic organizer for comparing and contrasting multiple ideas. As students conduct research for their arguments, they can complete the diagram and use it as a prewriting tool to focus on evidence for either side of their claim. Teachers should encourage students who are ready to formulate their own graphic organizers, or select a prepared organizer suited for comparing perspectives from the list of links in figure 3.12 (page 49) or use other resources.

Element 30: Using Academic Games

Academic games are quick remedies for disengagement and provide students with a fresh look at content. Figure 7.10 depicts the self-rating scale for this element.

Score	Description
4: Innovating	I engage in all behaviors at the Applying level. In addition, I identify those students who do not exhibit increased interest and intrigue in the content I present in class and design alternate activities and strategies to meet their specific needs.
3: Applying	Along with adequate guidance and support, I engage students in activities that involve academic games and monitor the extent to which students exhibit increased interest and intrigue in the content I present in class.
2: Developing	I engage students in activities that involve academic games and provide adequate guidance and support.
1: Beginning	I engage students in activities that involve academic games but do not provide adequate guidance and support, such as establishing clear roles and procedures for students and involving inconsequential competition.
0: Not Using	I do not engage students in academic games.

Figure 7.10: Self-rating scale for element 30—Using academic games.

Teachers can consider the following strategies for incorporating academic games into instruction.

- What is the question?
- Which one doesn't belong?
- Vocabulary review games

What Is the Question?

Teachers can create a *Jeopardy!*-like game in which they develop clues organized in categories to which teams of students respond. To address writing skills, categories could include vocabulary, parts of speech, sentence structures, genres, formatting, purposes for writing, text structure, or literary devices. As well, clues could revolve around subject-matter content that students use as the basis for their writing, for example, in science, options pertain to findings in a lab experiment, structural components of a lab report, types of ecosystems or energy sources, weather and climate, or cycles (life cycle of a plant, water cycle, and so forth).

Students could also create the clues and orchestrate the game. Rather than the actual game in which contestants frame their responses in a question format, teachers can allow students to merely answer a question with a straightforward response.

Which One Doesn't Belong?

In this game, teachers create four clues—three of which are correct and one that does not belong. Students read the set of clues, determine the incorrect one, and explain orally or in writing why it is different. Teachers can use this form of engagement as students hone vocabulary words, writing skills, content information, or process steps. When they respond, teachers encourage students to use context clues and elimination techniques to arrive at an answer if it is not initially forthcoming and they are stalled. As with the hand signal strategy (element 24, page 120), students can create clues to administer to their classmates. Figure 7.11 features examples of this strategy. Some teachers use this strategy with handheld electronic devices or online platforms (websites or applications like Kahoot!). For primary grades, teachers can feature three or four word or picture cards and ask students to identify which one does not belong in the group. For example, show sight words, words with short or long vowel sounds, uppercase letters (with one lowercase), real characters (with one fictionalized character), complete sentences (with one fragment), pairs of rhyming words, examples of detailed student drawings (with one void of detail), and so forth.

Which One Doesn't Belong?
Word: _Serenity_
1. _Serenity_ and _tranquility_ are synonyms. 2. A rock star, a carpenter, and a garage mechanic practice serenity each day in their jobs. 3. A serene place is a tropical island marked by peacefulness. 4. One who values serenity might be someone who prefers being alone.
Word: _Mellifluous_
1. something that sounds sweet and smooth 2. angry; harsh sounding 3. relating to words or sounds 4. The mellifluous words were honey to my ears.
Topic: Whales
1. An orca, also called a killer whale, is part of the dolphin suborder. 2. A killer whale can live up to ninety years. 3. Whales are not mammals. 4. An orca can eat sea turtles, penguins, and even sharks.
Topic: Methods of Characterization
1. What a character looks like 2. What a character thinks and feels 3. What others say about the character 4. What point of view the author uses
Topic: Rules for Commas
1. Use to separate two simple sentences. 2. Use between coordinate adjectives to replace the word _and_. 3. Use after a dependent clause. 4. Use with items in a series.

Figure 7.11: Which one doesn't belong? examples.

Vocabulary Review Games

Teachers need to assist students in adding words to their existing lexicon when composing various written products. For example, students learn subject-matter terms to incorporate into research and informational papers, descriptive vocabulary to make characters come alive, or words to evoke mood. In elementary or secondary classrooms, teachers or students can create games to help master these words, such as bingo, concentration, or a matching game. The game Which one doesn't belong? in the previous section can also work here. Or teachers can create game cards to use or prepare a game board expressly for vocabulary as in figure 7.For this game, teachers make word cards to use as the focus for each clue taken from the literary or nonfiction complex text students are reading in class. For the primary level, add pictures and read the prompts from the game aloud. Students play in small groups; each student has an object to use to advance through the board, such as a penny, elbow macaroni piece, or paper clip. Additionally, teachers furnish a die. For each turn, students choose a word card, roll the die, place their game piece the number of spaces indicated by the die, and respond to the game prompt. Students can make their own games and play them with classmates.

Element 31: Providing Opportunities for Students to Talk About Themselves

When students have opportunities to talk about themselves in relationship to academic content, it creates connections for them that are inherently engaging. It also fosters a sense of inclusion as they feel more welcome in the class. Figure 7.12 depicts the self-rating scale for this element.

Score	Description
4: Innovating	I engage in all behaviors at the Applying level. In addition, I identify those students who do not appear to be more motivated to participate in classroom activities and design alternate activities and strategies to meet their specific needs.
3: Applying	I engage in activities that provide students with opportunities to talk about themselves without significant errors or omissions and monitor the extent to which students appear to be more motivated to participate in classroom activities.
2: Developing	I engage in activities that provide students with opportunities to talk about themselves without significant errors or omissions.
1: Beginning	I engage in activities that provide students with opportunities to talk about themselves but do so with errors or omissions, such as not making links with the content I present in class and not providing adequate time for students to talk about themselves.
0: Not Using	I do not engage in activities that provide students with opportunities to talk about themselves.

Figure 7.12: Self-rating scale for element 31—Providing opportunities for students to talk about themselves.

We offer multiple strategies for this element in figure A.1 in appendix A (page 156). Here we elaborate on the strategy of making informal linkages during class discussion.

Teachers make it a priority to get to know the interests, experiences, and learning preferences of their students through surveys, discussions, or other means. By doing so, they forge connections between the subject-matter content and students' lives and make learning more interesting and personal. Instituting community circles and offering writing contest suggestions are concrete examples of this strategy.

To connect with students and promote relationships among students, to review content, and to practice speaking and listening skills (such as eye contact, body language, and voice projection), teachers in any content area can hold a twenty- to forty-minute community circle routinely either once a week or once a

START	What is this word's part of speech? How do you know?	Give two nonexamples of this word.	
		Give two examples of this word.	Place word cards here.
Draw a picture or symbol for this word.	Does this word have two different meanings? What are they?	Use the word in a sentence to show you know what it means.	
Find this word in a book. Find the context clues, or are they missing?	Act out this word.		
This word is like _____ because _____ .			
What is a word that means the opposite of this word?			END

Figure 7.13: Vocabulary game board (elementary).

Visit go.SolutionTree.com/instruction for a free reproducible version of this figure.

month. To conduct this strategy, teachers plan questions in advance to give to students so they can prepare their responses. During the community circle, students and the teacher sit in a circle. One student can volunteer to begin and holds a talking stick; the stick rotates clockwise as each student in the circle—and the teacher—shares responses to a prompt. A student can pass, but the stick eventually comes back around.

At the beginning of the year, the prompts can center on students getting to know each other personally. Teachers can offer sentence starters like these.

- Most people here may not know that I . . .
- My idea of a perfect day would include . . .
- One thing my family or friends would say about me is . . .
- I admire _____ because . . .

Throughout the year, the teacher can use a combination of prompts—personal, classroom content, thematic, and problem-solving questions. For content, teachers can pose a question asking for students to share an example from their writing, such as: *What is your strongest example of sensory detail in your paper?* Or, *What is one statistic or fact that you use in your argument as supporting evidence?* As another option, they can pose a text-dependent question, such as the following: *Do you agree or disagree with Jimmy Valentine's actions at the end of O. Henry's (1903) "A Retrieved Reformation"? Provide one reason to support your position.* Or this, related to social studies content: *Do you think the Puritans were selfish or selfless? Provide one reason to support your position.* Thematic question examples include:

- What does it mean to be American?
- What are the qualities of an ideal leader or citizen?
- How should power and responsibility be distributed in society?
- Should fracking be permitted?

For a problem-solving question, a teacher might ask, "It has come to our attention that many sixth graders are being bullied. What can you as eighth graders do to make younger students feel safer on campus?" Once students participate, they can transfer and extend their ideas by writing in journals or academic notebooks. If the responses center on content, teachers can use what students write as formative assessments to inform their instruction.

When teachers are aware of students' goals, capabilities, and interests, they can make suggestions for students to enter their writing in a particular contest, such as those in the list that follows. When doing so, teachers need to be mindful of the deadline dates, submission guidelines (word count, formatting, and other information), and required fees (if any) for entries. Some are geared to students only; others are open to anyone.

- **Hippocampus (www.hippocampusmagazine.com):** This online magazine accepts submissions for memoirs, personal essays, and flash creative nonfiction (or a work of creative nonfiction in an experimental format).
- **Letters About Literature (www.read.gov/letters):** A contest for students in grades 4–12 in which they read a book, poem, or speech and write to the author (living or dead) about how the book affected them personally
- **The *New York Times*'s Learning Network (www.nytimes.com/section/learning):** A variety of contests are available for thirteen- to nineteen-year-olds, such as for editorials, vocabulary videos, poetry, rap, summer reading (responses to what students found most interesting in the *New York Times*), editorial cartoons, and reviews (of books, video games, concerts, restaurants, art exhibits, and more).
- **River of Words (www.stmarys-ca.edu/center-for-environmental-literacy/river-of-words):** This contest, for five- to nineteen-year-olds (excluding nineteen-year-old college students),

focuses on the watershed theme. The creators designed it to help youth explore the natural and cultural history of their surroundings and express themselves through art or poetry. It accepts solo and collaborative poems in English, Spanish, and American Sign Language.

- **Sarah Mook Poetry Contest (www.sarahmookpoetrycontest.com/home):** This is a poetry contest for students in grades K–12 held as a memorial for a young poet named Sarah.
- **Scholastic Art & Writing Awards (www.artandwriting.org/the-awards/categories):** Students in grades 7–12 can submit writing in all sorts of categories, such as critical essay, drama script, flash fiction, poetry, science fiction, and more. There are also entries for art categories including ceramics, fashion, jewelry, painting, and other creative endeavors.
- *The Sun* **(http://thesunmagazine.org/about/submission_guidelines/readers_write):** This online magazine accepts submissions for essays, interviews, fiction, and poetry.
- **Teen Ink (www.teenink.com/Contests):** This site offers a host of contest opportunities including cover art, fiction, nonfiction, and poetry. It also sponsors writing contests on topics, such as environment (solutions and ideas about a problem facing the planet), educator of the year (nominate an amazing teacher in your life), community service (how you make the world a better place), and more.
- **Winning Writers (https://winningwriters.com):** This clearinghouse site for writing contests and services provides links to the best literary contests along with their rules. By subscribing to their free email newsletter, you'll learn more about each contest including which ones are suitable for writers at the beginning, intermediate, and advanced stages of their careers. Plus, it cautions writers about contests and services that may take advantage of or scam them.

Element 32: Motivating and Inspiring Students

Ultimately, the highest form of engagement occurs when students are intrinsically motivated and inspired. Figure 7.14 depicts the self-rating scale for this element.

Score	Description
4: Innovating	I engage in all behaviors at the Applying level. In addition, I identify those students who do not appear to be developing a sense of self-agency and design alternate activities and strategies to meet their specific needs.
3: Applying	I engage in activities to motivate and inspire students without significant errors or omissions and monitor the extent to which students appear to be developing a sense of self-agency.
2: Developing	I engage in activities to motivate and inspire students without significant errors or omissions.
1: Beginning	I engage in activities to motivate and inspire students but do so with errors or omissions, such as not allowing enough time for the activities and not communicating the importance and relevance of these activities to students.
0: Not Using	I do not engage in activities to motivate and inspire students.

Figure 7.14: Self-rating scale for element 32—Motivating and inspiring students.

In figure A.1 in appendix A (page 156), we list various strategies for motivating and inspiring students. Here we highlight the following specific strategies.

- Possible selves activities
- Gratitude journals

Possible Selves Activities

Teachers can instill within students the notion that they can develop into writers and pursue a career in the field. There are innumerable opportunities to write and make a living at it. Teachers can share options that match specific students' interests and burgeoning talents, such as technical writer, writer for health professions, journalist for a print or online publication, advertising copywriter, blog writer, reviewer for food or arts, grant writer, author of children's books, novelist, biographer, or other careers in this wide field. Once they feel inspired and have seen some options, students can research other possibilities of writing as a profession. Perhaps teachers can connect students to local professionals who can serve as mentors, or arrange for them to meet a trusted person in the field virtually.

Gratitude Journals

Being grateful helps people adopt a positive state of mind, and teachers can help facilitate the power of positive thinking by asking students to create a gratitude journal to catalog such a mindset. To do so, they can ask individuals, small groups, or the whole class to record what they are thankful for electronically or by hand. Students can write daily, weekly, or monthly. Not only does this present an opportunity to further practice writing, it also brings a grateful attitude to the forefront of their minds.

Teachers can begin the activity by asking students to list basic materials that they appreciate, like types of food, items related to their home, or school supplies. Later, they can catalogue their talents, activities, interests, and hobbies. They can continue to write in more detail about other topics, such as something in nature or their community; abilities or character traits they possess; people, pets, groups, subjects, and places that they are grateful exist; or situations or experiences that presented themselves (for example, a dance they performed, a vacation they went on, an award they won, or a party they planned or attended). With each entry, teachers encourage students to respond to these and other questions: *Why are you grateful for _____? How does it (he, she, they) make you feel? What would life be like without _____? How would you describe _____?* Teachers can invite students to take advantage of practicing skills like word choice, descriptive detail, and forms of figurative language to further probe their thinking about the content of their entry.

 GUIDING QUESTIONS FOR CURRICULUM DESIGN

This design question focuses on engagement: *What engagement strategies will I use to help students pay attention, be energized, be intrigued, and be inspired?* The following questions, which are aligned to each of the elements in this chapter, guide teachers to plan instruction.

- **Element 23:** What will I do to notice when students are not engaged and react?

  _____

  _____

  _____

  _____

- **Element 24:** What will I do to increase students' response rates?

  _____

  _____

  _____

  _____

- **Element 25:** What will I do to increase students' physical movement?

  _____
  _____
  _____
  _____

- **Element 26:** What will I do to maintain a lively pace?

  _____
  _____
  _____
  _____

- **Element 27:** What will I do to demonstrate intensity and enthusiasm?

  _____
  _____
  _____
  _____

- **Element 28:** What will I do to present unusual information?

  _____
  _____
  _____
  _____

- **Element 29:** What will I do to engage students in friendly controversy?

  _____
  _____
  _____
  _____

- **Element 30:** What will I do to engage students in academic games?

  _____
  _____
  _____
  _____

- **Element 31:** What will I do to provide opportunities for students to talk about themselves?

  _____
  _____
  _____
  _____

- **Element 32:** What will I do to motivate and inspire students?

  _____
  _____
  _____
  _____

Conclusion

Engagement encompasses various levels in this order of gradation from basic to highest degrees: getting students' attention, producing energy, stimulating intrigue, and motivating and inspiring students intrinsically. Several elements and embedded strategies help teachers design and conduct lessons that foster engagement. They would clearly not use all elements in a single unit of instruction but would frequently—if not daily—notice when students are disengaged or unresponsive. When this occurs, teachers can increase response rates, use physical movement, maintain a lively pace, or demonstrate intensity and enthusiasm. Organizing the classroom layout and understanding students' backgrounds and interests contribute to some aspects of engagement.

CHAPTER 8

Implementing Rules and Procedures and Building Relationships

As we mention in this book's introduction, *The New Art and Science of Teaching* framework features the three overarching categories (*feedback*, *content*, *context*), ten teacher actions, forty-three elements, and over 330 accompanying strategies. Teachers intentionally select elements and embedded strategies to build a well-rounded, effective instructional program based on a unit's learning goals of what students should come to know, understand, and do. Since our focus in this text is on writing and to some degree reading, this chapter highlights only one of the five elements within the category of Implementing Rules and Procedures and one element within the category of Building Relationships.

- **Element 34:** Organizing the physical layout of the classroom
- **Element 39:** Understanding students' backgrounds and interests

We encourage readers to study *The New Art and Science of Teaching* (Marzano, 2017) to take advantage of learning about all the strategies related to each category so they are fully aware of what contributes to excellence in teaching.

Element 34: Organizing the Physical Layout of the Classroom

The physical environment of the classroom can help stimulate students' sense of order or hinder their perception of it. Figure 8.1 depicts the self-rating scale for this element.

Score	Description
4: Innovating	I engage in all behaviors at the Applying level. In addition, I identify those students who do not appear to enjoy and use the resources within the classroom and design alternate activities and strategies to meet their specific needs.
3: Applying	I engage in activities to make the physical layout of the classroom appealing and supportive of learning and monitor the extent to which students both enjoy and use the resources within the classroom.

Figure 8.1: Self-rating scale for element 34—Organizing the physical layout of the classroom.

continued →

Score	Description
2: Developing	I engage in activities to make the physical layout of the classroom appealing and supportive of learning without errors or omissions.
1: Beginning	I engage in activities to make the physical layout of the classroom appealing and supportive of learning but do so with errors or omissions, such as not displaying enough student work and not referencing the displayed work during class time.
0: Not Using	I do not engage in activities to make the physical layout of the classroom appealing and supportive of learning.

This element is associated with the following specific strategies. In this section, we describe those that have direct application to writing.

- Displaying student work
- Considering classroom materials
- Considering computers and technology equipment
- Placing student desks
- Planning areas for group work

Displaying Student Work

When teachers display student work, they send the message that what students do has value. Plus, it is their classroom, so sharing student work contributes to a supportive environment. Perhaps teachers in a team or within a school commit to posting essential questions as a unifying feature and student work revolves around these questions along with their embedded themes and concepts, which reinforces critical thinking. Displaying work is also an opportunity to capture learning and a vehicle to incorporate the pieces into instruction. When determining what to select, sometimes teachers collect pieces from all students; other times it's a representative sample of exemplary work. Teachers might obtain students' permission or offer them choices for what to display from among a selection of writing pieces they have generated.

In elementary grades, teachers can tack up myriad student work on the walls, such as pictures with captions, thank you notes, formal letters, lists, or pages from a class book students produce, like a picture dictionary or an alphabet book. Or students might write an All About Animals or All About Plants report and select their favorite pages from it to display; for example, a favorite page might include a labeled diagram, types of animals or plants in a species, a glossary, or interesting facts. Additionally, teachers might assign an All About Me project in which students can showcase a self-portrait or a picture of themselves along with information that they can share with others.

In any grade, teachers can exhibit poems, posters, collages, storyboards, brochures, timelines, book covers, graphic organizers, and vocabulary projects. They can share work students create from any stage of the writing process instead of just the finished product, for example, graphic organizers used in prewriting or notecards from research students conduct. They might post these on a temporary basis only as students likely need these pieces in front of them when they compose, but displaying them for a while can further peers' learning and spawn new ideas.

Besides exhibiting two-dimensional projects on the walls or door panels, teachers can also hang three-dimensional objects, such as mobiles, portfolios, or project cubes using classroom supplies like file folders with prongs or rings. When students produce a project cube, they dedicate each side of a square or rectangular box to a subtopic and highlight salient content that they gleaned through words and pictures or symbols. For example, a small group of students might create a project cube around a realistic fiction novel whereby each side highlights a change the protagonist experiences throughout the story, or perhaps focuses on the author's use of literary devices. Or, students demonstrate their understanding of informational text by producing a project cube whereby each side features a different ecosystem. Be sure the students either leave the top empty (to hang the cube) or the bottom (to display it on a shelf).

The displays can also serve as an instructional tool during the unit as students document, review, and reflect on what they learn during a unit. Teachers can feature a combination of student work, pictures of students engaged in activities, student and teacher reflections, and collaborative pieces that students and teachers create, such as word walls, a poster of the writing process, or a graphic organizer depicting a process relevant to a current unit. Teachers encourage students to revisit any display and add new information.

Many teachers regularly feature a unit or semester theme on the walls. After the unit or theme focus, teachers replace old samples of student work with new pieces so the classroom showcases fresh material. Additionally, to avoid a distracting environment, teachers maintain uncluttered walls and ceilings by managing the amount of student work posted. Furthermore, teachers choose purposefully so that what they display enhances the environment, reinforces learning, supports sharing, and fosters a sense of pride.

Considering Classroom Materials, Computers, and Technology Equipment

When students prepare for and compose a piece of writing, they can do so by hand, electronically, or using a combination of both. For example, they might create a web by hand during prewriting, access the internet for research, and then use an electronic device to type their drafts. To appeal to this variety of methods in preparation and composition, teachers ensure that they make learning materials easily accessible, label them (if feasible or needed), and organize them in a dedicated place in the classroom or an identifiable location elsewhere. Plus, teachers must account for students' use of computers or other technology and prepare accordingly, matching learners with task needs so the purpose of using these devices and equipment is clear.

Students will need materials for editing and revising their writing, so teachers should make these available in a centrally located place that students can easily access. If students compose by hand, these and other items can be helpful: colored pencils or highlighters, highlighting tape, scissors, staplers, or paper clips. If students accompany their writing with illustrations, then they will need drawing tools available. On the walls, teachers can display support material for all ages and levels of learners, including English learners, such as various word walls (for example, adjectives or words to use instead of *said*), alphabet charts, sentence frames and templates, proofreaders' marks (see table 6.1, page 103), formats for works cited documents, and more. These can also be available digitally for those students who wish to access them on electronic devices, or distributed in a handout. Classroom materials also encompass teaching tools, for example, small dry-erase boards and markers for students to practice writing skills or pocket charts for primary students to manage independent learning or to manipulate parts of a sentence.

Computers and technology equipment are part and parcel of many classrooms; therefore, teachers need to account for where this equipment will reside in the classroom and how technology can support learning goals. For example, students can use software programs to generate graphic organizers, compose text on computers, access the internet for research, share their work in an online community with members of a public or controlled private group, or chat via Skype or Google Hangouts to get feedback, and publish their finished products on a legitimate website.

Placing Student Desks and Planning Areas for Group Work

Teachers strategically position student desks—whether standing desks or traditional seated ones—to facilitate learning individually, in pairs, in small groups, and during whole-class instruction. Students and teachers must all be able to easily and quickly maneuver around desks to confer with each other, access materials, and avoid safety hazards. When they ask students to meet in small groups or partnerships, teachers should consider how to arrange desks and where in the classroom students meet so they can accommodate space and location. This advanced planning can maximize learning time.

There are many occasions during the writing process when students meet with others. While brainstorming, for example, they bounce ideas off classmates, collect ideas, flesh out a complicated storyline, or solicit suggestions for research. During the revision stage, feedback is critical to success. Teachers, peers, members of a digital community of writers, parents or guardians, and other family members can all provide support and feedback to students as they revise their work. When students work with fellow classmates, they can collect such information verbally in a face-to-face meeting within the classroom or electronically. When students meet in person with one or two classmates or with the teacher, designating a part of the room where conferences can take place is helpful. Since students will engage in discussion, it is best if they can move away from others who prefer relative quiet while working independently.

Element 39: Understanding Students' Backgrounds and Interests

Understanding students' backgrounds and interests goes a long way in developing positive relationships between the teacher and students. When teachers conduct activities that uncover each student's accomplishments, likes, and dislikes, students feel highly regarded. Figure 8.2 depicts the self-rating scale for this element so teachers can gauge their performance.

Score	Description
4: Innovating	I engage in all behaviors at the Applying level. In addition, I identify those students who do not appear to perceive that the teacher genuinely likes them and design alternate activities and strategies to meet their specific needs.
3: Applying	I engage in activities to understand students and monitor the extent to which students perceive that I am genuinely interested in them.
2: Developing	I engage in verbal and nonverbal behaviors to indicate affection for students without significant errors or omissions.
1: Beginning	I engage in activities to understand students' backgrounds and interests but do so with errors or omissions, such as exhibiting these behaviors with some but not all students and engaging in these behaviors in a perfunctory manner.
0: Not Using	I do not engage in activities to understand students' backgrounds and interests.

Figure 8.2: Self-rating scale for element 39—Understanding students' backgrounds and interests.

Of the assortment of strategies for understanding students' backgrounds and interests that we identify in figure A.1 in appendix A (page 156), we elaborate on the following specific strategies in this section.

- Student background surveys
- Opinion questionnaires
- Familiarity with student culture
- Six-word autobiographies

Student Background Surveys

For teachers to get to know students on a personal level, they can issue a survey to collect information about students' lives at the beginning of the school year or course. This helps teachers connect with their pupils to determine their likes and dislikes, interests and activities, concerns and aspirations, family composition and dynamics, and more.

These background surveys might reveal a sensitive situation worth noting. Specifically, teachers need to be mindful of students' situations to avoid anything that might embarrass or humiliate them, leaving them vulnerable. For example, while writing, students might be reticent to get feedback from classmates on a brainstorming piece in preparation for a memoir or to share a journal entry if the topic is too personal. Instead, students can share with teachers privately.

The surveys can also support teachers in curriculum design. For instance, teachers can plan classroom instruction with students' favorite activities in mind or use examples from favorite television shows to illustrate characters' motivations that influence a plot. If there are cultural traditions that many students observe, teachers can ask them to write descriptively about their experiences or compare and contrast different traditions.

Opinion Questionnaires

Opinion questionnaires, as opposed to student background surveys, connect more deeply to classroom content. In this strategy, teachers collect information to better understand students' perspectives, interests, and levels of competency about classroom topics. These are the kinds of questions teachers might include.

- On a scale of 1 to 5, rate your comfort level with each of these areas related to writing—spelling, grammar, using new vocabulary, text structure, and so forth. (In this example, teachers would format each line for students to circle or check off their number on a rating scale.)
- What are your favorite writing topics?
- Do you prefer to give feedback to classmates in a face-to-face situation or electronically, like through Google Docs? If electronically, what tool do you like to use?
- Do you enjoy writing? If so, why? If not, what do you think gets in your way?
- What type of writing do you prefer to compose—narrative or expository?
- Check off any of these genres that you are interested in writing this year in class.
  - ☐ Mysteries
  - ☐ Realistic fiction
  - ☐ Myths
  - ☐ Fairy tales
  - ☐ Newspaper articles
  - ☐ Argumentation essays
  - ☐ Research reports
  - ☐ Historical journals
  - ☐ Other (Write in another genre not mentioned.)
- What argumentation essay topic would you like to investigate?
- What informational report topic would you like to research?
- What is your experience with the writing process—prewriting, drafting, editing, revising, publishing, and reflecting? For example, have you used all stages? Did the writing process help you, and how so? What stage makes you feel most and least comfortable?

For very young elementary students, teachers can conduct an oral questionnaire. For example, they ask students to say what they feel they are experts in and whether they can support others in these areas, such as spelling words correctly, using a dictionary, writing a fable, handwriting, finding synonyms, drawing with details, writing complete sentences, and so forth. Teachers might even include character education traits like taking turns, sharing, or helping others. Using their input, teachers compile a Classroom Resource book that catalogs names of students alongside their skilled areas. When students are stuck, they refer to this class resource and find students who can help them get unstuck.

Familiarity With Student Culture

Tapping into current trends and cultural phenomena that pique students' interests helps to engage them. Therefore, teachers can incorporate popular music, movies, and television shows (available on network, cable, or streaming), as well as specific actors, singers, or bands into their curriculum. For instance, in a poetry unit, teachers can invite students to quote their favorite contemporary song lyrics that exemplify a figure of speech at the focus of instruction, such as metaphor or simile, or a poetic device like rhyme or assonance. Or, as students learn about the elements of literature in preparation for writing narratives—character, setting, plot, point of view, and theme—teachers can assign the task of watching a show from a favorite series and writing a short piece highlighting evidence of these literary elements to share with the class. Specifically, they can identify the theme and cite dialogue or actions to support it, identify a personality trait of a character and share evidence, or predict what will happen next in the plot based on part of the episode that leads them to this conjecture. Students who watch the same episode can confer. In another example, students can write an opinion piece or argumentation essay citing evidence that a favorite current musician's style, genre, or lyrics qualify him or her as the most influential, talented, or iconic figure today.

Six-Word Autobiographies

In a narrative unit, teachers introduce nonfiction narrative genres centered on authors writing about themselves—autobiographies, memoirs, or personal narratives. In preparation for students crafting their own pieces and to glean insight about them, teachers can ask students to write about themselves in exactly six words. Early elementary students might list six words or draw pictures or symbols that exemplify them; elementary and secondary writers can create a succinct sentence or poem. Teachers can ask students to create a short poem comprised of several six-word lines as a more comprehensive expression of themselves, as in the sample that follows. When finished, small groups convene and elaborate with each other on anything they care to share.

Conscientious of others, I administer support.

When jubilant, I dance and sing.

Sometimes hastily, I finish homework poorly.

With prideful energy, I exercise regularly.

My exceptionally awesome father died recently.

GUIDING QUESTIONS FOR CURRICULUM DESIGN

The design questions in this chapter focus on implementing rules and procedures and building relationships: *What strategies will I use to help students understand and follow rules and procedures?* and *What strategies will I use to help students feel welcome, accepted, and valued?* The following questions, which align to each of the elements in this chapter, guide teachers to plan rules and build relationships.

- **Element 34:** What will I do to make the physical layout of the classroom most conducive to learning?

_____
_____
_____
_____
_____
_____
_____
_____
_____
_____
_____

- **Element 39:** How will I demonstrate that I understand students' backgrounds and interests?

_____
_____
_____
_____
_____
_____
_____
_____
_____
_____
_____

Conclusion

Strategies associated with the physical layout of the classroom enable movement about the classroom easy, make materials accessible, showcase students' work, and account for technology equipment. By attending to the physicality, teachers can enhance students' sense of order which contributes to their learning. Additionally, teachers can seek to understand students' backgrounds and interests, which help to build students' perception that their teacher and peers respect them. This, too, can elevate learning as students feel valued and connected. To develop teachers' competency in the art and science of this profession, the next chapter offers suggestions.

CHAPTER 9

Developing Expertise

As the previous chapters illustrate, *The New Art and Science of Teaching Writing* offers a comprehensive framework that can help writing teachers develop their expertise and, in turn, increase their students' learning. This relationship between teacher expertise and student learning is well established. For example, in one of the most rigorous studies of the relationship between teacher effectiveness and student achievement, Barbara Nye, Spyros Konstantopoulos, and Larry V. Hedges (2004) estimate that the difference in student achievement between a teacher who is "average" and a teacher who is "very effective" is about 13 percentile points in reading and 18 in mathematics. They note, "These effects are certainly large enough to have policy implications" (Nye et al., 2004, p. 253).

This relationship underscores the importance of helping teachers continually develop their expertise. The more skilled teachers become, the more their students learn. It's as simple as that. Fortunately, there is a great deal of research and theory on how to improve one's expertise in any complex domain such as teaching (see Ericsson & Charness, 1994; Ericsson, Krampe, & Tesch-Romer, 1993; Marzano, 2010). The process involves at least four steps, which we addressed in detail in this chapter.

1. Conduct a self-audit.
2. Select goal elements and specific strategies.
3. Engage in deliberate practice and track progress.
4. Seek continuous improvement by planning for future growth.

Step 1: Conduct a Self-Audit

The first step in developing one's expertise is to conduct a self-audit. Teachers of writing can easily accomplish this using the self-rating scales that we present for each element in the model covered in this text. Recall that we designed each of those scales in the format shown in figure 9.1 (page 148). The purpose of conducting a self-audit is to determine one's strengths and weaknesses. Strengths are celebrated; weaknesses become the focus of developing expertise.

Score	Description
4: Innovating	I adapt strategies and behaviors associated with this element for unique student needs and situations.
3: Applying	I use strategies and behaviors associated with this element without significant errors and monitor their effect on students.
2: Developing	I use strategies and behaviors associated with this element without significant errors but do not monitor their effect on students.
1: Beginning	I use some strategies and behaviors associated with this element but do so with significant errors or omissions.
0: Not Using	I am unaware of the strategies and behaviors associated with this element or know them but don't employ them.

Figure 9.1: General format of the self-rating scale.

As we explain in the introduction, customized scales accompany the elements in this book. We recommend that each year, teachers score themselves using these scales. In effect, each year teachers should construct a profile of their strengths and weaknesses. They can consider any elements on which they have scores of Applying or Innovating as strengths. Any elements on which teachers have scores of Not Using, Beginning, or Developing are candidates for improvement.

Teachers can use the self-audit form in figure 9.2 to record the results of the self-audit.

Element	4	3	2	1	0
1. Providing scales and rubrics					
2. Tracking student progress					
3. Celebrating success					
4. Using informal assessments of the whole class					
5. Using formal assessments of individual students					
6. Chunking content					
7. Processing content					
8. Recording and representing content					
9. Using structured practice sessions					
10. Examining similarities and differences					
11. Examining errors in reasoning					
12. Engaging students in cognitively complex tasks					
13. Providing resources and guidance					
14. Generating and defending claims					
15. Previewing strategies					
16. Highlighting critical information					
17. Reviewing content					
18. Revising knowledge					
19. Reflecting on learning					
20. Assigning purposeful homework					
21. Elaborating on information					

Element	4	3	2	1	0
22. Organizing students to interact					
23. Noticing and reacting when students are not engaged					
24. Increasing response rates					
25. Using physical movement					
26. Maintaining a lively pace					
27. Demonstrating intensity and enthusiasm					
28. Presenting unusual information					
29. Using friendly controversy					
30. Using academic games					
31. Providing opportunities for students to talk about themselves					
32. Motivating and inspiring students					
33. Establishing rules and procedures					
34. Organizing the physical layout of the classroom					
35. Demonstrating withitness					
36. Acknowledging adherence to rules and procedures					
37. Acknowledging lack of adherence to rules and procedures					
38. Using verbal and nonverbal behaviors that indicate affection for students					
39. Understanding students' backgrounds and interests					
40. Displaying objectivity and control					
41. Demonstrating value and respect for reluctant learners					
42. Asking in-depth questions of reluctant learners					
43. Probing incorrect answers with reluctant learners					

Figure 9.2: Self-audit for *The New Art and Science of Teaching* framework.

*Visit **go.SolutionTree.com/instruction** for a free reproducible version of this figure.*

Step 2: Select Goal Elements and Specific Strategies

Once teachers have conducted a self-audit, they identify elements that they will focus on for their personal and professional development over the upcoming year. We recommend that teachers choose from one to three elements per year. If a supervisor, evaluator, or instructional coach is involved in the process, then this individual should have some say in what a teacher selects. That is, he or she might require a beginning or floundering teacher to work on two elements and allow the teacher to select one. Sometimes the school or district has adopted a focus, in which case one element might be a collective mandate and teachers choose the others pertinent to their level of expertise and areas needing improvement. To illustrate, assume a teacher selects the following elements on which she has scored herself as Developing, Beginning, and Not Using respectively.

- **Element 6:** Chunking content
- **Element 11:** Examining errors in reasoning
- **Element 16:** Highlighting critical information

While there might be a number of other elements on which the teacher has assigned herself a relatively low score, these are the ones she wishes to focus on in the coming year. At a more granular level, the teacher then identifies specific strategies to target as a means of improvement. Recall that each element contains multiple strategies; for example, element 16—highlighting critical information—encompasses the following strategies.

- Repeating the most important content
- Asking questions that focus on critical information
- Using visual activities
- Using narrative activities
- Using tone of voice, gestures, and body position
- Using pause time
- Identifying critical-input experiences
- Using explicit instruction to convey critical content
- Using dramatic instruction to convey critical content
- Providing advance organizers to cue critical content
- Using what students already know to cue critical content

From this list, the teacher might select the strategy of repeating the most important content.

Step 3: Engage in Deliberate Practice and Track Progress

After identifying specific strategies within each selected focus element, the teacher now engages in deliberate practice. As its name implies, *deliberate practice* involves focusing on explicit goals and monitoring incremental progress toward those goals. Again, the self-rating scales should be of service when gauging progress.

In our example, the teacher initially scored herself as Not Using relative to the element of highlighting critical information. She then handpicked the strategy: repeating the most important content. This implies that she really doesn't even know how the strategy might manifest itself in the classroom. Therefore, she engages in some internet searches and finds a few examples described in downloadable documents as well as some video examples of how teachers use this teaching tool. Additionally, she might ask colleagues how they have incorporated it in their classrooms with success. Once she decides that she has enough information about the strategy, she is ready to try it out in her own classroom. She now has moved to the Beginning level on the self-rating scale.

The Beginning level means that a teacher is attempting to use a strategy but makes some significant errors. On a day during which our teacher tries out the strategy, she might solicit the support of a colleague—such as an instructional coach, fellow teacher, or administrator—to observe her with the express purpose of offering feedback on the use of this target strategy. She implements the strategy over again; each time she puts aside time to reflect on what she did well and what she could have done better. After about four attempts at using the strategy along with self-reflection, the teacher concludes that she is using it without making any significant errors. She is now at the Developing level.

To move to the Applying level, the teacher asks herself, "What do I expect to see students doing if this strategy is working well?" The answer is obvious to her. After she has presented new information to students, they should understand and remember what was most important out of all the information she has presented to them. To obtain a sense of this, she decides to ask students to respond to exit slips with the question, *What was most important about what we covered in today's class?* To her pleasant surprise, most of the students can accurately identify the critical content. She is now at the Applying level.

To advance to the Innovating level, the teacher examines the reactions of her students in even more depth by briefly talking to those students who still seem to have trouble identifying critical information even after she uses the strategy. She soon realizes that as English learners, simply repeating the content doesn't help them get over the language barrier. She decides to include some graphic and pictographic representations of the content along with her verbal repetitions and soon finds that it helps bridge the gap for these students. She is now at the Innovating level relative to this strategy.

A tracking chart like the one in figure 9.3 can help a teacher track his or her progress.

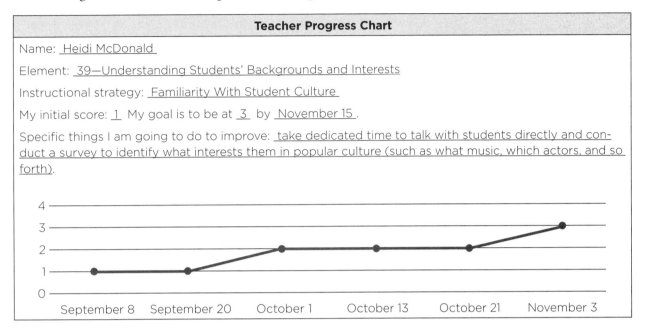

Figure 9.3: Teacher progress for the strategy of identifying cultural backgrounds.

Step 4: Seek Continuous Improvement by Planning for Future Growth

The final step in the development process is for teachers to keep selecting elements and strategies on which to work and improving their practice in those elements and strategies. Even if a teacher becomes competent in all elements of *The New Art and Science of Teaching* model, there are still multiple strategies within each element on which to improve. In effect, the model can provide teachers with new challenges and new levels of expertise throughout their entire career.

Conclusion

Developing expertise is not a function of talent or serendipity. Rather, it is a product of focus and hard work over time. The four steps we provide in this chapter should address the criterion of focus. The criterion of hard work over time is a product of teacher commitment. Hopefully, the resources provided in this book help elicit such commitment.

Afterword

The New Art and Science of Teaching (Marzano, 2017) presents a comprehensive model of teaching that organizes all or most of the instructional strategies available to teachers. The science reference is predicated on the fact that these strategies are founded on decades of research and theory and contribute to effective teaching. The art component indicates that factors other than research attribute to student learning, such as which strategies are used together and how teachers use them for express purposes. This analogy can help elucidate this point:

> Instructional strategies are best likened to techniques an artist might develop and refine over years of practice. The artist then uses these techniques to create works that are not only unique and complex but elegantly focused. The more skill the artist exhibits with available techniques, the better his or her creations. Likewise, the more skill the classroom teacher has with the instructional strategies that research and theory have uncovered over the decades, the better the teacher will be able to create lessons that optimize student learning. (Marzano, 2017)

It is the duty, the call to action, and the mission of educators everywhere to meet students where they are and elevate them to the next level of learning. This is an awesome task indeed and extremely rewarding when students move from not knowing to awareness. As teachers endeavor to undertake this responsibility, they need tools, resources, and support to help guide them so they can be the best possible conduit of learning for their charges. *The New Art and Science of Teaching Writing* presents myriad strategies to assist teachers in this work. We invite all teachers to raise their own bar of professional capacity so they can, in turn, open the door for the students they are so fortunate to lead.

Appendix A
Framework Overview

We have further divided each of the three overarching categories—feedback, content, and context—into ten teacher actions. These categories give rise to forty-three elements which, on a more granular level, comprise 333 associated instructional strategies. Figure A.1 (page 156) presents a comprehensive list of the forty-three elements and their associated strategies. The instructional strategies that appear in bold typeface are those that we feature in this book as they relate to writing instruction and to some degree reading since these areas of literacy are closely linked.

The New Art and Science of Teaching Framework Overview

Category	Teacher Actions	Desired Student Mental States and Processes	Design Questions	Forty-Three Elements	Strategies (We address the bolded strategies in this book.)
Feedback	**Chapter 1: Providing and Communicating Clear Learning Goals**	1. Students understand the progression of knowledge they are expected to master and where they are along that progression.	How will I communicate clear learning goals that help students understand the progression of knowledge I expect them to master and where they are along that progression?	**1. Providing scales and rubrics** — How will I design scales or rubrics?	**1. Clearly articulating learning goals** **2. Creating scales or rubrics for learning goals** **3. Implementing routines for using targets and scales** **4. Using teacher-created targets and scales** 5. Creating student-friendly scales 6. Identifying individual student learning goals
				2. Tracking student progress — How will I track progress?	7. Using formative scores **8. Designing assessments that generate formative scores** 9. Using individual score-level assessments **10. Using different types of assessments** 11. Generating summative scores 12. Charting student progress 13. Charting class progress
				3. Celebrating success — How will I celebrate success?	**14. Status celebration** **15. Knowledge gain celebration** **16. Verbal feedback**
	Chapter 2: Using Assessments	2. Students understand how test scores and grades relate to their status on the progression of knowledge they are expected to master.	How will I design and administer assessments that help students understand how their test scores and grades relate to their status on the progression of knowledge I expect them to master?	**4. Using informal assessments of the whole class** — How will I informally assess the whole class?	17. Confidence rating techniques **18. Voting techniques** **19. Response cards** 20. Unrecorded assessments
				5. Using formal assessments of individual students — How will I formally assess individual students?	**21. Common assessments designed using proficiency scales** 22. Assessments involving selected-response or short constructed-response items **23. Student demonstrations** 24. Student interviews 25. Observations of students **26. Student-generated assessments** 27. Response patterns

The New Art and Science of Teaching Framework Overview

Category	Teacher Actions	Desired Student Mental States and Processes	Design Questions	Forty-Three Elements	Strategies (We address the bolded strategies in this book.)
Content	**Chapter 3: Conducting Direct Instruction Lessons**	3. When content is new, students understand which parts are important and how the parts fit together.	When content is new, how will I design and deliver direct instruction lessons that help students understand which parts are important and how the parts fit together?	**6. Chunking content** How will I chunk the new content into short, digestible bites?	**28. Using preassessment data to plan for chunks** 29. Presenting content in small, sequentially related sets **30. Allowing for processing time between chunks**
				7. Processing content How will I help students process the individual chunks and the content as a whole?	**31. Perspective analysis** **32. Thinking hats** 33. Collaborative process 34. Jigsaw cooperative learning 35. Reciprocal teaching **36. Concept attainment** 37. Think-pair-share 38. Scripted cooperative dyads
				8. Recording and representing content How will I help students record and represent their knowledge?	39. Informal outlines **40. Summaries** 41. Pictorial notes and pictographs 42. Combination notes, pictures, and summaries **43. Graphic organizers** 44. Free-flowing webs **45. Academic notebooks** 46. Dramatic enactments **47. Mnemonic devices** 48. Rhyming pegwords 49. Link strategies
	Chapter 4: Conducting Practicing and Deepening Lessons	4. After teachers present new content, students deepen their understanding and develop fluency in skills and processes.	After presenting content, how will I design and deliver lessons that help students deepen their understanding and develop fluency in skills and processes?	**9. Using structured practice sessions** How will I use structured practice?	**50. Modeling** **51. Guided practice** 52. Close monitoring 53. Frequent structured practice 54. Varied practice 55. Fluency practice **56. Worked examples** 57. Practice sessions prior to testing

Figure A.1: *The New Art and Science of Teaching* framework overview.

continued →

The New Art and Science of Teaching Framework Overview

Category	Teacher Actions	Desired Student Mental States and Processes	Design Questions	Forty-Three Elements	Strategies (We address the bolded strategies in this book.)
Content	Chapter 4: Conducting Practicing and Deepening Lessons	4. After teachers present new content, students deepen their understanding and develop fluency in skills and processes.	After presenting content, how will I design and deliver lessons that help students deepen their understanding and develop fluency in skills and processes?	10. Examining similarities and differences How will I help students examine similarities and differences?	**58. Sentence-stem comparisons** **59. Summaries** 60. Constructed-response comparisons **61. Venn diagrams** **62. T-charts** 63. Double-bubble diagrams 64. Comparison matrices 65. Classification charts 66. Dichotomous keys **67. Sorting, matching, and categorizing** 68. Similes 69. Metaphors 70. Sentence-stem analogies 71. Visual analogies
				11. Examining errors in reasoning How will I help students examine errors in reasoning?	**72. Identifying errors of faulty logic** **73. Identifying errors of attack** **74. Identifying errors of weak reference** **75. Identifying errors of misinformation** 76. Practicing identifying errors in logic **77. Finding errors in the media** **78. Examining support for claims** **79. Judging reasoning and evidence in an author's work** **80. Identifying statistical limitations** 81. Using student-friendly prompts **82. Anticipating student errors** 83. Avoiding unproductive habits of mind
	Chapter 5: Conducting Knowledge Application Lessons	5. After teachers present new content, students generate and defend claims through knowledge application tasks.	After presenting content, how will I design and deliver lessons that help students generate and defend claims through knowledge application?	12. Engaging students in cognitively complex tasks How will I engage students in cognitively complex tasks?	**84. Experimental-inquiry tasks** 85. Problem-solving tasks 86. Tasks to examine the efficiencies of multiple methods of problem solving **87. Decision-making tasks** 88. Investigation tasks 89. Invention tasks **90. Student-designed tasks**

The New Art and Science of Teaching Framework Overview

Category	Teacher Actions	Desired Student Mental States and Processes	Design Questions	Forty-Three Elements	Strategies (We address the bolded strategies in this book.)
				13. Providing resources and guidance — How will I provide resources and guidance?	**91. Using proficiency or scoring scales** **92. Providing resources** **93. Providing informational handouts** **94. Teaching research skills** 95. Conducting interviews 96. Circulating around the room 97. Collecting informal assessment information **98. Offering feedback** 99. Creating cognitive dissonance
				14. Generating and defending claims — How will I help students generate and defend claims?	**100. Introducing the concept of claims and support** **101. Presenting the formal structure of claims and support** **102. Generating claims** **103. Providing grounds** **104. Providing backing** **105. Generating qualifiers** **106. Formally presenting claims**
Chapter 6: Using Strategies That Appear in All Types of Lessons		6. Students continually integrate new knowledge with old knowledge and revise their understanding accordingly.	Throughout all types of lessons, what strategies will I use to help students continually integrate new knowledge with old knowledge and revise their understanding accordingly?	**15. Previewing strategies** — How will I help students preview content?	107. Informational hooks **108. Bell ringers** **109. What do you think you know?** 110. Overt linkages 111. Preview questions 112. Brief teacher summaries 113. Skimming 114. Teacher-prepared notes **115. K-W-L strategies** 116. Advance organizers 117. Anticipation guides 118. Word splashes **119. Preassessments**

continued →

The New Art and Science of Teaching Framework Overview

Category	Teacher Actions	Desired Student Mental States and Processes	Design Questions	Forty-Three Elements	Strategies (We address the bolded strategies in this book.)
Content	Chapter 6: Using Strategies That Appear in All Types of Lessons	6. Students continually integrate new knowledge with old knowledge and revise their understanding accordingly.	Throughout all types of lessons, what strategies will I use to help students continually integrate new knowledge with old knowledge and revise their understanding accordingly?	16. **Highlighting critical information** How will I highlight critical information?	120. Repeating the most important content 121. Asking questions that focus on critical information **122. Using visual activities** 123. Using narrative activities 124. Using tone of voice, gestures, and body position 125. Using pause time 126. Identifying critical-input experiences 127. Using explicit instruction to convey critical content 128. Using dramatic instruction to convey critical content **129. Providing advance organizers to cue critical content** 130. Using what students already know to cue critical content
				17. **Reviewing content** How will I help students review content?	131. Cumulative review **132. Cloze activities** 133. Summary 134. Presented problem **135. Demonstration** 136. Brief practice test or exercise 137. Questioning **138. Give one, get one**
				18. **Revising knowledge** How will I help students revise knowledge?	**139. Academic notebook entries** **140. Academic notebook review** **141. Peer feedback** **142. Assignment revision** 143. The five basic processes **144. Visual symbols** **145. Writing tools**
				19. **Reflecting on learning** How will I help students reflect on their learning?	**146. Reflective journals** 147. Think logs **148. Exit slips** 149. Knowledge comparisons 150. Two-column notes

The New Art and Science of Teaching Framework Overview

Category	Teacher Actions	Desired Student Mental States and Processes	Design Questions	Forty-Three Elements	Strategies (We address the bolded strategies in this book.)
				20. Assigning purposeful homework How will I use purposeful homework?	151. Homework preview 152. Homework to deepen knowledge 153. Homework to practice a process or skill **154. Parent-assessed homework**
				21. Elaborating on information How will I help students elaborate on information?	155. General inferential questions **156. Elaborative interrogation** 157. Questioning sequences
				22. Organizing students to interact How will I organize students to interact?	158. Group for active processing 159. Group norm creation **160. Fishbowl demonstration** 161. Job cards 162. Predetermined buddies to help form ad hoc groups 163. Contingency plan for ungrouped students 164. Grouping students using preassessment information 165. Pair-check **166. Think-pair-share and think-pair-square** 167. Student tournaments 168. Inside-outside circle 169. Cooperative learning **170. Peer-response groups** 171. Peer tutoring 172. Structured grouping 173. Group reflecting on learning

continued →

The New Art and Science of Teaching Framework Overview

Category	Teacher Actions	Desired Student Mental States and Processes	Design Questions	Forty-Three Elements	Strategies (We address the bolded strategies in this book.)
Context	Chapter 7: Using Engagement Strategies	7. Students are paying attention, energized, intrigued, and inspired.	What engagement strategies will I use to help students pay attention, be energized, be intrigued, and be inspired?	23. Noticing and reacting when students are not engaged What will I do to notice and react when students are not engaged?	174. Monitoring individual student engagement 175. Monitoring overall class engagement 176. Using self-reported student engagement data **177. Re-engaging individual students** 178. Boosting overall class energy levels
				24. Increasing response rates What will I do to increase students' response rates?	179. Random names **180. Hand signals** **181. Response cards** 182. Response chaining 183. Paired response 184. Choral response 185. Wait time 186. Elaborative interrogation 187. Multiple types of questions
				25. Using physical movement What will I do to increase students' physical movements?	188. Stand up and stretch 189. Vote with your feet 190. Corners activities 191. Stand and be counted **192. Body representations** **193. Drama-related activities**
				26. Maintaining a lively pace What will I do to maintain a lively pace?	**194. Instructional segments** 195. Pace modulation 196. The parking lot **197. Motivational hooks**

The New Art and Science of Teaching Framework Overview

Category	Teacher Actions	Desired Student Mental States and Processes	Design Questions	Forty-Three Elements	Strategies (We address the bolded strategies in this book.)
				27. Demonstrating intensity and enthusiasm What will I do to demonstrate intensity and enthusiasm?	198. Direct statements about the importance of content 199. Explicit connections 200. Nonlinguistic representations **201. Personal stories** 202. Verbal and nonverbal signals 203. Humor 204. Quotations **205. Video clips**
				28. Presenting unusual information What will I do to present unusual information?	**206. Teacher-presented information** 207. WebQuests **208. Fast facts** 209. Believe it or not 210. History files **211. Guest speakers** and firsthand consultants
				29. Using friendly controversy What will I do to engage students in friendly controversy?	212. Friendly controversy 213. Class vote 214. Seminars **215. Expert opinions** 216. Opposite point of view **217. Diagrams comparing perspectives** 218. Lincoln-Douglas debate 219. Town-hall meeting 220. Legal model
				30. Using academic games What will I do to engage students in academic games?	**221. What is the question?** 222. Name that category 223. Talk a mile a minute 224. Classroom feud **225. Which one doesn't belong?** 226. Inconsequential competition 227. Turning questions into games **228. Vocabulary review games**

continued →

The New Art and Science of Teaching Framework Overview

Category	Teacher Actions	Desired Student Mental States and Processes	Design Questions	Forty-Three Elements	Strategies (We address the bolded strategies in this book.)
Context	**Chapter 7: Using Engagement Strategies**	7. Students are paying attention, energized, intrigued, and inspired.	What engagement strategies will I use to help students pay attention, be energized, be intrigued, and be inspired?	**31. Providing opportunities for students to talk about themselves** What will I do to provide opportunities for students to talk about themselves?	229. Interest surveys 230. Student learning profiles 231. Life connections **232. Informal linkages during class discussion**
				32. Motivating and inspiring students What will I do to motivate and inspire students?	233. Academic goal setting 234. Growth mindset cultivation **235. Possible selves activities** 236. Personal projects 237. Altruism projects **238. Gratitude journals** 239. Mindfulness practice 240. Inspirational media
	Chapter 8: Implementing Rules and Procedures	8. Students understand and follow rules and procedures.	What strategies will I use to help students understand and follow rules and procedures?	**33. Establishing rules and procedures** What will I do to establish rules and procedures?	241. Using a small set of rules and procedures 242. Explaining rules and procedures to students 243. Generating rules and procedures with students 244. Modifying rules and procedures with students 245. Reviewing rules and procedures with students 246. Using the language of responsibility and statements of school beliefs 247. Posting rules around the room 248. Writing a class pledge or classroom constitution 249. Using posters and graphics 250. Establishing gestures and symbols 251. Modeling with vignettes and role playing 252. Holding classroom meetings 253. Implementing student self-assessment

The New Art and Science of Teaching Framework Overview

Category	Teacher Actions	Desired Student Mental States and Processes	Design Questions	Forty-Three Elements	Strategies (We address the bolded strategies in this book.)
				34. Organizing the physical layout of the classroom What will I do to make the physical layout of the classroom most conducive to learning?	254. Designing classroom décor **255. Displaying student work** **256. Considering classroom materials** 257. Placing the teacher's desk **258. Placing student desks** 259. Planning areas for whole-group instruction **260. Planning areas for group work** 261. Planning learning centers **262. Considering computers and technology equipment** 263. Considering lab equipment and supplies 264. Planning classroom libraries 265. Involving students in the design process
				35. Demonstrating withitness What will I do to demonstrate withitness?	266. Being proactive 267. Occupying the whole room physically and visually 268. Noticing potential problems 269. Using a series of graduated actions
				36. Acknowledging adherence to rules and procedures What will I do to acknowledge adherence to rules and procedures?	270. Verbal affirmation 271. Nonverbal affirmation 272. Tangible recognition 273. Token economies 274. Daily recognition form 275. Color-coded behavior 276. Certificates 277. Phone calls, emails, and notes
				37. Acknowledging lack of adherence to rules and procedures What will I do to acknowledge lack of adherence to rules and procedures?	278. Verbal cues 279. Pregnant pause 280. Nonverbal cues 281. Time-out 282. Overcorrection 283. Interdependent group contingency 284. Home contingency 285. High-intensity situation plan 286. Overall disciplinary plan

continued →

The New Art and Science of Teaching Framework Overview

Category	Teacher Actions	Desired Student Mental States and Processes	Design Questions	Forty-Three Elements	Strategies (We address the bolded strategies in this book.)
Context	Chapter 9: Building Relationships	9. Students feel welcome, accepted, and valued.	What strategies will I use to help students feel welcome, accepted, and valued?	**38. Using verbal and nonverbal behaviors that indicate affection for students** — How will I use verbal and nonverbal behaviors that indicate affection for students?	287. Greeting students at the classroom door 288. Holding informal conferences 289. Attending after-school functions 290. Greeting students by name outside of school 291. Giving students special responsibilities or leadership roles in the classroom 292. Scheduling interaction 293. Creating a photo bulletin board 294. Using physical behaviors 295. Using humor
				39. Understanding students' backgrounds and interests — How will I demonstrate that I understand students' backgrounds and interests?	**296. Student background surveys** **297. Opinion questionnaires** 298. Individual student-teacher conferences 299. Parent-teacher conferences 300. School newspaper, newsletter, or bulletin 301. Informal class interviews **302. Familiarity with student culture** 303. Autobiographical metaphors and analogies **304. Six-word autobiographies** 305. Independent investigations 306. Quotes 307. Comments about student achievement or areas of importance 308. Lineups 309. Individual student learning goals
				40. Displaying objectivity and control — How will I demonstrate objectivity and control?	310. Self-reflection 311. Self-monitoring 312. Emotional triggers 313. Self-care 314. Assertiveness 315. A cool exterior 316. Active listening and speaking 317. Communication styles 318. Unique student needs

The New Art and Science of Teaching Framework Overview

Category	Teacher Actions	Desired Student Mental States and Processes	Design Questions	Forty-Three Elements	Strategies (We address the bolded strategies in this book.)
	Chapter 10: Communicating High Expectations	10. Typically reluctant students feel valued and do not hesitate to interact with the teacher or their peers.	What strategies will I use to help typically reluctant students feel valued and comfortable interacting with me or their peers?	**41. Demonstrating value and respect for reluctant learners** How will I demonstrate value and respect for reluctant learners?	319. Identifying expectation levels for all students 320. Identifying differential treatment of reluctant learners 321. Using nonverbal and verbal indicators of respect
				42. Asking in-depth questions of reluctant learners How will I ask in-depth questions of reluctant learners?	322. Question levels 323. Response opportunities 324. Follow-up questioning 325. Evidence and support for student answers 326. Encouragement 327. Wait time 328. Tracking responses 329. Inappropriate reactions
				43. Probing incorrect answers with reluctant learners How will I probe incorrect answers with reluctant learners?	330. Using an appropriate response process 331. Letting students off the hook temporarily 332. Using answer revision 333. Using think-pair-share

Visit go.SolutionTree.com/instruction for a free reproducible version of this figure.

Appendix B
List of Figures and Tables

Visit **go.SolutionTree.com/instruction** for free reproducible versions of figures and tables with an asterisk.

Figure I.1: The teaching and learning progression. 2

Table I.1: Teacher Actions and Student Mental States and Processes 3

Table I.2: Design Questions 3

Table I.3: Elements Within the Ten Design Areas 5

Figure I.2: General format of the self-rating scale. 7

Figure 1.1: Self-rating scale for element 1—Providing scales and rubrics. 12

Figure 1.2: Sample proficiency scale for generating narratives (grade 8).* 12

Figure 1.3: Sample proficiency scale for generating narratives (grade 2).* 13

Figure 1.4: Sample proficiency scale for revision (grade 8).* 14

Figure 1.5: Sample proficiency scale for generating sentences (grade 2).* 15

Figure 1.6: Argumentation writing analytic rubric, secondary level.* 17

Figure 1.7: Opinion writing analytic rubric elementary level.* 20

Figure 1.8: Process to determine median and mode.. 22

Figure 1.9: Argumentation writing checklist (secondary).*. 23

Figure 1.10: Opinion writing checklist (primary).*. 24

Figure 1.11: Self-rating scale for element 2—Tracking student progress. 25

Figure 1.12: Self-rating scale for element 3—Celebrating success. 26

Figure 2.1: Self-rating scale for element 4—Using informal assessments of the whole class. . . 29

Figure 2.2: Self-rating scale for element 5—Using formal assessments of individual students. . . 32

Figure 3.1: Self-rating scale for element 6—Chunking content. 37

Figure 3.2: Secondary figurative language preassessment.* 38

Figure 3.3: Upper elementary figurative language preassessment.* 39

Figure 3.4: Elementary figurative language preassessment.*. 40

Figure 3.5: Self-rating scale for element 7—Processing content.. 41

Figure 3.6: Perspective analysis examples.* 42

Figure 3.7: Thinking hats.* 43

Figure 3.8: Parallelism activity (upper elementary).*. 45

Figure 3.9: Parallelism activity (secondary).* 45

Figure 3.10: Self-rating scale for element 8—Recording and representing content. 46

Figure 3.11: Story summary template and example: *Wonder*.* 47

Figure 3.12: Graphic organizers.* 49

Table 3.1: Coordinating Conjunctions 50

Figure 3.13: Compound sentence examples (elementary)*. 52

Figure 3.14: Sentence examples (upper elementary).* 52

Figure 3.15: Sentence examples (secondary).*. 52

Figure 4.1: Self-rating scale for element 9—Using structured practice sessions.. 56

Figure 4.2: Modeling example.*. 57

Figure 4.3: Student character sketches.* 58

Figure 4.4: Self-rating scale for element 10—Examining similarities and differences. . . . 61

Figure 4.5: Diamante template and example: *Wonder*.* 63

Figure 4.6: Sorting exercise sentence excerpts 1.* 64

Figure 4.7: Sorting exercise sentence excerpts 2.* 64

Figure 4.8: Self-rating scale for element 11—Examining errors in reasoning. 65

Figure 4.9: Types of errors in arguments. 66

Figure 4.10: Thesis and aligned topic sentences.* 68

Figure 5.1: Self-rating scale for element 12—Engaging students in cognitively complex tasks. . . 71

Figure 5.2: Sample secondary templates and tasks.* 73

Figure 5.3: Options for written products.* 74

Figure 5.4: Self-rating scale for element 13—Providing resources and guidance. 76

Figure 5.5: Narrative feedback sheet.* 79

Figure 5.6: Argumentation feedback sheet.* 80

Figure 5.7: Prepositional phrase cards.* 81

Figure 5.8: Self-rating scale for element 14—Generating and defending claims.. 82

Figure 5.9: Argumentation characteristics.* 83

Figure 5.10: The structure of an argument.. 83

Figure 5.11: Introducing the structure of an argument to elementary students.* 84

Figure 5.12: Counterargument sentence frames.*. 86

Figure 6.1: Self-rating scale for element 15—Previewing strategies. 90

Figure 6.2: K-W-L chart.*. 92

Figure 6.3: Narrative preassessment.* 94

Figure 6.4: Elements of literature web.* 94

Figure 6.5: Fairy tale preassessment.* 95

Figure 6.6: Self-rating scale for element 16—Highlighting critical information. 96

Figure 6.7: Paragraphing poster.* 97

Figure 6.8: Paragraphing bookmark.* 97

Figure 6.9: Self-rating scale for element 17—Reviewing content 98

Figure 6.10: Cloze activity examples. 99

Figure 6.11: Cloze activity with author's excerpt. 99

Figure 6.12: Self-rating scale for element 18—Revising knowledge. 101

Table 6.1: Proofreading Marks* 103

Figure 6.13: Narrative revision sheet, secondary level.* 104

Figure 6.14: Personal narrative revision sheet 1, elementary level.* 107

Figure 6.15: Personal narrative revision sheet 2, elementary level.* 108

Figure 6.16: Self-rating scale for element 19—Reflecting on learning. 109

Figure 6.17: Self-rating scale for element 20—Assigning purposeful homework. 110

Figure 6.18: Suggestions for parents or guardians in assisting student writers.* 111

Figure 6.19: Self-rating scale for element 21—Elaborating on information. 112

Figure 6.20: Self-rating scale for element 22—Organizing students to interact 113

Figure 7.1: Self-rating scale for element 23—Noticing and reacting when students are not engaged. 120

Figure 7.2: Self-rating scale for element 24—Increasing response rates. 120

Figure 7.3: Hand signal examples.* 122

Figure 7.4: Self-rating scale for element 25—Using physical movement. 123

Figure 7.5: Tableau assignment sheet with teacher directions and potential student responses.* 124

Figure 7.6: Self-rating scale for element 26—Maintaining a lively pace. 125

Figure 7.7: Self-rating scale for element 27—Demonstrating intensity and enthusiasm. . . . 126

Figure 7.8: Self-rating scale for element 28—Presenting unusual information. 127

Figure 7.9: Self-rating scale for element 29—Using friendly controversy. 129

Figure 7.10: Self-rating scale for element 30—Using academic games. 130

Figure 7.11: Which one doesn't belong? examples. 131

Figure 7.12: Self-rating scale for element 31—Providing opportunities for students to talk about themselves. 132

Figure 7.13: Vocabulary game board (elementary).* 133

Figure 7.14: Self-rating scale for element 32—Motivating and inspiring students. 135

Figure 8.1: Self-rating scale for element 34—Organizing the physical layout of the classroom . 139

Figure 8.2: Self-rating scale for element 39—Understanding students' backgrounds and interests. 142

Figure 9.1: General format of the self-rating scale. 148

Figure 9.2: Self-audit for *The New Art and Science of Teaching* framework.* 149

Figure 9.3: Teacher progress for the strategy of identifying cultural backgrounds. 150

Figure A.1: *The New Art and Science of Teaching* framework overview.* 156

References and Resources

Aliki. (2015). *My five senses*. New York: Harper Collins.

Andrews, M. (n.d.). *After 27 rejections, Dr. Seuss almost burned his unpublished book. Fortunately, he didn't!* Accessed at www.elitereaders.com/dr-seuss-rejection-story on May 14, 2018.

Arbeiter, M. (2017, August 31). *11 things you might not know about* Lord of the Flies. Accessed at http://mentalfloss.com/article/62962/11-things-you-might-not-know-about-lord-flies on May 14, 2018.

Austen, J. (1996). *Pride and prejudice.* London: Penguin Books.

Babbitt, N. (1975). *Tuck everlasting.* New York: Square Fish.

Bloom, J. (2012, September 26). *Literary devices.* [Video file]. Accessed at www.youtube.com/watch?v=uCMniNKxLFk on February 5, 2018.

Blume, J. (n.d.). *Rejection.* Accessed at http://judyblume.com/writing/rejection.php on February 5, 2018.

Brookhart, S. M. (2013). *How to create and use rubrics for formative assessment and grading.* Alexandria, VA: Association for Supervision and Curriculum Development.

Brown, M. W. (1977). *The important book.* New York: HarperCollins.

Busari, S. (2017, February). *How fake news does real harm* [Video file]. Accessed at www.ted.com/talks/stephanie_busari_how_fake_news_does_real_harm on February 5, 20

Cameron, A. (1981). The pudding like a night on the sea. In *The stories Julian tells.* (pp. 1–16). New York: Alfred A. Knopf.

Civil War Trust. (2014). *Civil War Trust 2014 annual report.* Accessed at www.battlefields.org on June 8, 2018.

Collier, J. L., & Collier C. (1984). *My brother Sam is dead.* New York: Simon & Schuster.

de Bono, E. (1985/1999). *Six thinking hats.* New York: Little, Brown.

Doerr, A. (2014). *All the light we cannot see.* New York: Simon & Schuster.

Dweck, C. S. (2006/2008). *Mindset: The new psychology of success.* New York: Random House.

Eliot, T. S. (1939). "The song of the Jellicles." Accessed at www.best-poems.net/t_s_eliot/the_song_of_the_jellicles.html on March 20, 2018.

Ericsson, K. A., & Charness, N. (1994). Expert performance: Its structure and acquisition. *American Psychologist, 49*(8), 725–747.

Ericsson, K. A., Krampe, R. T., & Tesch-Romer, C. (1993). The role of deliberate practice in the acquisition of expert performance. *Psychological Review, 100*(3), 363–406.

Fox, M. (1984). *Wilfrid Gordon McDonald Partridge.* Gosford, New South Wales, Australia: Omnibus Books.

Gibbons, G. (2005). *Owls.* New York: Holiday House.

Glass, K. T. (2012). *Mapping comprehensive units to the ELA Common Core standards, K–5.* Thousand Oaks, CA: Corwin Press.

Glass, K. T. (2013). *Mapping comprehensive units to the ELA Common Core standards, 6–12.* Thousand Oaks, CA: Corwin Press.

Glass, K. T. (2017a). *The fundamentals of (re)designing writing units.* Bloomington, IN: Solution Tree Press.

Glass, K. T. (2017b). *(Re)designing argumentation writing units for grades 5–12.* Bloomington, IN: Solution Tree Press.

Glass, K. T. (2018). *(Re)designing narrative writing units for grades 5–12.* Bloomington, IN: Solution Tree Press.

Haley, A. (Writer). (1977). *Roots: The saga of an American family* [Television miniseries]. Hollywood, CA: ABC.

Hattie, J., & Yates, G. (2014). *Visible learning and the science of how we learn.* New York: Routledge.

Henkes, K. (2006). *Kitten's first full moon.* New York: Simon & Schuster.

Henry, O. (1903). "A retrieved reformation." Accessed at https://americanenglish.state.gov/files/ae/resource_files/a-retrieved-reformation.pdf on March 26, 2018.

Jackson, S. (1948). "The lottery." Accessed at http://fullreads.com/literature/the-lottery on March 21, 2018.

Lamott, A. (1995). *Bird by bird: Some instructions on writing and life.* New York: Random House.

Lionni, L. (1991). *Swimmy.* New York: Random House.

Literacy Design Collaborative. (2014, December). *LDC task template collection version 3.0.* Accessed at https://ldc-production-secure.s3.amazonaws.com/resource_files/files/000/000/044/original/LDC_Task_Template_Collection_Version_3.0.pdf on February 9, 2018.

Marzano, R. J. (2006). *Classroom assessment and grading that work.* Alexandria, VA: Association for Supervision and Curriculum Development.

Marzano, R. J. (2007). *The art and science of teaching: A comprehensive framework for effective instruction.* Alexandria, VA: Association for Supervision and Curriculum Development.

Marzano, R. J. (2010). Developing expert teachers. In R. J. Marzano (Ed.), *On excellence in teaching* (pp. 213–246). Bloomington, IN: Solution Tree Press.

Marzano, R. J. (2012). Art & science of teaching / teaching argument. *Educational Leadership, 70*(1), 80–Accessed at www.ascd.org/publications/educational-leadership/sept12/vol70/num01/Teaching-Argument.aspx on March 26, 2018.

Marzano, R. J. (2017). *The new art and science of teaching.* Bloomington, IN: Solution Tree Press.

Marzano, R. J., Marzano, J. S., & Pickering, D. J. (2003). *Classroom management that works: Research-based strategies for every teacher.* Alexandria, VA: Association for Supervision and Curriculum Development.

Marzano, R. J., Pickering, D. J., & Pollock, J. E. (2001). *Classroom instruction that works: Research-based strategies for increasing student achievement.* Alexandria, VA: Association for Supervision and Curriculum Development.

Marzano Resources. (2016). *Generating and defending claims.* Centennial, CO: Author.

National Governors Association Center for Best Practices & Council of Chief State School Officers. (2010). *Common Core State Standards for English language arts and literacy in history/social studies, science, and technical subjects.* Washington, DC: Authors. Accessed at www.corestandards.org/assets/CCSSI_ELA%20Standards.pdf on September 22, 2016.

ndonnenwerth1. (2015, August 18). *Figurative language in pop culture 2015* [Video file]. Accessed at www.youtube.com/watch?v=C7wYKVwsJ64 on February 5, 2018.

Nye, B., Konstantopoulos, S., & Hedges, L. V. (2004). How large are teacher effects? *Educational Evaluation and Policy Analysis, 26*(3), 237–257.

Pfister, M. (1992). *The rainbow fish.* New York: NorthSouth Books.

Palacio, R. J. (2012). *Wonder.* New York: Alfred A. Knopf.

Polacco, P. (1998a). *Mrs. Mack.* New York: Penguin Group.

Polacco, P. (1998b). *Thank you, Mr. Falker.* New York: Philomel Books.

Reeves, D. (2016). *FAST grading: A guide to implementing best practices.* Bloomington, IN: Solution Tree Press.

Rhode Island Department of Education. (n.d.). *Calibration protocol for scoring student work: A part of the assessment toolkit.* Accessed at www.ride.ri.gov/Portals/0/Uploads /Documents/Teachers-and-Administrators-Excellent-Educators /Educator-Evaluation/Online-Modules/Calibration_Protocol_for_Scoring_Student_Work.pdf on March 1, 2018.

Rhode Island Department of Education. (2013). *Writing calibration protocol.* Accessed at www.ride.ri.gov/Portals/0 /Uploads/Documents/Common-Core/RIDE_Calibration_Process.pdf on March 1, 2018.

Richards v. Thurston, 424 F.2d 1281 (1st Cir. 1970).

Ryan, P. M. (2000). *Esperanza rising.* New York: Scholastic.

Simms, J. A. (2016). *The critical concepts (Final version: English language arts, mathematics, and science).* Centennial, CO: Marzano Resources.

Simms, J. A. (2017). *The critical concepts.* Centennial, CO: Marzano Resources.

Stanford Center for Assessment, Learning and Equity (SCALE). (n.d.). *Selecting anchor papers: A guide.* Accessed at www.performanceassessmentresourcebank.org/resource/10491 on June 8, 2018.

Steinbeck, J. (1965). *Of mice and men.* Accessed at http://nisbah.com/summer_reading/ff_mice_and_men_steinbeck.pdf on March 26, 2018.

tickletales. (2012, April 23). *Kitten's first full moon* by Kevin Henkes [Video file]. Accessed at www.youtube.com/watch?v=w5paT0hDx-c on March 26, 2018.

White, E. B. (1952/1980). *Charlotte's web.* New York: HarperCollins.

Wiggins, G. (2012). Seven keys to effective feedback. *Educational Leadership, 70*(1), 10–Accessed at www.ascd.org /publications/educational-leadership/sept12/vol70/num01/Seven-Keys-to-Effective-Feedback.aspx on September 2, 2016.

Zarefsky, D. (2005). *Argumentation: The study of effective reasoning* (2nd ed.). Chantilly, VA: The Teaching Company.

Index

A

academic games, using, 130–132
academic notebooks, 49–50, 101
advance organizers, 98
argumentation
    characteristics, 83
    identifying errors in, 66–67
arguments, structure of, 83–84
argument writing
    example of, 17–19
    feedback sheet, 80–81
    student checklist, 23–24
Art and Science of Teaching: A Comprehensive Framework for Effective Discussion, The (Marzano), 1
assessments
    formal, of individual students, 32–33
    guiding questions, 33–34
    obtrusive, 26
    preassessment, 38–39, 92–95
    student-generated, 33
    student progress, tracking, 25–26
    unobtrusive, 25–26
    whole-class informal, 29–31
assignment revision, 101–102
autobiographies, 144

B

backing, providing, 85
bell ringers, 90–91
Bergson-Michelson, T., 77
Bloom, J., 125
bookmarks, 49–50, 96, 97
Brookhart, S. M., 21

C

cause-and-effect claims, 85
chunking content, 37–39

claims
    backing, providing, 85
    formally presenting, 86
    generating and defending, 82–86
    grounds, providing, 85
    qualifiers, generating, 86
    types of, 84–85
Classroom Assessment and Grading That Work (Marzano), 1
Classroom Instruction That Works: Research-Based Strategies for Increasing Student Achievement (Marzano, Pickering, and Pollock), 1
classroom layout, organizing, 139–142
Classroom Management That Works: Research-Based Strategies for Every Teacher (Marzano, Marzano, and Pickering), 1
cloze activity, 98–99
cognitive tasks, engaging students in, 71–75
common formal assessments, of individual students, 32–33
concept attainment, 43–45
content
    See also direct instruction lessons; knowledge application lessons; lessons, practicing and deepening
    use of term, 2, 3, 4
context
    See also engagement strategies; expertise, developing; relationships, building; rules and procedures
    use of term, 2, 3, 4, 119
controversy, using friendly, 129–130
Critical Concepts, The (Simms), 12

D

decision-making tasks, 72
declarative knowledge, procedural versus, 55
definitional claims, 84
deliberate practice, using, 149
demonstrations, student, 33, 99–100
depth of knowledge (DOK), 30
direct instruction lessons

chunking content, 37–39
elaborating on information, 112–113
guiding questions, 53–54, 115–116
highlighting critical information, 96–98
homework, assigning purposeful, 110–112
previewing strategies, 89–95
processing content, 39–45
recording and presenting content, 46–53
reflecting on learning, 109–110
reviewing content, 98–100
revising knowledge, 100–108
student interaction, organizing, 113–115
displaying student work, 140–141

E
elaborating on information, 112–113
elements, 3–5
    See also specific names
engagement, use of term, 119
engagement strategies
    academic games, using, 130–132
    allowing students to talk about themselves, 132, 134–135
    controversy, using friendly, 129–130
    enthusiasm and intensity, demonstrating, 126–127
    guiding questions, 136–137
    information, presenting unusual, 127–129
    motivation techniques, 135–136
    noticing when students are not engaged, 120
    pacing, maintaining a lively, 124–125
    physical movement, using, 123–124
    response rates, increasing, 120–123
enthusiasm and intensity, demonstrating, 126–127
errors, examining reasoning, 65–68
exit slips, 26, 110
experimental-inquiry tasks, 72
expertise, developing
    continuous improvement, 149–150
    deliberate practice, using, 149
    self-audit, conducting a, 147–148
    strategies and elements, 148–149
expert opinions, 130

F
factual claims, 84
fast facts, 128
feedback, 2, 3, 4
    See also assessments; learning goals
    offering, 77–81
    peer, 101, 114–115
figurative language preassessments, 38–39, 40
fishbowl demonstration, 114
formal assessments of individual students, 32–33
friendly controversy, using, 129–130

G
games, using academic, 130–132
genre characteristics and expectations, 49
give one, get one, 100
Glass, K., 77
Google Search Education, 77
grammar, conventions and formatting, 49
graphic organizers, 48–49, 67, 68, 77, 96–97, 129, 140
grounds, providing, 85
group work, planning areas for, 142
growth mindset, 27
guest speakers, 128–129

H
hand signals, 121–123
Hattie, J., 27
Hedges, L. V., 147
highlighting critical information, 96–98
Hippocampus, 134
homework, assigning purposeful, 110–112

I
informal assessments, whole-class, 29–31
information
    elaborating on, 112–113
    presenting unusual, 127–129
    teacher-presented, 128
instructional segments, 125
instructional strategies. *See* elements
intrinsic motivation, 135

J
journals
    gratitude, 136
    reflective, 109

K
Kahoot!, 131
knowledge
    procedural versus declarative, 55
    revising, 100–108
knowledge application lessons
    claims, generating and defending, 82–86
    cognitive tasks, engaging students in, 71–75
    elaborating on information, 112–113
    guiding questions, 87, 115–116
    highlighting critical information, 96–98
    homework, assigning purposeful, 110–112
    previewing strategies, 89–95
    reflecting on learning, 109–110
    resources and guidance, providing, 75–81
    reviewing content, 98–100
    revising knowledge, 100–108
    student interaction, organizing, 113–115
Konstantopoulos, S., 147
K-W-L strategy, 91–92, 98

L

learning, reflecting on, 109–110
learning goals
  guiding questions, 28
  scales and rubrics, providing, 11–24
  student progress, tracking, 25–26
  success, celebrating, 26–27
learning targets. *See* learning goals
lessons, direct instruction.
  See direct instruction lessons
lessons, knowledge application.
  See knowledge application lessons
lessons, practicing and deepening
  elaborating on information, 112–113
  guiding questions, 68, 115–116
  highlighting critical information, 96–98
  homework, assigning purposeful, 110–112
  previewing strategies, 89–95
  procedural versus declarative knowledge, 55
  reasoning errors, examining, 65–68
  reflecting on learning, 109–110
  reviewing content, 98–100
  revising knowledge, 100–108
  similarities and differences, examining, 61–65
  structured practice sessions, 55–60
  student interaction, organizing, 113–115
Letters About Literature, 134
Literacy Design Collaborative (LDC), 72–75
literature web, elements of, 94, 96, 97

M

Marzano, J. S., 1
Marzano, R. J., 1, 2
mnemonic devices, 50–53
mode and median, determining, 21–22
modeling, 56–57
motivation
  intrinsic, 135
  techniques, 135–136
motivational hooks, 125
movie and film clips, using, 126–127

N

narratives
  examples of generating, 12–15
  feedback sheet, 79–80
  preassessment, 94
  revision sheets, 105–108
National Geographic, 127
New Art and Science of Teaching, The (Marzano), 1, 2–5, 119
  framework overview, 153–165
New York Times Learning Network, 134
New York Times Magazine, 127
Nye, B., 147

O

obtrusive assessments, 26
opinion questionnaires, 143–144
opinion writing
  example of, 20–21
  student checklist, 24

P

pacing, maintaining a lively, 124–125
paragraphing, 96, 97
parallelism, 43–45
PBS LearningMedia, 127
peer feedback, 101, 114–115
peer-response groups, 114–115
personal stories, 126
perspective analysis, 41, 42
physical classroom layout, organizing, 139–142
physical movement, using, 123–124
Pickering, D. J., 1
policy claims, 84–85
Pollock, J. E., 1
practice sessions, structured, 55–60
preassessments, 38–39, 92–95
prepositional phrase cards, 81
previewing strategies, 89–95
procedural knowledge, declarative knowledge versus, 55
ProCon.org, 33
proficiency scales
  for common assessments, 32
  examples of generating narratives, 12–15
  examples of generating sentences, 15–16
  providing, 11–24, 76
  strategies for providing, 11–12
proofreading, 102, 103

Q

qualifiers, generating, 86
questionnaires, opinion, 143–144

R

reasoning errors, examining, 65–68
reflecting on learning, 109–110
relationships, building
  guiding questions, 145
  student backgrounds and interests, understanding, 142–144
research skills, teaching, 77
resources and guidance, providing, 75–81
response boards, 31, 123
response cards, 26, 123
response rates, increasing, 120–123
reviewing content, 98–100
revising knowledge, 100–108
River of Words, 134–135
rubrics
  components of, 16–17

example of argument writing, 17–19
example of opinion writing, 20–21
mode and median, determining, 21–22
strategies for providing, 11–12
rules and procedures
    guiding questions, 145
    physical classroom layout, organizing, 139–142

S

SAG-AFTRA Foundation, 125
Sarah Mook Poetry Contest, 135
scales. *See* proficiency scales
Scholastic Art & Writing Awards, 135
self-audit, 147–148
self-rating scales, 6–7
sentence patterns, 49
sentences, examples of generating, 15–16
sentence-stem analogies/comparisons, 61
similarities and differences, examining, 61–65
Simms, J. A., 12
sorting, matching, and categorizing, 62–65
sponge activities, 90
Storyline Online, 125
student backgrounds and interests, understanding, 142–144
student demonstrations, 33, 99–100
student-designed tasks, 72–75
student-generated assessments, 33
student interaction, organizing, 113–115
student mental states and processes, 2–3
student progress, tracking, 25–26
students, allowing them to talk about themselves, 132, 134–135
student work, displaying, 140–141
success, celebrating, 26–27
summaries, 46–48, 62
Sun, The, 135
surveys, interest, 143

T

T-charts, 62
teacher actions and student mental states and processes, 2–3
technology, 141
Teen Ink, 135
think aloud, 57
thinking hats, 41–43
think-pair-share, 114
think-pair-square, 114

U

unobtrusive assessments, 25–26
USC Shoah Foundation, 127

V

value claims, 84
Venn diagrams, 62, 129
video clips, 126–127
visual activities, using, 96–97
visual symbols, using, 102, 103
vocabulary lists, 49
vocabulary review games, 132, 133
voting techniques, 30–31

W

What Do You Think You Know?, 91
What Is the Question?, 130–131
Which One Doesn't Belong?, 131
whole-class informal assessments, 29–31
Wiggins, G., 78
Winning Writers, 135
writing samples, resources for student and published, 60, 77
writing tools, 102, 104–108

Y

Yates, G., 27
YouTube, 125, 127

Solution Tree

Solution Tree's mission is to advance the work of our authors. By working with the best researchers and educators worldwide, we strive to be the premier provider of innovative publishing, in-demand events, and inspired professional development designed to transform education to ensure that all students learn.

LEARN. TEACH. LEAD.

ASCD is a global nonprofit association dedicated to the whole child approach that supports educators, families, community members, and policy makers. We provide expert and innovative solutions to facilitate professional development through print and digital publishing, on-site learning services, and conferences and events that empower educators to support the success of each child.